# Finance for
# Nonfinancial Managers

## Other titles in the Briefcase Books series include:

To learn more about titles in the Briefcase Books series go to
**www.briefcasebooks.com**

# Finance for Nonfinancial Managers

## Second Edition

## Gene Siciliano

New York  Chicago  San Francisco  Athens
London  Madrid  Mexico City  Milan  New Delhi
Singapore  Sydney  Toronto

1 2 3 4 5 6 7 8 9 0 QFR/QFR 1 0 9 8 7 6 5 4

ISBN        978-0-07-182436-1
MHID        0-07-182436-7

e-ISBN      978-0-07-182437-8
e-MHID      0-07-182347-5

**Library of Congress Cataloging-in-Publication Data**
Siciliano, Gene.
  Finance for nonfinancial managers / by Gene Siciliano. — Second edition.
    pages cm
  Includes index.
  ISBN 978-0-07-182436-1 (alk. paper) — ISBN 0-07-182436-7 (alk. paper)  1.  Financial statements.  I. Title.
  HF5681.B2S4873 2015
  658.15'11—dc23                              2014018963

This is a CWL Publishing Enterprises book developed for McGraw-Hill Education by CWL Publishing Enterprises, Inc., Madison, Wisconsin, www.cwlpub.com.

Product or brand names used in this book may be trade names or trademarks. Where we believe there may be proprietary claims to such trade names or trademarks, the name has been used with an initial capital or it has been capitalized in the style used by the name claimant. Regardless of the capitalization used, all such names have been used in an editorial manner without any intent to convey endorsement of or other affiliation with the name claimant. Neither the author nor the publisher intends to express any judgment as to the validity or legal status of any such proprietary claims.

McGraw-Hill Education products are available at special quantity discounts to use as premiums and sales promotions, or for use in corporate training programs. To contact a representative, please visit the Contact Us pages at mhprofessional.com.

# Contents

# Acknowledgments

Since writing the first edition of this book, I brought two more books into circulation. I've come to realize that I enjoy writing and that it comes easily to me. Countless newsletters and published articles attest to the fact that I seem to have lots to say on the subject of financial communications. That's a good thing for an author. But I also learned early in the process that I couldn't do it alone unless I wanted to self-publish and fill my garage with books, something that doesn't hold much appeal for me. Thanks to John Woods of CWL Publishing Enterprises and two other publishers along the way, I never had to go that route.

I'm particularly indebted to Alexander Auerbach, founder of a successful Los Angeles–based public relations and marketing services consultancy, for his talented assistance in editing the final draft of this book and to Daniel Feiman and Ed Story, two of my gifted associates who provided valuable assistance with several key chapters of the first edition. Their generous contributions are reflected in this version as well. Also, a thank you goes out to Dave Berkus, noted entrepreneur and serial investor who gave me carte blanche to quote his proven thinking for entrepreneurs. His wisdom appears in the chapters on cash flow and entrepreneurship. Over the life of the book, I've gotten many comments and suggestions from readers, business associates, and instructors who have used the book for classes in entrepreneurial finance. I have considered every comment as I crafted this edition, and I hope I've done justice to all your input. It is deeply appreciated.

Finally, all those efforts would have been in vain if my beloved partner, Karen Dellosso, hadn't been willing to let me stretch already-long work-days into even longer workdays as this book came into existence—twice.

Thank you all. I really appreciate you.

# Introduction

**W**hy should you buy this book? There are certainly others to choose from, each with a viewpoint that reflects the author's background and opinions. Why this one? Why this particular author's background and opinions? The answer is *financial comprehension*: This book is a communication manual for nonfinancial managers.

I believe there is a great need for better communication between financial and nonfinancial professionals, a need for a better tool to help the nonfinancial manager understand the language of finance, and for the financial professional to learn the terminology that has meaning for the nonfinancial manager. I believe this book can enable that better communication. That is, in fact, its purpose.

Why me? First, I spent eight years of my early working life as a practicing CPA. I felt the frustration that comes from not speaking the same language as my clients and the difficulty in getting the information I needed from people who didn't understand why I requested the information or what I would do with it. Then there were my 14 years as a financial officer inside several companies where I was responsible for finding a common language so I could provide business managers with what they needed to run their departments, divisions, and corporations. Since then I have spent more than 25 years as an advisor to business managers and entrepreneurs on financial matters.

Over each of those career phases, I've become known for my ability to translate complex or esoteric financial concepts into plain language. I understand better than most both the accountant's and the business manager's viewpoints. Not surprising, they often speak different languages, and the results are usually less than satisfactory for both. This book can facilitate a better understanding between them, since their common objective is the greater success of the enterprise that employs them both. This second edition, 10 years after the original edition was published, is evidence that my purpose is being achieved, at some level at least.

There are more than a few books on bookstore shelves—including digital versions—that attempt to achieve a similar purpose. But few have demonstrated a decade-long staying power. Mine has, and to me, financial communication is a topic I believe this book deals with very effectively.

So, what should you hope to get from this book?

- The viewpoint of an author who speaks the language of finance, but thinks more like a line manager than an accountant;
- Examples of typical financial reports, with plenty of explanations—in comprehensible English—that will help you understand those same kinds of reports when you see them in your company;
- Examples of financial reports you may not yet have seen in your company, but that you might want to, because they could give you valuable information; and
- Help in mastering the tools of finance where they can be useful to you, without wasting your time with explanations of the deep details that will likely never benefit you.

If you are now or intend to become a manager in charge of a profit center or perhaps the owner of your own business, you need a working knowledge of a lot of the information in this book. You are or may become:

- The person your staff looks to for guidance in budgets and other financial management matters;
- The person your boss or the home office expects to consistently achieve your assigned financial targets—or even the person who sets those targets;
- The person responsible for directing the finance and accounting functions that support your unit or company; and

- The person who can effectively explain to staff, boss, board of directors, and even outsiders the financial implications of the results you've achieved and the results you expect to deliver in the future.

Regardless of your path, your career success depends on doing these things reasonably well, and you cannot do that without a respectable knowledge of finance and accounting. Notice I didn't say a *thorough* knowledge and I didn't say you need to understand how accountants process detailed information. I didn't even say you had to get it right every time, because accountants don't, either. But you do need to be comfortable talking the language of finance at the nontechnical level so that you can communicate effectively in either direction. And that's why this book is still relevant after 10+ years.

## How to Use This Book

Chapter 1 sets the stage for the book. It discusses how events in today's business world have increased the need for financially savvy managers. Business managers and owners today must have both financial integrity and a degree of financial competence not previously expected of them. It's no longer good enough to keep poor accounting records in the belief that the accountants will clean it up at the end of the year so the company can file correct tax returns. There's no scanning a financial report to find the profit number for the month and ignoring the rest of the report. And it's no longer good enough for a manager to be ignorant of financial terminology if he or she wants to climb the corporate ladder, or even be demonstrably successful in their current job. You need more.

To those ends, allow me to introduce you to the Wonder Widget Company, a manufacturer and distributor of the most amazing line of widgets you'll find anywhere. They're economical to produce and sell, durable, and easy to replace when they wear out, which they are of course designed to do at some point so the company can sell more. But profit motive (and cynicism) aside, Wonder Widget has a pretty enlightened management team when it comes to sharing its financial position with its employees. The company long ago adopted a practice called Open Book Management, which means management regularly shares the company's financial reports with the employees, so everyone in the company feels they're seeing the results of their efforts reflected in the company's success. To achieve that, management takes pains to design the financial reports to be easy to read without sacrificing accuracy or usefulness. So I decided to use this company as an example of good reporting when most of the readers will be nonfinancial people. Like many of my clients. Like you.

Chapters 2 through 6 cover the basic financial reports you should typically see on a monthly basis, with lots of tips on reading, understanding, and using the information they contain. For that reason, as your first objective, I suggest you read, and perhaps reread, Chapters 2 through 6, in order, until you feel comfortable with them.

Then I suggest you proceed to Chapters 7 and 8, which delve into the "hidden information" that Wonder Widget and every company has. Each explores a specific analysis area in which basic financial information is reorganized and discussed in more depth to present that hidden information. The objective of these chapters is for you to know how to get to that information—get it into reports *and* understand what the reports are telling you.

Chapter 7 focuses on Wonder Widget's operating ratios, which are selected relational calculations based on numbers in the financial statements. The ratios show the relationship between two variables that may not be apparent from a casual reading of the statements, but that are important to assessing a company's financial health. We discuss some of the most common and useful ratios and how you can use them to better understand the underlying strength of whatever it is they measure. This is a chapter you might return to often as a handy reference.

Chapter 8 explains the essentials of cost accounting—how it works and why it's so important in helping a company control its gross profit margins. The purpose of cost accounting is to enable managers to know the true cost of the products or services their company sells so they can choose to sell more of the profitable ones and fewer of the unprofitable ones.

Chapters 9 and 10 present material not covered in the first edition. The content covers decision-making tools that every company needs when investing in growth or new products, or even when choosing between investment alternatives or enhancing existing products. Wonder Widget management performed all these activities at one time or another. They used investment return analysis to determine the best use of the company's investment capital, and they used breakeven analysis to decide how much to invest in new product development, how to price products, and how to set goals for their sales department, all decisions that require focused financial analysis.

Chapters 11 and 12 explore the critical management function of planning, including operational planning and budgeting. These sections are placed near the end of the book so that you first acquire an understanding of the types of things you typically plan for—profits, cash flow, and financing the business—before you get into the planning itself. Chapter 11 discusses business planning—the importance of planning, the difference between strategic planning and operational planning, using vision and mission as the starting point for planning strategy, and setting long-term and short-term goals. Chapter 12 considers budgeting, that is, how to best allocate the company's resources to achieve the goals set out in the business plan.

Chapter 13 explains the fundamentals of financing a business—getting the capital to launch it and the working capital to operate it. This is an important area for growing businesses everywhere, because growth consumes capital, often at a pace faster than a growing business can create that capital internally. This chapter looks at both debt and equity financing, explains some of the techniques used to get the needed capital, and discusses some of the advantages and disadvantages of each.

Finally, for those of you starting your own business or hoping to, Chapter 14 discusses some basics of attracting capital to a new venture. This is a path chosen by more and more budding entrepreneurs as they see untapped opportunities created by the digital age and by managers in large companies that experience layoffs. They come to understand what I tell the consultants I mentor: The only real job security comes from the business you build for yourself. (But that's another story for a different book.)

It's my hope that you'll refer to sections of this book many times over, long after you've finished your "first read." By using this book as an ongoing reference, you'll reinforce the book's lessons and find new ways to use it with each reading.

## Special Features

Titles in the Briefcase Books series are designed to give you practical information written in a friendly, person-to-person style. The chapters deal with tactical issues and include lots of examples. They also feature numerous sidebars that give you different types of specific information. Here's a description of the sidebars you'll find in this book.

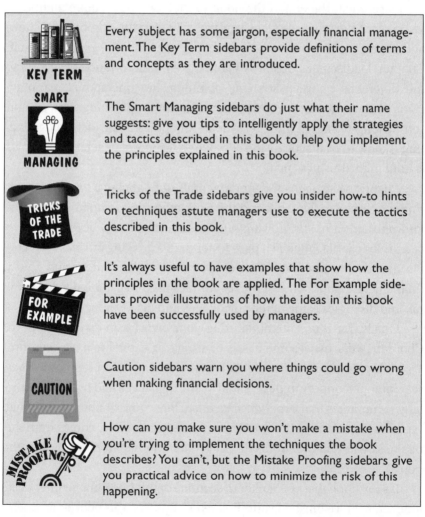

**KEY TERM**

Every subject has some jargon, especially financial management. The Key Term sidebars provide definitions of terms and concepts as they are introduced.

**SMART MANAGING**

The Smart Managing sidebars do just what their name suggests: give you tips to intelligently apply the strategies and tactics described in this book to help you implement the principles explained in this book.

**TRICKS OF THE TRADE**

Tricks of the Trade sidebars give you insider how-to hints on techniques astute managers use to execute the tactics described in this book.

**FOR EXAMPLE**

It's always useful to have examples that show how the principles in the book are applied. The For Example sidebars provide illustrations of how the ideas in this book have been successfully used by managers.

**CAUTION**

Caution sidebars warn you where things could go wrong when making financial decisions.

**MISTAKE PROOFING**

How can you make sure you won't make a mistake when you're trying to implement the techniques the book describes? You can't, but the Mistake Proofing sidebars give you practical advice on how to minimize the risk of this happening.

**TOOLS**

The Tools sidebars provide specific directions for implementing the techniques described in the book in a systematic fashion.

# Counting the Beans: Why Good Financial Information Is Critical to You

T he young adults of every generation believe the business environment in which they work is tougher than ever before. Today we are no exception. And those who follow us will likely be no exception. Well, guess what? Everybody's right!

## Managing a Company in Today's Business Environment

As business gets more competitive, more global, more technologically driven, it gets easier for others to compete with you. It gets harder to be successful by just doing OK. It gets harder to launch a good product and enjoy the benefits of your innovation for long without serious competition. And, yes, it does get tougher to make a living. In our parents' time, performance that was good enough to get by and make a decent living isn't good enough today. You may have read that many of us will fail to achieve the relative standard of living that our parents did because of this tougher world. It was recently reported that U.S. workers don't begin to earn a median-wage income (about $42,000) until they are 30 years old (*The Wall Street Journal*, September 30, 2013). Of course, if you've been alive for the past 10 or 15 years, you also know that there are unprecedented opportunities to create new wealth, new products, new companies, and new fortunes. It's unlikely that our forefathers could have imagined fortunes being made, and lost, as quickly as they were in the last decade.

So it's hard to dispute that times are more challenging now. The question is: What can you do about it? The answer: You can't do much about the times, but you can do a lot about how you prepare for them. And that's what this book is about.

When I was a youngster, my father owned and ran a small grocery store that supplied the neighbors with their daily household needs. This was long before supermarkets killed the mom-and-pops that existed then in every neighborhood. When school was over, I went to the store to help out my parents. My first job was opening cases of packaged goods, pricing the packages, and stocking the shelves. Then I packed groceries and delivered them to customers, sometimes after taking their order over the phone and personally filling it. (Yes, that was how many small stores did business back then.) Then I graduated to cutting meat in the fresh meat department. When I was in junior high school, I was working the cash register, opening the store in the morning, and finally, running the store when my parents went on a rare vacation. By the time I was in high school, I had run every aspect of a small business, including setting up and closing out the cash register and doing the bookkeeping at the end of the day.

In today's business terms, I had worked in Shipping/Receiving, Warehousing and Inventory Control, Production, Sales, Delivery, Billing and Collection, Accounting, and General Management.

Uncommon today? Yes, and yet that kind of diverse background is exactly what's increasingly demanded of today's up-and-coming professionals. Not necessarily in delivering groceries, but in many other ways. Managers in companies large and small—including directors, vice presidents, and general managers—are finding their particular specialties aren't going to carry them to the finish line as they might once have. Today's report card on performance includes finance, and that has caught many managers by surprise.

A generation ago, senior managers and company executives were challenged by the arrival of the personal computer and their lack of knowledge of this new tool. No matter how firmly they knew their own particular areas of expertise, the young professionals coming into the business often made their bosses look old-fashioned with their mastery of this impressive and intimidating technology. Soon, those young professionals had children, whose computer acumen after being on the planet for only a few years made even their savvy parents sit up and take notice. And so it goes. We need more knowledge of more subjects to succeed. Technology and finance are making demands on us in new ways virtually every year.

Now finance and accounting impact many companies in ways managers outside the financial department never thought about. The accounting scandals at the start of this century (Enron, Worldcom, and others) showed that financial incompetence or carelessness or simply lack of integrity could wipe out the efforts (and jobs) of thousands of loyal, hard-working employees. Then the financial meltdown of 2008–2010 showed that even the financial "experts" didn't always know what they were doing. Their mistakes (or willful ignorance) contributed to the near-collapse of the financial system, throwing the global economy into the deepest recession since the Great Depression. The report card, it seems, has become more important than it ever was when we were in school. Today's business "report card" is its financial report.

Today we're finding that we need to know how to read that report card just to keep our jobs, let alone advance in our careers. Boards of directors now need to delve into a company's financial reports to a degree never before contemplated. They need to understand—and even challenge—financial terminology and accounting methods they might previously have taken for granted. CEOs now must be completely aware of what their people are doing and the financial ramifications, because saying they didn't know is no longer an acceptable excuse. Managers within a company, large or small, must understand the basic rules of accounting and finance well enough to avoid getting into trouble while aggressively trying to make their goals. Those who aspire to become managers may not even get a start up the ladder until they can demonstrate this kind of knowledge. So you see, the need for a basic understanding of finance touches everyone.

Financial scandals make headlines, but they aren't going to make anyone learn more about finance and accounting. What's the real reason to

**KEY TERM** **Budget** A projection of the detailed income and expenses that are esti- mated to occur in a speci- fied future period, usually prepared on a month-to-month basis for up to a year. Each item of income and expense is listed, along with the amount each is expected to add to or subtract from the profit for the period.

know this stuff? Consider the new manager who is asked to prepare a budget for his or her department.

How do you begin to pull together a budget? How about sales? Do you start with what you hope you can sell? What you're sure you can sell? What you sold last year or last month? What management will believe?

OK, if that's too confusing, maybe you could start with expenses. What do you need to spend? What you spent last year or last month? What you hope you can get approval to spend? Do you know what everything will cost?

Just knowing where to begin is a challenge. And then how do you decide how much money or staffing you'll need to reach your goals or that your boss wants you to achieve?

Whew! Why can't the finance department do this for you?

The truth is, they can't. Oh, sure, finance can prepare something that looks like a budget, and in many companies that's what happens. But then it's not really your budget; it's theirs. If you miss the target finance sets, well, it's not really your problem, now, is it? As managers we know that each department understands its unique needs and capabilities bet- ter than anyone else. And we know from Management 101 that a goal must be accepted—better yet, owned—by the people who actually will do the work for there to be a strong commitment to achieving it. Simply put, that's why each department within the organization must do its own budget and, therefore, why its managers must learn to budget effectively. And, yes, you'll need to be able to answer, at some level, all the questions I've raised above. Happily, Chapter 12 in this book will help you do that.

# The Role of the Finance Department
## The Two Sides of Finance

The Finance Department has two distinct jobs to perform in most companies: managing the company's financial resources (finance) and recording and reporting all its financial transactions (accounting). Today many small and midsized companies don't establish separate Finance and Accounting departments. A company might instead have

> **Chief Financial Officer (CFO)** The job title of the executive in charge of all the financial activities in all large companies and most midsized ones. Smaller companies might instead place their financial activities under a vice president for finance or a controller, depending on how they define the responsibilities of these people.
>
> **KEY TERM**

a chief financial officer (CFO) who performs or oversees the company's finance functions and accounting activities. Larger companies are likely to have separate departments for finance and accounting that report to the CFO.

## Finance

The Finance Department may be responsible for an assortment of functions, depending on the company. It might oversee insurance and risk management, contract pricing and administration, internal auditing, investor relations, and more. At a minimum, Finance is likely responsible for treasury activities (cash management, etc.), often under the direction of an executive with the title of treasurer or vice president for finance. His or her role likely includes cash management, bank relations, investments, and everything having to do with making sure the organization has enough cash to pay its employees and its bills, and productively investing excess cash.

> ### DON'T JUDGE THE EXECUTIVE BOOK BY ITS COVER
> While we've tried to give you a general idea of what job titles might do which jobs, these are generalizations that do not apply to every company, and maybe not yours. Some companies are more liberal than others in granting titles. Others might employ less commonly used titles such as director of finance or vice president of administration or even manager of accounting for the head financial executive in their organization. If you need to determine exactly who does what, obtain an organization chart or ask someone in Human Resources or Finance. It could spare you embarrassment or, even worse, getting the wrong information.
>
> **CAUTION**

Major activities like mergers and acquisitions, attracting investment capital, and internal management of public stock offerings usually fall within the Finance Department's responsibility, because that's all about making sure the company has enough cash to carry out its plans. When a company decides to sell its stock in the public marketplace for the first time—in an initial public offering (IPO)—it almost always places the task of coordinating that transition in the hands of the Finance Department.

## Accounting

The accounting job is typically done by the Accounting Department, led by an accounting manager, controller, comptroller, or someone with a similar title. These folks record all the transactions that occur as the company does its business and then prepare reports that help them, company management, and outside constituencies understand the financial impact of those transactions.

The accountants maintain the accounting software, process all the paperwork that documents transactions that have occurred, and record them into the company's general ledger. Most of these transactions are recorded in dollars and cents, or the appropriate foreign currency for operations outside the United States. Some transactions keep track of other units of measure besides currency, such as the number of pieces of inventory in the warehouse, the number of vehicles in the company fleet, and so on.

**General ledger** The principal accounting record to which all company transactions are recorded and summarized. The general ledger is the record from which information for the basic financial reports is drawn. These reports vary greatly in look and wording among organizations. General ledgers were once huge books maintained with carefully handwritten entries, but today nearly all entries are documented with computer software.

**KEY TERM**

Of course, keeping records of financial transactions tucked away in some computer serves no one unless we can get access to the information when we need it. So, from all those transaction records the accountants prepare a variety of reports. Some are for people outside your company, such as government agencies, your bankers, investors, and stockholders. But the reports that are most important to running the company are those the accountants prepare for company managers, for it is these reports that managers use to understand their company's financial past and present, and make decisions about its financial future.

As you will learn later in this book or as you may already have discovered the hard way, the readability of those reports is a huge factor in their value. To put it another way, you can't use a report you don't understand, no matter how valuable the information it contains.

Unfortunately, some managers view the computerized financial reports produced by their company's accounting programs as technical, irrelevant, and nearly useless in their decision making. (We discuss some of these reports in depth in Chapters 3 and 4.) Managers often have good reason to feel that way, it seems to me, because these basic financial reports were designed for use by outsiders! Their primary purpose is to give a snapshot of a company's financial condition to people outside the company—bankers, government regulators, stock analysts, investors, and others who have no direct role in running the company. Despite this, these reports provide a summary of the company's monthly or quarterly operations. They present this information in a standard, consistent, and familiar format, which makes them credible and more useful. They also serve as the basis for more tailored and typically more useful reports, which we discuss later in this book. How do we do that? With a fictitious company that does everything right, of course.

## The Wonder Widget Company Is Our Guide

Learning is easier and more effective when students can picture the thing being learned in context with something already familiar to them. On the assumption that you are working in a company now—otherwise why would you care about this stuff?—the context that makes the most sense is a simulated company. Our imaginary company uses the tools we discuss, issues the reports we talk about, and is challenged to understand their financial data to run their company more effectively.

Allow me to introduce The Wonder Widget Company, a manufacturer of premium-quality widgets that are sold across the country by a team of strong in-house salespeople. Wonder Widget is privately owned, so we don't have to deal with its stock price or the public company reporting rules published by the Securities and Exchange Commission (SEC), which would needlessly complicate our lives as it does for today's public companies. Although I occasionally bring in a topic that mostly applies to public companies (e.g., stock price or equity financing), my assumption is that you want to learn about finance, not government regulations, stockholder lawsuits, and investor relations. Besides, the vast majority of companies in this country are privately owned, so chances are good that your employer is a privately owned company. Throughout this book, we follow Wonder Widget and learn how its managers deal with the financial issues they must address.

SMART

MANAGING

**YOU DON'T GET WHAT YOU DON'T ASK FOR**

Some accounting departments produce reports that they never distribute outside their department simply because no one has ever asked for them. These reports, perhaps produced as part of a standard computerized process or to serve a limited departmental purpose, might contain information that could be useful to you—indeed, it could be the information you've been trying to collect on the back of an envelope for months. If your Accounting Department doesn't know you want a report, it's unlikely to go looking for you when the report is printed. Tell Accounting what you would like to know and ask what kinds of reports are produced that don't get distributed. There just may be a gem hidden in the Accounting file cabinet or stored on the company's computer network.

## The "Rules" of Financial Reporting

The standard format for recording and reporting financial transactions in the United States is outlined in guidelines, or rules, called *Generally Accepted Accounting Principles* (*GAAP*). These guidelines are published by the accounting profession (with some gentle prodding from the U.S. government) and have been evolving ever since their origin in the aftermath of the 1929 stock market crash. They are intended to be the foundation upon which readers of these reports can gauge a company's progress, compare one company or one accounting period with another, and judge the financial effectiveness of a company's management efforts.

As we've seen, it doesn't always work out that way, but that's not necessarily because the rules are flawed. The job of creating comparable accounting and reporting standards for widely varied businesses is a daunting task for the folks who set the standards. The objective of each accounting rule is to record a transaction so that it makes economic sense for the company and for readers of the company's reports. Yet to achieve that objective, accountants in two dissimilar companies might need to record the same transaction differently. And that's just in the United States. Consider the additional complications of creating comparability for a company that operates in more than one country, or in some cases dozens of countries, each with regulators holding different views of what accounting rules should look like.

> **Generally Accepted Accounting Principles (GAAP)** A set of rules, conventions, standards, and **KEY TERM** procedures established by the Financial Accounting Standards Board (FASB) and its predecessors for reporting financial information in a consistent manner to facilitate understanding and comparison.

That's been the dilemma for financial reporting since companies started operating globally after the end of World War II. By the late 1900s the recognized need for international standards led to the creation of the International Accounting Standards Board (IASB), followed by various levels of collaboration between the United States and the European Union to try to agree on a common set of reporting rules. It's a work in progress, and likely will be for many more years, given the usual political and economic differences between the countries that most influence rule setting. The main reason for discussing it here is to make you aware that some financial reports of companies with multinational operations might employ IASB rules, while other companies reporting in the United States may employ GAAP under the U.S.-based FASB.

Why do you care? For most of us it's a minor issue because differences are often subtle and esoteric. But for those of you who are serious investors outside your work, comparisons between U.S. and foreign companies often have anomalies you should be aware of.

OK, let's get back to understanding the differences among U.S. companies operating under GAAP. Some of these differences are far from trivial.

### ARE ALL FORDS CREATED EQUAL?

**FOR EXAMPLE** Two companies purchase identical Ford Taurus automobiles. Company A will use its vehicle for occasional corporate visitors, so it's expected to last about five years. Company B will add its new Ford to its fleet of taxis, so the car is expected to last only about 18 months. Over which of the following periods of time would an accountant in each of these companies depreciate or expense the purchase?

- 5 years
- 18 months
- 3 years (an average)
- different periods in different companies, based on the vehicle's useful life in each company

The choice of how quickly to depreciate a car (or other asset) will affect the profits of the company that buys it. The choices companies make must reflect their particular circumstances. Wrong choices could lead to confusion and misstatement. However, setting one absolute rule for all companies would create different problems and perhaps greater confusion. This need for some flexibility is why we have generally accepted accounting *principles*, rather than *rules*. These principles have been the basis for reasonable estimates and unreasonable abuses for many years, with the abuses typically getting a lot more press.

Incidentally, the correct answer is the last choice.

We devote a fair amount of time in this book to helping you understand how to read and use these primary financial statements, prepared in accordance with GAAP. We also discuss special-purpose reports that company management may find useful for internal purposes. Our comments in all cases assume the use of GAAP, except where we specifically note exceptions.

## The Relationship of Finance and Accounting to the Other Departments

The Finance Department in every company has, in theory, two primary areas of responsibility:

1.  Finance must safeguard company assets by properly accounting for them, instituting internal controls to prevent their misuse or loss, and generally monitoring their proper use. In this role, Finance becomes a policing activity, making sure others don't damage the company through their actions.

2. Finance organizes all the data it collects about company transactions and presents that data in a form everyone in the company can use to most effectively manage their own functions and the company as a whole. In this sense, Finance provides information to help other departments—its customers—do their jobs, and ideally to do them better.

While these functions should generally carry equal importance for company management, they aren't always carried out with equal enthusiasm by financial departments. In some companies, financial departments focus more on assertive policing than on serving the users of financial information. Policy constraints and procedural labyrinths seem to be the predominant preoccupation of these accountants, to the frustration of many outside the Finance Department. Yet in other companies, the strong direction of operationally driven management can result in a financial department that's totally occupied with servicing a continuous flow of requests for ad hoc information, at the expense of the protection function. In these companies, folks outside of Finance get their needs met, but auditors and others outside the company may become concerned about the safety of the company's assets and the efficient use of its resources.

In a perfect world, then, these functions would be balanced in a way that serves the best interests of the company's owners. A financial department that implements adequate internal controls and enforces them with appropriate levels of enthusiasm would have time and resources to serve the reasonable information needs of the enterprise as well. However, in reality, finding this balance is one of the most challenging management jobs in the company.

# Manager's Checklist for Chapter 1

☑ Managers need to understand the rules of accounting and the boundaries of proper finance well enough to avoid getting into trouble as they aggressively pursue their goals.

☑ The Finance Department has two distinct jobs to perform in most companies: managing the company's financial resources (finance) and recording and reporting all its financial transactions (accounting).

☑ The standard format for recording and reporting financial transactions is outlined in guidelines, or rules, called Generally Accepted Accounting Principles (GAAP).

☑ One of the greatest challenges for management is to balance the two primary responsibilities of the Finance Department: (1) to safeguard the assets of the company by properly accounting for them and monitoring their use, and (2) to organize information from transactions and present it in reports that help managers function more effectively.

# The Structure and Interrelationship of Financial Statements

Every corporation has, from the moment it's formed, an indefinite life under the law. The corporate laws of every state grant a corporation the right to perpetual existence to enable management to take strategic actions that will have a long-term impact on the company's survival and growth. These include making long-term contracts and issuing certificates of ownership (stock) that don't expire.

But perpetual existence is only a legal concept. In reality, most companies follow a pattern of birth, rapid growth, slowing growth, plateau or no growth, decline, and demise (Figure 2-1). That is, unless they've learned how to evolve, i.e., adapt, to a changing world.

Companies that react effectively to change can minimize or even avoid decline and demise, but those are natural phases in the lifecycle. There are companies whose names are as familiar to you as they were to your grandparents; these are the ones that learned how to extend their lifecycle.

Unfortunately, most new companies follow the more typical pattern, most eventually closing their doors. If you were even a moderate investor in the dot-com era of the '90s, you likely are able to rattle off a half-dozen names of once-promising companies that no longer exist (hopefully not because you owned their stock). Outside the technology industry there were also many companies that didn't have the right stuff to remain inde-

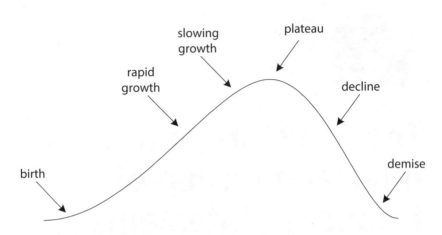

**Figure 2-1.** The lifecycle of a company

pendent and have fallen. The list continued to grow as the 21st century got under way. Household names that are rapidly fading into history include TWA, Worldcom, Enron, Arthur Andersen, and more recently, Tower Records, Circuit City, Sharper Image, and Borders Bookstores. The economic upheavals of the last 15 years or so have proven fatal to companies that had been around for decades. That includes a few financial names that seemed long-lived: Lehman Brothers, Countrywide, Washington Mutual, Wachovia, and of course the biggest scam in history, Madoff Investment Securities.

Many more companies that didn't actually close their doors were acquired at fire sale prices by other companies and lost their separate existence, becoming merely a unit of a larger, more successful company. You can still see names like Texaco, RCA, Merrill Lynch, and Chrysler, but none of these companies exist today as a standalone entity.

Yet good companies continue to grow through successive periods of renewal, rebirth, and resurgence. Multiple examples of these can be found in names we recognize—IBM, Intel, and Apple, to name a few.

A few excellent companies, by contrast, seem to be forever resurgent. While they may occasionally pause in their progress, they never seem to actually go into decline. Examples include General Electric, Southwest Airlines, Walmart, and Microsoft.

A major similarity among these companies, perhaps the overriding one, is their ability to react to change. Change impacts a company's ability to capture and hold its market, grow its business, profitably sell its products, and ultimately, survive and prosper (Figure 2-2).

**Figure 2-2.** The lifecycle of a well-managed company

My 25-plus years of consulting experience tell me that the tendency of most business activity is to find those processes that seem to work and then repeat them over and over as long as they continue to function. This is considered efficient and is a proven technique for maximizing profitability. However, every company or department manager must learn to differentiate between those business processes that must evolve, like research and development, and those that should remain stable. *Financial accounting is one of those processes that needs a high degree of stability.* Financial statements are a key source of information managers need to help them decide how to keep their companies evolving, re-inventing themselves, and remaining profitable in a rapidly changing world.

## Tracking a Company's Lifecycle

As we have learned in the past few years, financial accounting needs more stability and less creative accounting than it has experienced to give it adequate credibility in the eyes of the users of financial information. Managers rely on financial reports prepared from accounting data to guide their business decisions. Investors rely on those same reports to guide their investment decisions. Government relies on many of the same reports to collect taxes, enforce our laws, and protect the company's investors, employees, and customers. Thus the recorders of a company's financial data carry a heavy responsibility to provide information that is, in a word, ARTistic—*Accurate, Relevant,* and *Timely.*

While accounting rules change to respond to changing business models and new types of business transactions, those changes must reflect the responsibility accounting has to all its constituents: to produce information that they can rely on. As you will read, that isn't always easy, but it's every bit as important as it sounds. That's why accounting as a business process should remain fairly *stable*, evolving only after careful consideration of the implications of reporting transactions differently than they might have been recorded previously. Remember that a major use of financial information is to make comparisons with similar information from earlier periods. If the accounting methods are different, the comparisons and, hence, conclusions may be flawed. As we have learned from the reports of financial shenanigans in recent years, it is too easy to create incorrect conclusions if the rules allow too much flexibility.

---

**TRICKS OF THE TRADE**

### ARTistic Financial Reports

Unlike the "creative" financial reporting adopted by formerly major companies in the news in the past few years, ARTistic reports are the cornerstone of sound reporting; that is, financial information that's:

- **Accurate**—Prepared with sufficient accuracy to be relied upon, and yet without requiring such a high degree of accuracy as to make them too expensive or too time-consuming to produce. This balance concept in financial reporting is called *materiality*. Generally, a transaction is considered to be material if the financial report reader would be likely to be influenced by knowing it. Materiality is usually evaluated in terms of the amount of money involved, relative to the whole.
- **Relevant**—Presented in a format that is useful to those who must use the information. A detailed listing of transactions with no totals or explanation might be accurate, but it's of little use to anyone and, so, likely irrelevant for most business purposes.
- **Timely**—Produced in time to be useful to those who need it. A totally accurate, relevant report that comes out many months late is of little value because managers likely will have had to make decisions before it was available.

---

In addition to stability, one of the key characteristics of the accounting process is *repeatability*. The accounting process achieves the highest degree of accuracy, relevance, and timeliness by use of its repetitive methodologies, enabling accountants to process the most data at the least cost. The most common repetitive process in the accounting world is the monthly closing cycle. A company goes through the traditional monthly routine of "closing the books" to see how the company is doing in terms of its financial objectives, including profitability. That accounting cycle, and the information value it produces, is perhaps best demonstrated by *not* going to a football game.

## Accounting Is Like a Football Game on Your DVR

Imagine yourself at home on a November Saturday evening. You're looking forward to watching the football game that was played earlier in the day while you were doing chores. You digitally recorded the entire game and now you want to watch it and enjoy all the nuances of the action. You bring up the recording, settle back into your easy chair, and press Play.

In the very first big play of the game, your team's quarterback takes the snap, steps back, and deftly throws the ball to a receiver 30 yards downfield. Just as the receiver reaches out to catch the ball, a defender's hands block him and prevent the catch. You're out of your seat in an instant, demanding the referee call interference and penalize the defender. Then you realize you can replay the action and see if there was any illegal pushing. You stop the video, go back to the moment of the play, and freeze the action so you can study it in detail. Even though the action didn't stop, your recorder gives you the ability to pause and review any segment of the play action. Notice on the stopped video that the ball is frozen in mid-air and the players reaching for it are similarly frozen in time, feet high off the ground. You can see exactly where everything was at that moment—the players, the referee, and even the players in the background who were part of the action elsewhere on the field. In a real sense, it's a snapshot of a game moment, a single instant in the 60 minutes of playing time.

Grudgingly satisfied that there was no interference, you restart the recording. Your team marches down the field, nicely mixing running and passing, until it has a first down on the visitor's 8-yard line. In a well-executed running play, your team's running back takes the ball and charges through the pack, only to be tackled at the goal line. Did he get over or not? The referee says no. Once again, you stop the recording, back up a few seconds, and review. This time you're sure the ref is blind, because you've made your own analysis of the data and are convinced the score should now be 6–0 in favor of your team.

Keep in mind that the game was played hours earlier, before you got a chance to watch it, and it went on continuously for three hours (counting pileups, commercials, and halftime). Despite your ability to stop the recording whenever you chose, in reality, the game never stopped. Your tools enabled you to look back and analyze the action in as much depth as you wanted, because your DVR had recorded all the details of the game. In picture form, that might look like Figure 2-3.

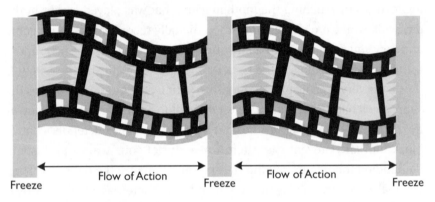

Freeze  ◄——— Flow of Action ———►  Freeze  ◄——— Flow of Action ———►  Freeze

**Figure 2-3.** Flow of the action

As you can see in Figure 2-3, the action flows throughout the recording, but your periodic Pause commands to your remote resulted in an artificial stop in the action. When you press Play, the action resumes exactly where it left off, as if the Pause had never happened. Each vertical bar on the chart represents the freeze frame actions you took in an otherwise continuous flow of activity.

Now consider the financial transactions that occur every day in your company. Employees arrive, do their work, and get paid. The company buys products and services, pays for them, adds its value to what it buys, and delivers the products or services to its customers. Then it bills those customers and collects what they owe, enabling it to pay its own bills. This flow of activity is continuous every business day, all year long, for as many years as the company is in business. Once a month the Finance Department produces a report that starts on the first day of each month and ends on the last day of that month. The accountants have found a way to stop the action for their purposes, even though it never stops in reality, so they could report on the results for each period of "the game." The accountants succeeded because they, too, "recorded" the action. Think of the accounting books as an Accounting Transaction Recorder, or ATR. Now we might change the labels of Figure 2-3 to those shown in Figure 2-4 and see some similarities between the two recordings.

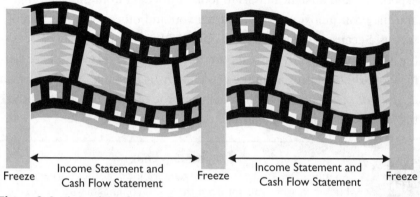

| Freeze | Income Statement and Cash Flow Statement | Freeze | Income Statement and Cash Flow Statement | Freeze |

**Figure 2-4.** Flow of the financial action

As you can see, Record starts when the business starts and the Pause status is captured in the company's balance sheet at the end of each period. Then there is a continuous flow of action, captured in the company's income statement and its statement of cash flow. The action never stops, but periodically, usually once a month, the accountants press Pause on their recorders so they can analyze in detail the progress the company has made. They then give you an income statement and statement of cash flow that total the changes that happened during the month-long activity. You also get a balance sheet, which shows where everything was on the last day of the month, when the accountants pressed Pause: how much the company was owed by customers, how much cash it had in the bank, how much it owed to creditors at that moment, and more. Much like the paused play in the football game, the balance sheet is a snapshot of a single instant in the life of the company.

What's the big difference here? For the football game, you had to do your own analysis, using only your eyesight and your knowledge of the game. Of course, you can get extra value from hearing the announcers, particularly the ex-coach-turned-announcer, because they always describe things that their experience and keen eyes picked up that you didn't. The better you know the game, of course, the more useful information you can get from what the announcer says, although most will miss the nuances.

In your company, by comparison, the accountants likely have in-depth experience and analytical tools to look at the data from different angles, and they can prepare reports that tell you and others what the analysis reveals. Because you are using the financial Record and Replay devices—the ATR—you can study those reports at your leisure and even ask for clarification without losing a minute of company "game time." You could read the reports yourself without their help, but you probably couldn't produce the reports without their help, because you don't have an ATR.

**TRICKS OF THE TRADE**

## THE INSIDE EDGE

The more you know about the game of football, the more valuable the insights you get from the game commentary, even though most viewers will miss most of the nuances. Not surprising, the analogy carries over to financial reports. The more familiar you are with the concepts of accounting and finance, the more of the "hidden" information you'll get from your company's financial reports and the less time it will take you to get it, even though others may miss the point entirely.

# The Chart of Accounts: A Collection of Buckets

If you've seen a chart of accounts, you probably wondered why the accountants hold this list in such high regard. You might hear comments like, "It's not in the chart of accounts. We don't know where to put it." Or, "We can't process your invoice without an account number." While to many nonfinancial managers, these phrases might seem intended primarily to retard the progress of commerce, that's really not their purpose—honest!

The entire recording process of any accounting system requires a basic organization of data; for example, the payment of vendor invoices can be summarized and clearly reported as to what was done, why it was done, and what organization(s) benefited from those expenditures. That basic organization is called a *chart of accounts.*

You might think of the organizing system for your company's accounting data as a collection of buckets, or accounts, with each bucket holding a particular kind of data. There is probably a bucket for each asset the company owns and a bucket for each debt the company owes. There is also a bucket

> **Chart of accounts** A systematic listing of all the general ledger account names (and associated numbers) **KEY TERM** used by a company, arranged in the order in which they normally appear in financial statements—customarily Assets, Liabilities, Owners' Equity (or Stockholders' Equity), Revenue, and Expenses. The purpose of the chart of accounts is to enable the classification of transactions into groups of similar transactions to make reporting and analysis easier and more productive.

for each product or service the company sells and one for each type of expense the company might incur as it sells its products or services. A company might have 200 or more buckets to hold all the transaction data about each asset and liability and each income and expense category. Some companies have many more in order to capture data even more precisely in the interest of greater accuracy.

The chart of accounts is an organized, comprehensive list of all those buckets. Each bucket, in turn, is labeled with its appropriate account number and arranged by the kind of data it holds, so that accountants can quickly find the right bucket to store a new piece of data about a particular asset or liability. These buckets are then arranged and rearranged during the accounting process and their contents are counted and checked—usually monthly—to produce reports that summarize the data they contain.

Take a quick look at the abbreviated chart of accounts in Figure 2-5, to get an idea of what it might look like in a typical company. We discuss and define the major categories in the chart of accounts in Chapters 3 and 4, when we talk about the basic financial statements. You don't need to memorize what the chart of accounts looks like, as long as you remember its importance in categorizing raw accounting data into useful information.

Notice that accountants use a numbering convention to differentiate assets from liabilities and income from expenses. There are endless vari-

| Account Number | Account Description |
|---|---|
| | **Assets** |
| 1000 | Cash |
| 1100 | Short-Term Investments |
| 1200 | Accounts Receivable—Trade |
| 1250 | Allowance for Uncollectable Accounts |
| 1500 | Fixed Assets |
| 1510 | Land and Buildings |
| 1520 | Machinery and Equipment |
| 1530 | Accumulated Depreciation |
| 1600 | Deposits |
| 1900 | Long-Term Investments |
| | **Liabilities** |
| 2100 | Accounts Payable—Trade |
| 2200 | Accrued Payroll and Benefits |
| 2220 | Accrued Payroll |
| 2230 | Accrued Payroll Taxes |
| 2300 | Other Accrued Liabilities |
| 2500 | Contracts Payable for Leased Equipment |
| 2700 | Long-Term Notes Payable |
| | **Stockholders' Equity** |
| 3100 | Capital Stock |
| 3500 | Retained Earnings |
| | **Income** |
| 4100 | Sales of Widgets |
| 4110 | Sales of Super Widgets |
| 4120 | Sales Discounts and Allowances |

**Figure 2-5.** Wonder Widget chart of accounts (continued on next page)

| | Cost of Goods Sold |
|---|---|
| 6000 | Sales and Marketing Expenses |
| 6100 | Salaries and Wages |
| 6120 | Travel Expenses |
| 6130 | Telephone |
| 6200 | Advertising |
| 6300 | Trade Shows |
| 7000 | General and Administrative Expenses |
| 7100 | Salaries and Wages |
| 7200 | Insurance |
| 7300 | Postage and Mailing |
| 7400 | Professional Fees Paid |
| | ... and so on |

**Figure 2-5.** Wonder Widget chart of accounts (continued)

ations on account numbering, but all follow some similar kind of arrangement to facilitate transaction coding. Notice that some accounts are indented and numbered to indicate they are subordinate to others. These subaccounts provide a breakdown of the larger categories into smaller categories to save time and readily provide more detail later when users are analyzing the data.

If you have spending authority in your company, you may be asked to approve invoices from vendors. In some companies, that approval process includes assigning an account number to the invoice to advise the accountants into which bucket the transaction belongs. In other companies, a purchase order must be issued with all the account information that Accounting needs to process vendor invoices. If you are blessed to be in the latter group, you may never need to know anything more about the chart of accounts except that it exists.

## The General Ledger: Balancing the Buckets

You've probably heard the term *general ledger* and might even have joked that this must be the guy who secretly runs Accounting and issues all those reports no one can read. (Well, maybe not.) As mentioned in Chapter 1, the original general ledger was a large book with ruled pages into which all the transactions were carefully recorded by hand. It's now likely to be a computer file, but it still carries the traditional name, and it's still the place where all accounting transactions ultimately are recorded. It's also the data source for most of the basic financial statements that companies produce.

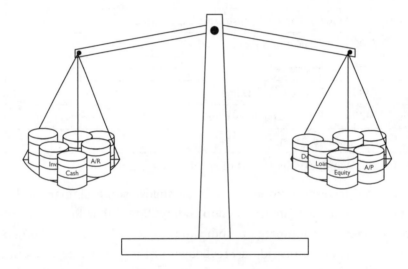

**Figure 2-6.** The balance sheet balances!

Think of the general ledger as an old-fashioned weight scale that's always in balance because its keepers always add or subtract equal and offsetting amounts to each side whenever they weigh something. All the buckets that appear in the chart of accounts are arranged in one or the other of the scales, depending on the account number on the bucket.

As each transaction occurs and is entered into the accounting system, the accountants refer to the chart of accounts to find the name and location of the correct bucket(s). Then they add to each bucket the appropriate amount that represents the financial effect of that transaction. When they add something to a bucket on the Asset side, such as a new delivery truck, they must finish the job in one of two ways to rebalance

## SURPRISE! THE BALANCE SHEET ALWAYS BALANCES!

One relationship is fundamental to financial accounting: Total assets must *always* equal the sum of total liabilities and total stockholders' equity. Thus, if a company is able to conduct its financial affairs in such a way that it can add assets without adding an equal amount of liabilities, it effectively increases the relative weight (i.e., value) of the company's ownership. Remember: The two sides must always balance, according to the formula that is always true under the rules of accounting:

**Total assets – Total liabilities = Stockholders' equity**

Now, what this means to you is this: The simplest way to increase Assets without increasing Liabilities by an equal amount is to make a profit.

**Stockholders' equity** The amount that would theoretically remain if all the assets were sold and all the liabilities were paid off, at the values shown in the company's general ledger. Stockholders' equity typically comprises the total amount

KEY TERM

invested in the company by its owners plus accumulated profits of the business since inception.

Stockholders' equity is not a reflection of the dollar amount that would be realized if the company were liquidated, however, because liquidation almost always produces a cash return that differs from the originally recorded amounts. For example, liquidated equipment would probably be sold at a sharp discount, sometimes at a fraction of the amount recorded in the general ledger. Thus, stockholders' equity is a guide—a reasonable approximation—rather than an accurate measure of the owners' relative share of the business. Other terms that mean the same include *owners' equity* (often used for a sole proprietorship or partnership), *net worth*, *capital accounts*, *equity*, and *surplus* (not-for-profit organizations).

the scale. Either they must take away something of equal value from a bucket on the Asset side, such as the cash that was paid for the truck, or they must add something to a bucket on the Liability side, like the bank loan for the money that was borrowed to purchase the truck.

The result of these entries is that the scale is still in balance—*and the company has a self-checking system to ensure the entire transaction has been recorded*. Assuming the accountants have picked the right account buckets, the details of each transaction are correctly captured and available for review at any time. Codes attached to each piece of data enable the accountants to connect all the data pieces that were added to the scale as part of that particular entry, should the entire transaction need to be reconstructed in the future. For example, those various codes enable Accounting to know what was bought, from whom, for how much, on what date, and where it will appear in the financial reports.

## Accrual Accounting: Say What?

The accounting rules outlined in GAAP (remember Chapter 1?) require most companies to keep their accounting records on what is called the *accrual basis*. In our everyday financial activities, such as when we balance our checkbook, we operate on a cash basis, meaning a transaction is recorded only when cash changes hands. Because *cash basis accounting* does not reflect debts that we owe others or others owe us, it's not considered indicative of economic reality. That's why most companies use accrual basis accounting. The only exceptions are very small businesses and some not-for-profit organizations.

Here's an example of accrual basis accounting: When the Sales Department obtains an order from one of your customers and the product is shipped to the customer, a sale has been consummated and it is recorded. This transaction will appear on the income statement even if not a single dollar has passed from the customer to your company, because the customer has an open account with the company. The transaction is recorded on one side by increasing Sales and on the other side by increasing Accounts Receivable, the amount due from your customer.

Later, perhaps the following month, your customer pays the amount owed, and your company receives the cash. That transaction will not appear on the income statement. It was already recorded as income when the sale was made. Under accrual accounting rules, the sale itself is considered the income-producing event. The act of collecting the money is just converting one asset—accounts receivable—into another asset—cash. That's a new transaction, but not one that produces a profit, since the dollar amount owed by the customer is replaced by an equal dollar amount of cash received from the customer.

This example demonstrates the essence of accrual basis accounting. Transactions are recorded when an economic event is deemed to have occurred. A sale is an economic event because a binding agreement has

> ## Don't Get Hung Up on Debits and Credits!
> In almost any discussion of accounting, you'll hear talk of *debits* and *credits*. Those elusive terms exemplify the technical jargon of accounting and (in my opinion) are not terribly useful for nonaccountants. You don't really need to know that debits increase Assets and decrease Liabilities, or that credits do the reverse. You only need to know the nature of the transactions that accomplish those things, and that has been well covered in this book. If you understand the idea of accrual accounting and the "buckets" discussed above, you don't need to worry about the debits and credits (unless you're applying for a job in Accounting, in which case this is the wrong book to be reading).

**CAUTION**

been reached: Your customer agreed to accept the merchandise and pay for it in due course, and your company shipped the merchandise based on your customer's promise to pay. That is an economic event: an offer made, accepted, and fulfilled.

The customer's payment is another economic event. It's related to the first, but it's nevertheless a new event. The customer might have chosen to delay payment or return the merchandise, but instead chose to pay for it. The second economic event doesn't affect Sales. However, it does affect the balance in the customer's accounts payable account, and it increases your company's cash receipts. So when this transaction is recorded, Accounts Receivable and Cash are the affected accounts. This transaction, although not shown on the income statement, is included in the statement of cash flow, which documents cash transactions other than those affecting income and expenses. If this explanation isn't clear, more information is presented in Chapters 5 and 6.

Having tossed around the names of financial reports that we haven't yet defined, let's take a moment to clarify those terms and add the next piece to this puzzle, called Finance, before we move on to the next chapter.

## The Principal Financial Statements Defined

Three primary financial statement formats appear in every company's annual report as well as in most internal monthly financial reports. We mentioned them briefly during the football game analogy, but I want to reintroduce them here, because in the next few chapters we discuss their contents and appearance in considerable detail.

## The Balance Sheet

The *balance sheet* is the report that shows the company's financial condition as of a particular date—usually the end of a month, a quarter, or a year. The report shows all the company's assets, typically valued at the cost to acquire them. In some cases assets are shown at whichever is lower, the actual cost or the current market value, if accounting rules indicate a permanent reduction in value below cost has occurred. Simi-

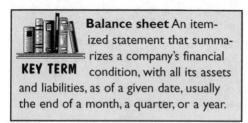

**Balance sheet** An itemized statement that summarizes a company's financial
**KEY TERM** condition, with all its assets and liabilities, as of a given date, usually the end of a month, a quarter, or a year.

larly, the company's liabilities are shown at either the amount(s) borrowed or owed. Some of these numbers are shown as exact amounts, and some may be estimates based on the best available information. The dollar difference between the reported values of the assets and the liabilities belongs to the owners of the company—it's their stockholders' equity interest. The balance sheet is discussed in detail in Chapter 3.

## The Income Statement

The *income statement* recaps all a company's activities intended to produce a profit. It shows the amount of sales, all the costs incurred in making those sales, and all the overhead costs incurred in running the company so it's able to deliver on its promises to customers. In this book we call it the income statement, but your company may call it something else. All companies that keep their accounting records on the accrual method produce a statement similar to this. The income statement is discussed in Chapter 4.

**Income statement** An accounting of revenue, expenses, and profit for a
**KEY TERM** given accounting period, usually a month, a quarter, or a year. Also known as *profit and loss (P&L) statement, statement of income and expenses*, and *operating statement*.

## Statement of Cash Flow

The income statement shows activities that were recorded using accrual basis accounting. However, companies that keep their books using accrual accounting still will have transactions that don't appear on the income statement, usually involving the exchange of cash. Let's say your company borrows money from the bank and puts the money into its checking account for later use. No income is created here, and no expense yet—until the loan interest begins to accumulate. So how do you get this on the books? And how do you report it? The answer is the *statement of cash flow*. This report shows the effect of all transactions that involve or influence cash but

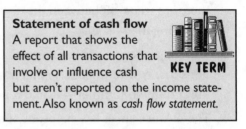

**Statement of cash flow**
A report that shows the effect of all transactions that involve or influence cash but aren't reported on the income statement. Also known as *cash flow statement*.

**KEY TERM**

don't appear on the income statement. Going back to our football game analogy, you'll recall we noted about Figure 2-4 that these two statements together would contain every transaction that occurs in a company between any two balance sheet dates. You learn more about the statement of cash flow in Chapter 6.

## Other Report Formats

A wide variety of other reports may accompany the basic statements in a financial report or may be prepared separately for special purposes. These often are more valuable in managing specific areas of the company's finances than the basic statements. Examples include reports on accounts receivable, accounts payable, and inventory. We don't have room in this book to cover all the possibilities, but we mention some of them in later chapters as they relate to the subject.

It's sufficient here to recognize that computerized accounting data today is almost universally maintained in database formats that give the Accounting Department the flexibility to produce report data in a wide variety of formats. If you feel a critical need for information that you're not getting from reports, visit the controller or the company bookkeeper; you might be surprised at how easily a responsive financial analyst can produce exactly what you need.

# Manager's Checklist for Chapter 2

☑ Financial reports must be reasonably accurate, formatted in a relevant way, and delivered in timely fashion in order to help managers make decisions about the company. For each ARTistic attribute, there is a trade-off between the degree of perfection and the cost of achieving it.

☑ The chart of accounts is an organized list of all the kinds of transactions that typically occur, so that transaction totals can be meaningfully grouped, summarized, and reported on financial statements.

☑ The balance sheet is a snapshot of a company's financial condition at a specific point in time, while the income statement and the statement of cash flow tabulate all the transactions that occurred during a period of time, i.e., between any two balance sheet dates.

☑ Accounting transactions are recorded in a balanced way, with each transaction affecting the scales equally to ensure that the transaction has been recorded completely and correctly. If the scales are always in balance, the balance sheet will always be in balance as well.

☑ Assets always equal the sum of liabilities and stockholders' equity. Put another way: Assets minus liabilities always equals stockholders' equity (owners' equity). As a result, increasing assets without increasing liabilities by a like amount increases equity. This is achieved in its simplest form when the company makes a profit.

☑ The accrual method of accounting is the standard for nearly all companies. Under the accrual method, transactions are recorded when an economic event has occurred, such as when a customer buys a product or the company purchases supplies. The results of these transactions generally are recorded as soon as the commitment to enter into the transaction has been consummated, not when cash is received or paid for the commitment, which might be much later.

# The Balance Sheet: Basic Summary of Value and Ownership

In Chapter 1 we compared the balance sheet to a snapshot. That was to give you an idea of its purpose, which is to show the financial condition of the business at a single point in time. Now let's talk about what the balance sheet is and what it looks like.

## Assets and Ownership—They Really Do Balance!

In this chapter we get into the nitty-gritty to help you understand the various line item labels that appear on a balance sheet, what they represent, and what you can learn from them.

### Introducing the Wonder Widget Company

Let's build our discussion on an example. Throughout this book, we use an imaginary company, the Wonder Widget Company, a manufacturer of a wonderful (and fictional) new product for home and garden. When we need an example, we look at our imaginary company's financial department to provide it.

Let's call first for a *statement of financial condition*, more commonly called a *balance sheet*.

Notice that the two sides of the balance sheet shown in Figure 3-1— Assets on the left and Liabilities and Stockholders' Equity on the right— are in balance, meaning they total the same amount. That's nice. But what's actually shown on this magically balanced report?

| ASSETS | |
|---|---|
| **Current Assets** | |
| Cash and Equivalents | $35,300 |
| | |
| Accounts Receivable | 1,059,700 |
| Less Allowances for Bad Debts | (64,000) |
| | 995,700 |
| | |
| Inventory | |
| Raw Materials | 311,000 |
| Work in Process | 65,000 |
| Finished Goods | 215,000 |
| | 591,000 |
| | |
| Prepaid Expenses | 45,000 |
| **Total Current Assets** | 1,667,000 |
| | |
| **Fixed Assets** | |
| Land and Buildings | 1,250,000 |
| Machinery and Equipment | 750,000 |
| Computers and Office Equipment | 250,000 |
| | 2,250,000 |
| Less Accumulated Depreciation | (972,000) |
| **Total Fixed Assets** | 1,278,000 |
| | |
| **Other Assets** | |
| Deposits *(held by others)* | 25,000 |
| Long-Term Investments | 276,000 |
| **Total Other Assets** | $301,000 |
| | |
| **Total Assets** | $3,246,000 |

**Figure 3-1.** Wonder Widget Company balance sheet (Assets)

Let's look at the line items on our balance sheet and discuss what they are and what they tell us about theWonder Widget Company. (On our balance sheet you will see some italicized comments in parentheses, for example, *(held by others)* next to the Deposits item under the Other Assets heading. These comments are there to help you understand the line item; they would not normally appear on the report.)

| LIABILITIES | |
|---|---|
| **Current Liabilities** | |
| Accounts Payable | $475,000 |
| Accrued Payroll | 57,000 |
| Other Accrued Liabilities | 31,000 |
| Income Taxes Payable | 54,000 |
| Notes Payable to Banks, Short-Term | 150,000 |
| Current Portion of Long-Term Debt | 52,000 |
| **Total Current Liabilities** | 819,000 |
| **Long-Term Liabilities** | |
| Lease (Purchase) Contracts | 125,000 |
| Long-Term Debt (*other than leases*) | 300,000 |
| Loans from Stockholders | 75,000 |
| | 500,000 |
| Less Current Portion of Long-Term Debt | (52,000) |
| Total Long-Term Liabilities | 448,000 |
| **Total Liabilities** | 1,267,000 |
| **Stockholders' Equity** | |
| Capital Stock | 50,000 |
| Contributed Capital | 1,750,000 |
| Retained Earnings | 179,000 |
| **Total Stockholders' Equity** | 1,979,000 |
| **Total Liabilities and Equity** | $3,246,000 |

Figure 3-1. Wonder Widget Company balance sheet (Liabilities and Stockholder's Equity)

# Current Assets—Liquidity Makes Things Flow

Simply put, *Current Assets* are those assets that either are cash or are expected to become cash "currently," that is, within the next 12 months. These assets produce most of the company's liquidity, and they are the main sources of the business' working capital. Figure 3-1 shows the most typical examples of current assets.

## Cash and Cash Equivalents

Cash itself is the most liquid asset of all and always the first item listed on any balance sheet. Cash includes Wonder Widget's checking

**Liquidity** The ability to meet current obligations with cash or other assets that can be quickly conSverted to cash in order to pay bills as they come due. In other words, the company has

**KEY TERM** enough cash or enough assets that will soon become cash so it's able to pay bills without running out of money.

**Insolvency** The opposite of *liquidity*; not having enough money to pay bills as they come due. Insolvency is often a precursor to a creditor revolt or even a bankruptcy filing.

accounts, cash reserves, and petty cash fund. *Cash Reserves* might be in the form of savings accounts, bank certificates, money market accounts, short-term investments, or similar cash-like assets.

Companies vary in their policies about listing all the details of their various cash accounts. Some simply show *Cash* or *Cash in Banks*, while others combine the details under a caption such as *Cash and Short-Term Investments* or the more common label used in our example, *Cash and Cash Equivalents*. The important thing about all the items in this section is that, if needed, they can be spent almost immediately.

## Accounts Receivable

Amounts due from customers and others usually appear next in the Current Assets section of the balance sheet. The largest of these is usually called *Accounts Receivable*; it typically means  amounts due from customers as a result of sales made on credit. It's expected that customers will pay for those sales within a relatively short time (typically 30–60 days), so they are classified as "current," even if some customer accounts may actually be past due.

In some industries, business practice permits a much longer collection period, sometimes 6–9 months or more. This practice enables makers of seasonal products to spread out their manufacturing over most of the year and induce their customers to take delivery of goods (but not pay for them) well before they'll be able to sell them, getting that inventory out of the manufacturers' warehouses and into their customers' warehouses.

During a recession, it's common for a company's customers to experience cash flow problems that make it difficult for them to pay promptly. This might result in collections that go beyond one year, although that isn't usually apparent from a glance at the balance sheet.

**LONG COLLECTION CYCLES BY INTENT**

The toy industry is a good example of long collection periods. Toy stores sell most of their merchandise during the last two months of the year. Yet toy makers maintain their manufacturing activities over the entire year and sell to their customers under special arrangements that allow the stores to pay for those purchases *after* they sell them. That mostly means after the holidays, perhaps many months after the goods were purchased and delivered to the stores. This practice is called *dating*, not in the "boy meets girl" sense, but rather meaning the due date for payment has been extended. Sellers that engage in this practice must make sure they have enough cash or borrowing capacity to operate while they wait for payment.

As a manager, you should remember that customers usually pay later than the terms your company originally granted them. The national average is estimated at about 45 days in normal economic times, longer than the customary 30-day terms printed on most suppliers' invoices. In a recession, that period can stretch to 90 days or more, leaving some suppliers in dire straits for lack of cash. So you can't always count on customers to pay their balances on time. This is one of the key cash flow planning issues companies must face in managing their resources effectively. If Wonder Widget's customers don't pay promptly, the company has less money to pay its suppliers and employees, and to replace goods it has sold.

A typical balance sheet may show other amounts owed to the company in addition to accounts receivable. They might include loans to employees or officers, tax refunds from the government, and other amounts due that are not the usual accounts with customers. In all cases, by classifying them as Current Assets, management is expressing the expectation that these amounts will be collected within a year.

## Allowance for Bad Debts

Closely related to Accounts Receivable is an account called Allowance for Bad Debts or some similar label, which is not always shown separately on the balance sheet. This is a *reserve*, an estimated amount the company sets aside for the possibility that some customer balances will never be collected and will have to be written off. Any company that sells on credit has these kinds of issues to deal with—granting credit and managing cus-

**KEY TERM**

**Write-off** Removing from the balance receivable from customers an amount judged to be uncollectible. Recorded by reducing the customer account receivable balance and reducing by an equal amount the allowance for bad debts. Companies that do not use an allowance for bad debts may instead create a bad debt expense at the time of write off. Also sometimes referred to as a charge off.

**Valuation adjustment account** An account created to reduce the value of another account, e.g., accounts receivable, without actually reducing directly the balance of that other account. Thus the full amount of accounts receivable is visible on reports as is the actual amount expected to be collected, which is the net or difference between, in this case, accounts receivable and the allowance for bad debts, its valuation adjustment account. See also accumulated depreciation later in this chapter, another example of a valuation adjustment account.

tomer relationships so that collection losses are as small as possible consistent with maximizing sales and with good business practice.

Because companies cannot tell at first who will pay and who won't, they often provide a reserve for such losses at the time sales are made, typically calculated as a percentage of all sales made in a given period. Such reserves can then absorb the cost of bad debt losses that may be recognized (written off) in future periods.

Companies build reserves by creating a *write-off to expense*. They then write off (recognize and record) uncollectible amounts against the reserve once they decide collecting the full amount due is unlikely. At

**TRICKS OF THE TRADE**

### Avoiding a Cash Management Pothole

Every company has to manage its accounts carefully to ensure it gets paid in full and there are no significant bad debt losses. However, because periodic fluctuations in collections are a normal risk of doing business, smart managers with responsibility for the company's cash accounts will arrange for credit lines with their banks so they can be sure they can meet their obligations to their creditors. A *credit line* is a commitment by the bank to lend a company a certain amount of money to tide it over until its customers pay their bills. The company borrows what it needs (within the credit limits) whenever it needs cash and repays the bank when it collects from its customers. Interest is charged only for the time the borrowed funds are in the company's hands. (The bank may also charge a service fee for making the credit line available.)

any point in time, the Allowance for Bad Debts is effectively a valuation adjustment account that reduces the total amount of customer accounts receivable on the books to the net amount the company expects to collect.

## Inventory

The next item on our balance sheet is *Inventory*, a term used for production materials, products purchased, or products manufactured and held by the company until sold.

A company that manufactures its products might show several categories of inventory, like those on Wonder Widget's balance sheet:

- **Raw Materials**—Whatever the company uses in the manufacturing process, before it begins to change them into something else. It might be whole logs for a sawmill or it might be electric motors for washing machines. The amount on the balance sheet is the cost of these materials, the amount the company paid to its suppliers to purchase them.

### FAILING TO CONTROL INVENTORY LOSSES CAN COST A BUNDLE!

CAUTION

Companies maintain inventories of their products so they can promptly satisfy customer demand for those products. The risk for any company is that it will keep inventory on hand that never sells or that sells only at a deep discount, for a variety of reasons, including the following:

- It has more inventory than its customers wanted (such as new cars at the end of the model year).
- It stocked items that its customers didn't want to buy (such as marked-down fashion clothing at the end of the season).
- The inventory became useless before anyone bought it (such as perishable food in the supermarket or a technology product that became obsolete as a result of a competitor's innovations).
- Inventory was lost or damaged or disappeared from theft or other causes and was not available to sell.

When there are losses, inventory is revalued at a new, net realizable amount, and the difference becomes an expense on the company's books. If not properly controlled, such expense can become a large and unpleasant shock to a company's profit expectations. Companies typically examine and count their inventory periodically—at least annually, and sometimes as often as monthly—to avoid unexpected losses in value.

- **Work in Process**—Products in the midst of the manufacturing process that no longer are raw materials but are not yet finished goods. The balance sheet includes raw material costs as well as some labor and related costs applied to these materials during the manufacturing process. We discuss this further when we talk about cost accounting in Chapter 8.
- **Finished Goods**—Fully manufactured products ready for sale to customers. The balance sheet shows all the costs needed to make the products, including labor and related overhead costs, such as factory rent, supervision, and product inspection.

By contrast, retailers, distributors, and trading companies usually purchase fully manufactured products, which they resell without processing them further. Their balance sheet most likely shows only a single line called Inventory.

## Prepaid Expenses

Prepaid Expenses, an unusual asset among Current Assets, will never, except in rare cases, be turned into cash, in spite of our statement above that such conversion is a typical characteristic of current assets. *Prepaid expenses* are exactly that—expenses that have been paid in advance and therefore won't have to be paid again. Thus, in a sneaky way they increase available cash in future months by enabling the company to avoid paying out that amount during the next 12 months. OK, so that's a stretch, but that's how it works—honest.

Let me give you an example. Every company buys insurance of various kinds, and nearly every type of insurance has a premium that must be prepaid, typically a year in advance. Since insurance can be a costly

---

**KEY TERM**

**Prepaid expenses** Amounts paid in advance to a vendor or creditor for goods and services. Because the purpose of the payments is to obtain benefits for the organization over time, the cost of these assets is charged against profits throughout the period, usually on a monthly basis. Prepaid expenses is a current asset because the company has paid for something and either someone is obligated to provide the company with services or it has purchased a supply of consumable goods, e.g., office supplies, that will be consumed and charged as an expense over an extended period.

item, companies allocate the cost of that protection over the period the company is protected. The company writes a check for 12 months of insurance protection and expenses the amount over the 12 months of protection, usually by charging 1/12 of the total to Expenses each month. The balance of the advance premium payment is considered an asset, and it rests in a prepaid expense account until it has been entirely written off to Expenses. Other examples of prepaid expenses are property taxes, income tax installments, or even marketing materials.

## Fixed Assets—Property and Possessions

Every company acquires physical assets that it uses to conduct its business—computers, manufacturing equipment, buildings, land, trucks, and so forth. Those assets are used for extended periods of time, usually years, and are thus not current assets in the sense of the items discussed above. These are usually called *Fixed Assets* or *Property, Plant, and Equipment* or—if no real estate or vehicles are owned—*Equipment and Furnishings*.

Because such assets are used for a number of years and are not held for resale to customers, they are not considered sources of liquidity or cash flow. They are, well, "fixed" in place until they are no longer useful. At that point, they are either sold or discarded, and then replaced.

---

**AVOID GETTING CAUGHT WITH YOUR ASSETS DOWN!**    SMART

MANAGING

In evaluating a company, look carefully at the relationship of the Fixed Assets to the Accumulated Depreciation shown on the balance sheet. If accumulated depreciation is a large percentage of total fixed assets and little remains to be written off, it may be a sign that the company is facing potentially heavy expenditures in the near future to replace aging or obsolete equipment. In an industry influenced by technology, such as automobile manufacturing, this may be even more of a concern. If instead the company decides to keep old equipment in place, it may incur higher maintenance and repair costs. Either way, these lines on the balance sheet could be a clue to future drains on cash flow or the need to borrow money for replacement purchases.

The smart strategy: Keep up maintenance programs on equipment with long service lives to avoid unnecessarily shortening their useful lives. When equipment must be replaced, use return on investment (ROI) calculations (see Chapter 9) to find the best way to finance the replacement.

---

Fixed assets may not move around much, but during their period of use their value declines substantially, often to zero by the end of their useful life. (The sole exception is land. It generally does not decline in value, and in fact is more likely to increase in value.) To recognize that reduction in value, a company will *depreciate*, or systematically write down, the cost of each fixed asset (except land) over the period that it's used in the business.

This reduction in value is charged to expense when recognized, under the label of Depreciation Expense on the income statement (see Chapter 4). On the balance sheet, the total amount written off to expense since a fixed asset was purchased appears under Accumulated Depreciation. This account is shown immediately after the original cost of the fixed assets as a deduction from the original cost, so that the net value of the fixed assets is readily apparent to anyone who reads the statement. Think of this as a valuation adjustment account similar to the Allowance for Bad Debts discussed earlier.

## Other Assets—The "Everything Else" Category

At the bottom of the Assets side on most balance sheets is a catchall category called, cleverly, *Other Assets*. These are company holdings that are neither current nor fixed. Assets in this category are not expected to become cash in the next 12 months, and they are not real estate, machines, or equipment used in the company's business operations. They may not even be directly related to the company's business.

For example, a deposit paid to a landlord from whom the company leases its offices would appear under other assets, since most such leases are multiyear commitments. (A lease deposit is not really a current expense to the company, because it can be either applied against final rent under the lease or returned to the tenant when the property is vacated. So a rent deposit may be disbursed at the beginning of the lease but not become expense until the end of the lease, if at all.)

An investment in another company would be listed here as well. Wonder Widget apparently has made at least one such investment. Putting this item in the noncurrent category indicates the company intends to hold this investment for an extended period. In other words, it's not a readily marketable security that's going to be sold as soon as the price goes up a few points.

## Current Liabilities—Repayment Is Key

The Liabilities side of the balance sheet also begins with the most current liabilities. Here, too, liquidity is the measure of the label "current," but in the case of liabilities it is *negative* liquidity—cash going *out* the door. Current liabilities are all the debts the company expects to pay within the next 12 months, the same period in which the current assets are expected to become cash.

The relationship between assets and liabilities is evident if you think about it for a moment. Current assets will become cash to pay off current liabilities. That's the principal of working capital in any company. If you look at Wonder Widget's balance sheet (Figure 3-1), you'll notice that current assets are about twice current liabilities. That's usually thought of as a good ratio to ensure that the cash is available when needed. You'll read more about that relationship in Chapter 7, when we discuss key performance indicators.

> **Working capital** A common but theoretical way to measure the amount of a company's ready liquidity. To calculate it, deduct current liabilities from current assets. Also called *Networking Capital*. For example, Wonder Widget's current assets total $1,667,000, and its current liabilities total $819,000. Thus it has working capital of $848,000.
>
> **KEY TERM**

### Accounts Payable

This account includes all the unpaid bills from all the company's suppliers and service providers. This is usually the largest item among a company's current liabilities. Accounts Payable is usually the first item listed under Current Liabilities.

Amounts in this category should be paid in accordance with trade terms printed on the invoices. Typically that's 30 days, or whatever other payment period is granted by the supplier. Sometimes companies take longer to pay their bills than the official period, as noted above for accounts receivable. In such cases, customers are, in essence, borrowing money from their trade creditors to help increase the financial resources at work in their company. This is called *leverage*, and we bring this up

**KEY TERM** **Leverage** The ability to borrow and thereby to put more money into a business than has been invested by its owners, thus earning more than its invested capital could earn alone.

**FOR EXAMPLE** **DELAY CAN PAY**
If a company can earn 12 percent annually by buying and reselling merchandise, it can earn almost 0.25 percent on every dollar that it can delay paying its creditors by a week. If this company has an average balance of $50,000 in accounts payable, it could earn about $125 a week, or over $6,000 a year. Of course, it may not be worth it if the company incurs additional charges or jeopardizes its standing with creditors.

again in Chapter 5 and in discussing ratios in Chapter 7. When Wonder Widget extends its payment period by delaying payments to its creditors, it benefits from the use of leverage. When Wonder Widget's customers do the same thing, its accounts receivable take longer to collect and it's on the wrong side of that leverage.

Often a company shows other amounts it owes under separate labels to make sure readers of the report know there are amounts due for these "special" liabilities. Wonder Widget's balance sheet shows income taxes payable as such a category.

**CAUTION** **THE CASH SQUEEZE—DON'T GET CAUGHT IN THE MIDDLE!**
Keep this in mind: Despite all the headlines around bank lending practices, venture capital investing, public offerings of stock, etc., the largest single source of operating capital for most businesses is the money they borrow from their creditors, that is, accounts payable. Almost every entrepreneur has a few stories about the struggles he or she went through to squeeze more working capital out of the balance sheet. This usually means increasing available cash by delaying payment to creditors, while at the same time trying to make sure their customers don't do the same to them.

Sometimes the squeeze play goes against you; the company can't collect its accounts receivable on a timely basis, and its creditors won't let it slow down its payments. The result can be a disastrous cash flow crunch. Companies in the construction industry often face this. Their customers hold up payment for unfinished loose ends on a project, while their subcontractors must be paid to prevent them from filing mechanic's liens on the property.

## Accrued Payroll

Next on Wonder Widget's statement of financial condition (an alternative name for balance sheet) is the *Accrued Payroll* account, which represents the amount earned by employees but not yet paid to them. Since employees are typically paid for time already worked, not in advance, almost every company has some amount of compensation earned by its employees but not yet paid to them. When a company keeps its accounting records on the accrual basis (refer to Chapter 5 for a discussion of accounting methods), such liabilities are recorded when they become owed, even though they don't actually have to be paid until later. An exception would be companies that pay employees on the last day of their workweek. In this case, at the end of a payday they would not owe any money to their employees—until the following day.

## Other Accrued Liabilities

Just as Wonder Widget records its payroll earned but not yet paid, a company usually has other such liabilities. These may be expenses the company has incurred but for which it has not yet received an invoice to record. To ensure the expense is recorded in the right accounting period, the company's accountants accrue the liability rather than wait for an invoice to arrive or a check to be issued. Examples might include large purchases for which the supplier has not yet invoiced the company or

**Loan covenant** Clauses in a loan agreement that require the borrower to do certain things (*affirmative covenants*) or not do others (*negative covenants*) during the term of the loan agreement. Some typical covenants include the following: **KEY TERM**

- The company must maintain adequate insurance.
- The company must furnish the lender with financial statements quarterly and annually.
- The company cannot allow other liens on company assets.
- The company cannot merge with another company or acquire another company.
- The company must make enough profit to cover loan payments.

Banks often monitor compliance with loan covenants quarterly, based on the financial statements, and sometimes require that a corporate officer or independent accountant issue a compliance certificate as evidence that no covenant violation has occurred.

interest expense on a loan that doesn't get invoiced but for which the bank will automatically charge the company.

## Notes Payable and Other Bank Debt

Loans from banks and other lenders that represent borrowed money, and not simply trade accounts with suppliers, are always shown separately. This is because loans and repayments typically have special terms. When you see Notes Payable to anyone, particularly banking institutions, you can be pretty sure the company has agreed to some limitations on its range of activity, called *covenants*, required by the lender as a way of trying to ensure the loan repayment.

While borrowing to finance the business is discussed in Chapter 10, keep in mind that when such loans appear on the balance sheet, you can expect to see other kinds of guarantees provided to the lender. These might include pledging assets as collateral, a personal guarantee of repayment by the owners of the company, or perhaps even a contingent claim on company ownership.

## Current Portion of Long-Term Debt

Refer to the discussion below of long-term debt. The "current" label represents the portion of that debt that must be repaid within the next 12 months.

# Long-Term Liabilities—Borrowed Capital

You might see a wide variety of long-term borrowings on a company's balance sheet, including the line items seen in Figure 3-1. Rather than describe all the items you might find listed under Long-Term Liabilities, let's look for a moment at the types seen on our sample balance sheet.

## Lease Contracts

The *Lease Contracts* label shows commitments made by a company in order to lease equipment or other assets at favorable payment terms, usually followed by a modest buyout option at the end of the contract. According to current U.S. accounting rules, when a lease contract is designed primarily to finance the intended purchase of the asset, the asset and the liability are recorded on the lessee's books and accounted for as if the asset had actually been purchased with a loan agreement instead of a lease contract. A lease can also be a long-term rental agreement in which there is no actual transfer of ownership, and therefore no recording of the asset and liability on the company's books. However, some leases are written more like purchase agreements, which is why they often appear on balance sheets, as in our example. There is some discussion among accounting rule makers to require even long-term rental agreements to be shown on the balance sheet, to alert readers that assets are being used, and liabilities incurred, even though no formal purchase agreement exists. A draft accounting rule was published in late 2013 which may ultimately make this change a requirement in public financial reports.

## Long-Term Debt

A company with financing needs that extend for years might opt to borrow money with a payment term that stretches out as far as possible, enabling the company to put the borrowed money to use and earn enough to more easily repay the loan. In such cases the loan's entire amount is reported as a Long-Term Debt, and the portion of that loan due to be paid within the next 12 months—meaning "currently due"—is shown under Current Liabilities. This is what Wonder Widget has done in our example.

## Loans from Stockholders

This is another special category of loan, most often seen on the balance sheets of privately owned companies operated by the owners. For some privately owned companies, this is how owners put money into the company when it needs cash and take it out when it's not needed. All too frequently, however, business conditions do not improve soon, so Loans from Stockholders may stay on the balance sheet for years. In fact, banks and other outside lenders may require that such loans remain unpaid as long as the company has outside loans. Thus, these amounts can end up looking more like owners' equity than loans to the company. This is often a frustrating reality for entrepreneurs and small business owners who had hoped to be repaid sooner.

# Ownership Comes in Various Forms

Owners' Equity or Stockholders' Equity (for a corporation) or Capital (for a proprietorship or partnership) is the owners' stake in the business. It includes what they have invested to launch, to finance, or to refinance the company, plus what the company has earned in profits since it was founded.

As already noted, it can also include amounts the owners have loaned to the business that they cannot get back due to some subsequent loan agreement with a bank or other lending source. Such loans are always shown in under Liabilities on the balance sheet, and never under Equity because they are not legally investment capital until and unless ultimate repayment is formally relinquished. Labels that may appear in this section include the following.

## Capital Stock and Contributed Capital

*Capital Stock* is the amount paid into the company by investors to purchase stock, at some nominal amount per share. It's usually a small part of what the investors actually paid, for legal reasons too complicated to discuss here. Let's just say that investors usually pay more for a share of stock than the amount shown under this label; the balance of the proceeds is reported under a heading such as Contributed Capital or a similar description. When combined, these two amounts represent the total amount formally contributed by owners and investors to finance the company.

---

**KEY TERMS**

**Capital stock** The amount paid into the company by investors to purchase stock at some nominal amount per share; the par value printed on each share of stock. *Par value* is an arbitrary dollar amount assigned to shares of stock for accounting purposes during the incorporation process, usually set as low as possible to minimize legal restrictions on the amount classified as par value. Many incorporations today assign no par value to their shares to avoid this problem entirely.

**Additional contributed capital** or **additional paid-in capital** The amount paid into the company by investors to purchase stock, above its par value. Also sometimes a general label that includes both capital stock and additional paid-in capital, especially when capital stock has been issued at no par value.

---

# Capital Stock Comes In Several Flavors

Occasionally a company has reasons to issue several kinds of capital stock, usually for the purpose of raising capital or restricting ownership rights of some stockholders compared to others. This occurs when

established, publicly traded companies or emerging companies raiser money from outside investors. In these cases we have to distinguish between common stock and preferred stock.

## Common Stock

*Common stock* is generally owned by the *residual owners*—those who own whatever value in the company is not committed to others. There are occasions when a company issues two or more classes of common stock. Some may have different voting rights without surrendering their residual profit-sharing rights. Other common stock might contain different participation in profits or voting. A good example is the stock of Berkshire Hathaway (remember Warren Buffett?). That company has Class A common shares with full voting rights, and Class B shares that participate in profits differently and have limited voting rights.

## Preferred Stock

*Preferred shares*, by contrast, are typically issued to investors who want a fixed return on their investment and are less interested in voting rights. Preferred shares typically have a fixed rate dividend that they will earn each year—4 or 5 or 6.25 percent, etc., and limited or no voting rights. And talk about variety: A large company may issue a number of classes or series of preferred shares at various times to raise money at different dividend, or *coupon*, rates to meet investor demands. Some types of preferred shares may even be convertible to common shares at the owner's option, and some may be subject to buyback at the issuer's option. Bank of America, for example, had 20 different issues of preferred stock outstanding at the end of 2012, each with different terms and different dividend rates.

## Retained Earnings

Every company, from its inception, develops a history of profits and losses. Profits add to retained earnings and losses reduce Retained Earnings. If a company operates with overall profitability, it accumulates a substantial amount of earnings over time. If it's a *propri-*

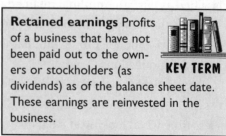

**Retained earnings** Profits of a business that have not been paid out to the owners or stockholders (as dividends) as of the balance sheet date. These earnings are reinvested in the business.

**KEY TERM**

*etorship* (unincorporated, one owner) or a *partnership* (unincorporated, two or more owners), these earnings are usually taxable to the owner(s) immediately, so the earnings are typically paid out to the owner(s) each year as dividends or distributions of profits.

However, if the company is a corporation, its owners are generally not taxed on the company's accumulated profits until the company chooses to distribute those earnings to its owners in the form of cash dividends. In the interim, the accumulated earnings not distributed to its owners are shown on the balance sheet as retained earnings.

Earnings are retained in the business for reasons other than to avoid paying taxes on them. These include enabling the business to retain cash for expansion or to purchase land, buildings, or equipment (fixed assets) to facilitate its operations. The company may also be building a "war chest" to enable it to buy other companies, protect itself against a possible catastrophe, or repurchase its own stock when prices are low.

Wonder Widget is a relatively new company, so its retained earnings are still low. Some companies actually have negative retained earnings, because they've lost more money than they've made over their existence. (This is the situation for many airlines, for example.) You can recognize this by the label Deficit in Retained Earnings. This is often an indication that you might not want to buy their stock now, as they may not yet have figured out how to make money in their business. (This was a story heard frequently in the aftermath of the 2000–2001 dot-com collapse.)

## Using This Report Effectively

The balance sheet is the status report of the company's financial health. It shows where the company is strong, such as good cash balances and low amounts of debt, and where it is weak, such as large amounts of debt classified as current, minimal retained earnings, etc.

Often the answers the balance sheet provides are your cue to ask, "Why?" It's a good idea to be familiar enough with the balance sheet to know which questions to ask.

Pay particular attention to the ratios and analysis tools that we discuss in Chapters 7 and 9. They are excellent ways to get more information in less time when looking at a balance sheet.

# Manager's Checklist for Chapter 3

☑ The balance sheet is the report of the company's financial condition at a specific moment. It provides valuable information about the success of the company's cash management practices, its history of profitability, and the adequacy of its invested capital. Often the most valuable information it provides is simply suggesting the right questions to ask.

☑ Current assets and current liabilities are closely related. Current assets are liquid and should be convertible to cash within a 12-month period. Current liabilities, in turn, must be repaid within that same 12-month period, usually from the cash raised by converting current assets. The difference between the two is called *working capital* or *net working capital*.

☑ A large amount of accounts receivable may look good on the balance sheet, but their collectability is the most important issue, and that's not always apparent by looking at the total. Look at the allowance for bad debts and customer-by-customer details to better understand the true quality of this line item.

☑ Inventory represents a constant management challenge and can be a high-risk area for losses unless inventory management practices are solid. Inventory can cost a company money in many ways including deterioration, obsolescence, and breakage.

☑ Accounts payable is the largest source of day-to-day financing for most companies. Delaying payment can provide temporary relief for cash-strapped companies, while causing accounts receivable collection problems for the creditors.

☑ All company assets have been paid for with capital that was provided either by creditors (liabilities) or investors (stockholders' equity).

# The Income Statement: The Flow of Progress

You'll remember we identified the Income Statement as a report that tallies the cumulative effect of all the income and expense transactions that occurred during a given period, i.e., between two balance sheet dates. Those transactions typically have the goal of producing a profit for the company. The income statement shows the company's success in achieving that objective.

## They Say Timing Is Everything—And They're Right!

The Income Statement is the report most nonfinancial managers readily recognize. They know it shows whether the business made a profit for the month, the quarter, or the year. In large companies and small ones, managers' bonuses are often based on profit results (too often, in my opinion, because most of them typically have little control over profit—but that's another subject). Others know it's the report most valued by CEOs, shareholders, bankers, and government regulators. Some managers recognize its format but call it by a different name such as *profit and loss (P&L) statement, statement of income and expenses,* and a few others.

Whatever you call it, it's usually acknowledged to be the most important report a company produces. (But hold your vote until you've read Chapter 6.) As such, it behooves us to take time to understand how it comes together and why that matters.

While nonfinancial people recognize the importance of the income statement, they don't always appreciate how transaction timing affects profit in any given period. In fact, they're often surprised that monthly reports don't show the effects of individual transactions that they expected to see, even though nothing has been missed or reported incorrectly. There are two culprits in this plot:

1. The passage of time between the date a transaction was first committed to a supplier or a customer and—through the processes of fulfillment, invoicing or billing, and recording—the date payment was made or received.

2. The confusion that sometimes arises as to when a transaction should properly be recorded under the accounting rules (recall GAAP from Chapter 1).

Regarding the first culprit—time—there's often a long sequence of events that must be completed before a transaction can be recorded. The

## THE WIDGET ISN'T SOLD—OR RECORDED— UNTIL IT WORKS

**FOR EXAMPLE** Imagine a new Wonder Widget salesperson is selling an advanced widget, the Super Widget 2000. The salesperson does a great job of selling the product's benefits and tells the customer the price includes full installation and training, with no commitment to pay until the widget works. So the customer places the order. The paperwork goes into Wonder Widget's Sales Office for processing, and the salesperson enthusiastically goes on to the next deal, hoping for a commission check before sunset. Meanwhile, the process of setting up the customer begins, including credit application, credit checking, shipping instructions, etc. Then the product finally ships to the customer. Done, right? Actually, it's just the beginning.

This Super Widget 2000 isn't "plug-and-play" like its predecessors; it requires installation, setup, debugging, and finally, training, all of which are part of the product package. By the time all that's completed, months have passed. The salesperson still has that sale on an open item list—I sold it, but they haven't paid me for it yet. The company can't hold the customer to the sale until the installed product is accepted. Under the rules of accounting, the sale can be recorded only when the customer is irrevocably committed *and* the company has delivered on its promises. Under Wonder Widget's commission plan, the commission is payable under the same circumstances: so, no sale, no commission.

final step of a transaction might be recorded days or even weeks after the initiating department has finished its role in the process, e.g., taking an order from a customer or ordering goods from a supplier. It might be even longer before the transaction is complete, e.g., the company collects from the customer or pays the supplier.

As for the second culprit—confusion—I recall an incident when I was the controller of a large company with a nationwide sales organization. A regional sales manager with budget responsibilities questioned a financial report that showed expenditures charged to his department in June, when he had made the deal with the supplier to provide the merchandise or services in April. "Why wasn't it taken out of my budget in April, when I spent the money?" he asked.

Expenses don't get recorded when they're committed, when the order is called in, when a purchase order is issued, or even when the supplier agrees to supply the goods or services ordered. Those events are simply requests or promises, all of which typically can be rescinded without penalty. So they're not irrevocable transactions that we can record. When the supplier acts on that promise to deliver, then we have an accounting event to record, and that's when the money is really spent.

Why would the sales manager even care about such accounting refinements? Well, first, he was being evaluated on his performance against budget, which is always a good tool for instilling budget consciousness. But mostly he wanted to be relieved of the need to keep track of money he had committed and (in his mind) spent. It's easy to understand his desire, since keeping track of such details is time-consuming. If the money were charged against his budget when it was committed, he would know how much he had left to commit or spend in later months.

The questions made sense to the sales manager, yet frustrated the accountants. They could never convince him they had accounted for it correctly (especially since they sometimes hadn't). Yet the best answer lay in better communication between the two groups about how accounting works and about when a promise becomes a commitment.

In today's digital environment, many companies have integrated enterprise accounting software that keeps track of purchase orders issued but not yet fulfilled, making it easier to track and report commitments

**SMART MANAGING**

**IF IT COUNTS TOWARD MY BONUS, IT MUST BE A SALE**
A good example of conflicting objectives that can cause misunderstanding is the answer to the question: When is it sold? One of the corporate scandals reported in the press a few years ago involved equipment service contracts the company recorded as equipment sales. Why? Probably because equipment sales go into profit immediately, while service contracts can be recorded only as the service is rendered, often over months or years. A sale recorded now counts for more than a sale that will be recorded next year, especially if you're trying to pump up earnings per share this quarter. A smart manager understands about conflicting objectives and the dangers that can result.

made for future goods and services. Even so, such commitments cannot be booked as expenses until the goods have been delivered and the purchase order satisfied. This is the flip side of the sales example above, but the same accounting rules apply. With that overview in mind, let's look at the line items on a typical income statement. As an example, let's use the most recent income statement of the Wonder Widget Company. Take a look at Figure 4-1 and then read on.

| | | |
|---|---:|---:|
| Sales | | 650,000 |
| Cost of Sales | | 475,000 |
| Gross Profit | | 175,000 |
| | | |
| Operating Expenses | | |
| Engineering | 25,000 | |
| Sales and Marketing | 76,000 | |
| General & Administrative | 37,000 | 138,000 |
| Operating Income | | 37,000 |
| Other Income and Expenses | | (5,000) |
| Income Before Taxes | | 32,000 |
| Income Taxes | | 12,800 |
| Net Income | | 19,200 |
| Earnings per Share | | $0.10 |
| Fully Diluted Earnings per Share | | $0.08 |

**Figure 4-1.** The Wonder Widget income statement

## Sales: Grease for the Engine

"Nothing happens until you sell something." This is the sale to customers of products and services *that the company regularly offers for sale in the normal course of business.* This means we don't include the sale of surplus equipment off the shop floor because that's not our business. We also don't include the sale of a building that we're no longer using (unless our business is buying and selling buildings). It does mean, as noted above, a completed sale, an irrevocable transaction for which the customer must pay.

Depending on your business, *sales* might be called different things on your income statement. Sales of services are often called *revenue*, although the terms mean pretty much the same thing, and there are no real differences in the rules between sales of products and sales of services. We use the terms interchangeably in this book.

---

### TRICKS THAT TEMPT MANAGERS INTO TROUBLE

When the outside world looks so intently at a company's sales for clues to its success, it's sometimes hard for company management to resist the temptation to cut corners in the interest of pleasing current and potential shareholders. Because some of the accounting rules seem to have room for interpretation, occasionally they get interpreted all the way into the next room. Here are some examples that you will want to look out for:

- Recording sales too soon, before the transaction is complete, e.g., such as when the quarter is ending and the CEO wants the company to look good.
- Recording sales too late, e.g., waiting until the next month or quarter because the CEO doesn't expect that quarter to look as good as this one and he or she wants to even out the quarters a bit.
- Recording sales that haven't really happened (yet), but that the CEO is sure will happen momentarily, and so why not slip them in a bit early.

---

## Cost of Sales: What It Takes to Earn the Sale

*Cost of Sales* represents all the costs of manufacturing or buying the products sold during the period, including raw materials, manufacturing labor, and related overhead costs (collectively these are called *Cost of Goods Sold*), and including the directly related selling costs, e.g., commissions, which are not typically included in the calculation of cost of goods sold. Figure 4-2 shows how the two terms differ in their calculation. Depending on which approach a company takes, its gross profit and gross margin percentage will be slightly different, although operating profit will be the same in either case.

Companies that purchase and resell goods intact (rather than manufacturing the products they sell) generally report the cost of purchased goods on this line rather than accumulating raw materials and direct labor costs.

To take this one step farther, companies that sell services rather than products usually report this line as Cost of Services rather than Cost of Sales. This subtle distinction has lost ground in recent years as some service companies have dispensed with the term altogether, opting instead to simply report Revenues, Operating Expenses, and Operating Profit.

One element of cost that is almost always represented in cost of sales, and in operating expenses as well, is Depreciation, described briefly in Chapter 3, and its close cousin, Amortization. These line items require extra comment because they don't flow to the income statement in the same way as other costs. As noted in the discussion of the balance sheet, *depreciation* describes the gradual decline in value of a capital asset—a building, machine, truck, or table that was purchased for its value to the business over a number of years. *Amortization* applies to the decline in value of *intangible* assets with a multiyear life, such as a website, a patent, or a license to use someone else's intellectual property.

---

**KEY TERM**

**Depreciation** The amount of expense that a company charges against earnings to write off the cost of a capital asset over the time it will benefit the company, without regard to how it was paid for and after considering age, wear, obsolescence, and salvage value.

Various methods are used to calculate this expense, most originating from favorable tax laws. If the expense is assumed to be incurred equally over the life of the asset, the method of depreciation is *straight line*, with the same amount recorded to expense in each period of the asset's life. If the expense is assumed to be incurred in decreasing amounts over the life of the asset, the method is *accelerated*, with a larger expense recorded in the early years than in the later ones. The former method is more common; the total cost of the asset is divided by the number of months it will be used and the result is charged to expense each month until the asset is retired or sold off.

| | |
|---|---:|
| Start with the inventory on hand at the beginning of the month, valued at the total actual cost to make or buy it. | $275,000 |
| Add the cost of all the inventory purchased during the month, which was intended to be used in making the company's products, either now or later. | 175,000 |
| Add the cost of the labor used to manufacture products during the month. | 265,000 |
| Add the other costs incurred by the company indirectly related to making its products, such as plant electricity, machine depreciation, supervisory salaries, and so on. | 321,000 |
| This is the total cost invested in inventory for sale during the month. | 1,036,000 |
| Deduct the total cost of inventory unsold at the end of the month. | (591,000) |
| This is Cost of Goods Sold for the month. | 445,000 |
| Add the costs incurred to get the products to the customer, such as delivery freight, commissions, etc. | 30,000 |
| This is the Cost of Sales for the month. | $475,000 |

**Figure 4-2.** Cost of Sales: How Wonder Widget calculates cost of sales

Purchasing a capital asset entails a cash expenditure but not the recording of an expense. Instead, the capital asset is placed on the balance sheet in the appropriate asset category and charged to expense gradually over its estimated useful life. Thus the expense charge for depreciation is one of the unusual items that doesn't result from a cash expenditure in the period that the charge appears—the cash was actually spent months or years ago—and for that reason you'll see it appear again in the discussion of cash flow (Chapters 5 and 6).

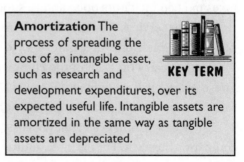

**Amortization** The process of spreading the cost of an intangible asset, such as research and development expenditures, over its expected useful life. Intangible assets are amortized in the same way as tangible assets are depreciated.

**KEY TERM**

## Gross Profit: The First Measure of Profitability

Gross profit is a key measure of profitability, one we discuss in more depth in Chapters 7 and 8. *Gross Profit* is the gain the company earns by selling its products after accounting for all elements of the cost of sales. Earning a gross profit is important, because the difference between sales and the cost of sales normally pays all the operating expenses discussed next. In other words, if you sell each widget at a loss, it's highly unlikely you'll make up the loss through volume.

---

**SMART**

**MANAGING**

### A DIFFERENT LOOK AT GROSS PROFIT: CONTRIBUTION PROFIT

While the traditional income statement that shows cost of sales and gross profit is most commonly seen in financial reports, there is great value in presenting Contribution Profit instead of gross profit, or as an additional P&L view. In this approach all direct costs are deducted from sales first, because they are costs directly incurred as a result of sales—costs that would not have occurred but for the sales. The result of deducting direct costs from sales is called *Contribution Profit*, meaning the profit directly contributed by those sales. Indirect costs and overhead are presented later on the income statement, indicating they would have occurred even if the sales had not occurred. Net income is the same in either case, of course. The greatest value of contribution profit comes in presenting it for individual product lines, thus showing the specific contribution to the bottom line that was produced by each product line.

---

## Operating Expenses: Running the Business

*Operating Expenses* includes all the business' operating costs—what it takes to keep the doors open and to support the sales of the company's products or services. Usually subcategories appear on the income statement, as we've done in Figure 4-1, to show the operating expenses incurred to carry on each of the company's major functional activities. These are typically engineering or R&D (research and development), sales and marketing, and general and administrative expenses.

There can be other categories of costs, depending on the nature of the company's business. For example, a drug company might carry separate categories for research and for product development because these are such significant cost areas for a company in that business. A distribution company that buys and sells products made by others would have no reason to have R&D costs, but might have a category called Distribution Expenses, because that's a significant area of expense for a distribution company.

Let's look briefly at what each of these expense categories typically include.

## Research and Development: Finding Something New

*Research and Development (R&D)* is money spent to create new products or to significantly improve existing products. The classic example is the drug company that spends millions in the laboratories exploring diseases for which there's no known cure, in the hope of an exciting discovery that will justify all the R&D expense. It doesn't always work out that way, of course, and most R&D expenditures are ultimately unproductive in terms of developing a marketable product. Still, a company that depends on a flow of new products to survive in the marketplace must allocate a portion of its annual spending to R&D if it is to stay in business.

Closely related are groupings of expenses that are often called *Engineering Expenses*. Some companies prefer this label, perhaps because they don't think of themselves as engaged in basic research, but rather in using engineering methodologies to improve what's already known about their business.

Farther down the line from basic research and engineering is an area called *Product Development*. This is the cost of taking the fruits of that research to develop products that can be sold, e.g., a cure for the common cold in simple pill form. Product development can also include expenditures intended to improve existing products, such as a better nasal spray or even a better dispenser for that nasal spray.

These are all costs that a company incurs to find something new to sell. A company that can afford to spend more for R&D has a better chance of staying ahead of its competitors. Having better products sooner than others should provide an edge, at least for a while. As you can see, a company will be motivated to allocate as much of its resources as possible to R&D in the belief that it will pay off in sales. R&D is a cost the company incurs before it will have the opportunity to make a sale and then as it's making sales, to ensure that sales will continue. In other words, R&D is a cost of doing business that must be financed out of the gross profit.

## Sales and Marketing Expenses: Positioning the Company to Sell Something

We noted earlier that the direct costs of making a sale, such as commissions for salespeople, are often reported as a part of the cost of sales. Beyond those costs directly related to making a sale, substantial effort and costs go into creating and maintaining a sales and marketing presence.

*Marketing Costs* are all those expenditures a company makes to find out what people want to buy from it, to interest people in its products, and to create prospects for the company's sales force. Typically, none of these costs are directly related to making a sale, yet they're necessary to create a steady flow of prospective buyers for the salespeople. Market research, brand development, website development and maintenance, advertising, and test marketing are examples of marketing costs.

*Selling Expenses*, by comparison, are the costs of actually selling the company's products and services. This includes putting salespeople in the field to call on prospects and get orders or on the telephone to take orders. It also includes distributing sales brochures, the shopping cart on that website, trade shows, and all the support costs of the sales organization. Sales and marketing, then, is another cost of doing business.

## General and Administrative Expenses: Running the Back Office and Paying the Rent

The third common category of expense is *General and Administrative Expense (G&A)*. This is sort of the "all other" category, because it includes everything not grouped under some other heading. If it's not production, research, development, engineering, sales, or marketing, then it must be G&A. Examples include executive salaries, Accounting and Human Resources personnel, many corporate and employee welfare costs, and all the costs of supporting the company's administrative organization. Yep, another cost of doing business.

# Operating Income: The Basic Business Bottom Line

The next important measure of overall profitability—*Operating Income*—is the profit that comes from doing what the company is in business to do. This key number is not yet the "bottom line" we so often refer to, but it's close. It's usually the result of the company's normal business activities, before unusual, nonrecurring, or financially related items that are often considered incidental to what the company is in business to do.

# EBITDA—He Bit Who?

Nowhere to be seen on Wonder Widget's income statement is the term seen so often on reports issued by a growing number of companies in recent years, Earnings Before Interest, Taxes, Depreciation, and Amortization. Folks who fancy buzzwords will appreciate the buzzword for this one—EBITDA, pronounced "ee-bit-dah."

*EBITDA* is a way to present operating income modified for readers who aren't concerned about the financially oriented charges that it excludes. Consider a profit center within a company—perhaps a division whose job is simply to produce operating income. The division general manager is not concerned with corporate office decisions about how to finance the business (that removes interest expense from the calculation of EBITDA), how long to depreciate its assets (that removes depreciation and amortization expense), or how to pay or defer its taxes (that removes income taxes). The resulting calculation is closer to a pure operating income at the unit level, perhaps where this measurement got its initial support.

Later on, of course, it began to appear on the income statements of companies with heavy investments in equipment and heavy debt loads, as

---

 **KEY TERM**   **Earnings before interest, taxes, depreciation, and amortization (EBITDA)** A financial measure for evaluating a company often used as an approximation of operating cash flow, it came into use during the dot-com era to more favorably present the results of technology companies that had incurred large capital costs—thus depreciation and interest expense—but as yet had little in the way of earnings to show for it.

---

a way to show their earnings without the burden of these financial charges. For our purposes, think of it as a different version of operating income.

But let's get back to what our income statement actually shows.

## Other Income and Expenses: Not Just Odds and Ends

Finally, we come to the *Nonoperating Items*, such as interest expense on borrowed money and profits or losses on selling nonbusiness assets that are likely to happen in the normal course of doing business but are not part of running the business. Typical examples include:

- Interest income and interest expense, considered financial costs and not operating costs (unless your company is an insurance company or a bank, for which the rules are different);
- Gain or loss on selling off equipment no longer used by the company;
- Gain or loss on the disposition of investments that were incidental to the business.

These items appear near the bottom of the income statement so that they don't detract from the reader's conclusions about how well the normal business of the company is going. While typically small in relation to the business operations, they are not necessarily minor. In fact, some of them can become very large in relation to net income, especially if the company's profit margins are modest. An example might be the sale of unused land the company has held for many years, often at a price many times greater than the value at which it was carried on the company's books. When such infrequent or one-time items grow very large, they are most likely labeled *Extraordinary Items* and are shown separately, sometimes even with a separate calculation of earnings per share to show their impact on the bottom line.

# Income Before Taxes, Income Taxes, and Net Income

We're coming to the bottom of the page, and we see a number often called *Pretax Income*. The formal label you will most often see is *Income Before Taxes*, although there are variations of that as well, for reasons that even I don't understand. In any event, they all mean the same thing—the income on which the company expects to pay tax, the amount on which its income tax estimate is based. Immediately following that comes the income tax estimate, usually called *Provision for Income Taxes* or something like that.

---

### PRETAX INCOME AND PROVISION FOR INCOME TAXES ARE USUALLY WRONG!

**CAUTION**

OK, not wrong because they were calculated incorrectly, but because they're rarely the actual amounts reported on the company's tax returns. They're estimates, and often not even based on the tax returns actually filed, but on a complex calculation that blends GAAP and the tax laws. So take these numbers with a grain of salt and don't expect to see them on the company's tax returns. No matter, though, because the difference isn't usually controllable.

---

The number that matters most comes last, *Net Income*. This is the real bottom line. It's the financial result of everything the company has done for the period being reported, after all the reasons, the excuses, the bragging, and the complaining. This is it—the final act, the last number you'll see. Well, almost.

# Earnings per Share, Before and After Dilution—What?

For a privately owned company and its principals, nothing matters after Net Income. But if your company is publicly traded and the financial statement is one of the quarterly or annual reports issued to stockholders and the news media, what seems to matter more than net income is a little thing called *Net Income per Share of Stock Owned by Stockholders*, better known as *Earnings per Share (EPS)*.

In this calculation, net income is divided by the number of shares held by all the owners. The result is the amount of that net income (or loss) that is allocable to each share of stock. This is a powerful number in the hands of a media representative, an investment advisor, or an investment banker touting an upcoming stock offering. Why so much attention? It's the easiest way an individual who owns 100 shares of General Motors stock can tell how his or her ownership participated in the company's huge earnings, just as effectively as the investor who owns 100,000 shares of GM. All those reporters and advisors have made EPS one of the principal gauges of a company's profit performance, and thereby, one of the principal indicators of the stock's possible price performance.

**KEY TERM** **Earnings per share fully diluted** Common stock earnings per share calculated as if all stock options and warrants were exercised and if all convertible preferred stock and convertible debt were converted into common stock, thus increasing the number of common shares that will share net income. Also termed *Fully Diluted Earnings per Share.*

The only problem is that there's no one number for EPS, with the result that many companies routinely report two such numbers: *Earnings per Share* and *Earnings per Share Fully Diluted.* Huh? Why two? Well, it's often the case that some company employees—and perhaps others—hold options to buy some of that stock, and they may be waiting for the right time. In the interim, they represent the possibility that there will be more people dividing up that net income than there are now. That is called *dilution.* Dilution can come in a variety of other ways, too, including:

- **Warrants,** a kind of option given to banks and other financial institutions as extra payment for a loan or a public stock offering;
- **Convertible preferred stock,** a class of shares that can be converted into common stock; and
- **Convertible bonds/debentures,** a debt that can be converted into common stock.

There is more to say about these types of financial instruments in Chapter 13.

## DILUTION CAN BE HAZARDOUS TO YOUR INVESTMENT

Let's suppose you bought 10,000 shares of XYZ stock and there are 100 million shares outstanding (including yours). Now, suppose the company reports net income of $100 million for last year. A little quick arithmetic shows us that's $1 per share of earnings for each of those 100 million shares outstanding. Now let's suppose that the *price/earnings ratio* in the marketplace is 20. That would make the likely value of each of your shares $20 and your investment would be worth $200,000. If you bought the stock for $18, you now have a $20,000 profit (on paper).

But wait! There are some stock option holders out there who could purchase 5 million shares of XYZ. They like the earnings report as much as you do, so they all exercise their options right after the report. Now there are 105 million shares outstanding to divide up that $100 million in income, so each share now has claim on only 95 cents of earnings, not $1. At the same P/E ratio of 20, your shares are now worth $19 each, not $20. Because of this dilution, your profit drops from $20,000 to $10,000—a drop of 50 percent.

As the "For Example" sidebar shows above, dilution can significantly affect earnings per share. Accounting rules say you must be able to easily see the effects on EPS if all those option holders exercise their options. Fully diluted earnings per share is almost always shown below the regular (primary) EPS on a public company's income statement. That way you can see what your smaller share of earnings would be under the worst case and make your investment decisions accordingly.

**Price/earnings (P/E) ratio** The relationship between a stock's price and its earnings per share, **KEY TERM** calculated by dividing the current price per share by the earnings per share for the most recent 12-month period. For example, a stock selling for $50 a share and earning $5 a share has a P/E ratio of 10. The ratio—the most common measure of how expensive a stock is—gives investors a rough idea of how much they're paying for earning power. Also termed *earnings multiple, P/E multiple*, or *multiple*.

## Using This Report Effectively

The income statement is a useful tool for understanding a company's performance in a high-level way. Internal income statements used by company managers are typically more useful than those generated for outsiders because they contain details not presented in the published, highly summarized versions. The best way to use an income statement is to put it alongside income statements for prior periods or against the expectations of the company (the budget) or against income statements of other, similar companies. It's by comparison against some benchmark that the income statement has its greatest value. This kind of comparison enables you to assign a performance grade that's not possible when you look only at a statement for a single period.

## Manager's Checklist for Chapter 4

☑ Don't be confused by all the line item labels on income statements. The labels are attempts to adapt to top management's preferences or to unique aspects of one company or industry compared with others. Look for the common thread; marketing is marketing, even if the label is a little different.

☑ Don't be fooled by accounting tricks. Remember that sales belong in the periods in which they were earned and completed, not necessarily where they make the company look good.

☑ Review the few, key numbers on an income statement: sales, gross profit, operating income or EBITDA, and net income. These are the numbers most often reviewed by those with an interest in the company to measure profit performance.

☑ The income statement is the most familiar measure of a company's performance over a period of time. The statement's usefulness increases substantially when compared with a benchmark, such as a budget, prior month, or prior year. The comparison enables you to better judge the company's performance.

# Profit versus Cash Flow: What's the Difference— and Who Cares?

**M**any participants in the workshops my firm leads are surprised to learn that instant profits and rapid growth aren't always cause for celebration. I tell them the story of how the Wonder Widget Company got started.

As a start-up, Wonder Widget was launched with $100,000 in cash and the hottest product in its market, the amazing Wonder Widget. The owners had sales and profits from the first month they had a product to sell! All they had to do was make the product and ship it to waiting customers who would pay enough to give Wonder Widget handsome margins from Day 1. And so the owners leased and outfitted a factory (no cash outlay initially), leased the production equipment and furnishings (still no initial cash outlay), bought the materials, hired the workers, made the product, and shipped it. They then mailed invoices totaling $50,000 to customers in their first month of sales. Amazing!

They paid their bills as they came due, and collected from customers in the normal course of doing business. Their customers were sometimes a bit slow, of course, but nothing out of the ordinary—the kind of 40- to 50-day payment patterns that most companies see today. And sales continued to grow, increasing by $50,000 every month, with no decline in margins and no serious competition. Profits climbed without a pause. The owners didn't have to worry about expanding their product line because everyone continued to want the product. So Wonder Widget just produced and shipped those widgets as fast as they could. This was a business your mother would love!

Yet a strange thing happened on the way to the bank. The owners were suddenly shocked to find they didn't have enough cash to pay their bills. They soon found they couldn't buy more materials to make more widgets. Then they couldn't make payroll. Finally creditors went to court and nearly had the company closed down. Instantly profitable Wonder Widget was insolvent six months after its doors opened!

I hope you're asking "How could that happen?" Good question. Let's try to answer.

To do that, we need to look at how cash typically flows through a company. As usual, Wonder Widget is our example.

## The Cash Flow Cycle

At the beginning of the cash cycle, nearly every business starts with— you guessed it—cash. But from that point on, the central purpose of the business is to convert that cash into other kinds of assets, to leverage or extend it with liabilities, and to ultimately turn it back into cash, but more cash than the business started with. This process continues indefinitely and simultaneously throughout the existence of a business.

> **KEY TERM**
> **Cash cycle** In general, the time between cash disbursement and cash collection. In manufacturing, this cycle consists of converting cash into raw materials, raw materials into finished goods, finished goods into receivables, and receivables back into cash. Also known as *cash flow cycle*, *cash conversion cycle*, and *operating cycle*.

In the final analysis, when a company closes its doors, the only real financial measure of its success is the difference between the amount of cash it started with and the amount it ended with, after considering cash distributed to its owners over the life of the business. However, during the life of a company we can't very well judge how much cash it would produce if it were closed and liquidated, so we measure success in terms of how it succeeds in conducting activities that ultimately produce cash, usually measured in terms of profits and other financial factors included in the monthly reports we discussed in Chapters 3 and 4.

Let's look at this cycle as it applies to Wonder Widget by referring to the diagram in Figure 5-1, in which activities are moving clockwise in an endless process as the business operates.

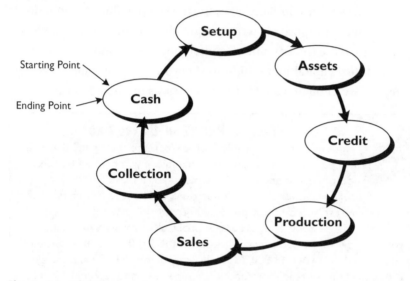

**Figure 5-1.** Cash flow cycle

When Wonder Widget started up, its first activities revolved around setup—renting facilities, installing phones and utilities, and the like. Most of this required the outlay of cash for rent deposits, phone service, utility deposits, and other, related costs.

Closely aligned with setup, and often simultaneous, was the purchase of assets to commence business operations. These included office equipment and computers for administrative purposes and factory equipment to manufacture widgets. For distributors, wholesalers, or retailers, those costs would include equipping warehouse space to stock the merchandise that they will buy and resell.

The most important asset for any business is people, of course, and Wonder Widget was probably hiring staff all along the way toward the start of production—to answer phones, to run the office, and to produce and sell their product. Of course, this can get expensive. If the owners had lots of cash, they might have paid for all these things by writing a check, using money from investors or cash they themselves invested in the beginning. Usually, however, prudent owners go to their bank or a finance company to get an extended period of time to pay for their larger purchases, such as machinery, furniture, and buildings.

That is where the company takes the next step in the cycle: obtaining credit. The main purpose of credit in a growing business is to enable the owners to increase the amount of capital they have working for them by using creditors' capital in addition to their own. This is called leverage, putting more capital to work for the business, as discussed in Chapter 3.

---

**FOR EXAMPLE**

### THERE'S PROFIT IN BORROWING

Borrowing money enables you to increase the capital that you can put to work for you. For example, if you have $1,000 that you can invest and earn 10 percent, you'll make $100 a year in profit. However, if you can borrow $4,000 more from a bank at 5 percent interest, you can now put $5,000 to work earning 10 percent, which will produce $500 a year. Your net profit, after paying $200 in interest to your lender, will be $300, much more than the $100 you'd have earned if you'd invested only your $1,000. You've leveraged your $1,000 and tripled its productivity. You'll read more about leverage in Chapters 7 and 13.

---

In any event, cash is still going out at this point, even though the company's use of credit may allow some delay in payouts. We know the Wonder Widget owners used credit to leverage their cash because unhappy creditors later took them to court.

Wonder Widget was now ready to begin production, manufacturing widgets. It began by using its inventories of materials, adding the labor of the workers and a host of other costs needed to complete the widgets. This process consumed even more cash—for workers' wages and related taxes, materials to replace those consumed in production, sales and marketing efforts to find customers for their products, delivery of products to customers, billing, administration, accounting, and so on. This is typically the period of greatest cash consumption: when a company is in full production but no cash is coming in yet. The company hasn't sold anything, or it has sold products but on credit, so the customers haven't yet paid. At the same time, production and all the related business activities mentioned above must continue.

Continuing with the remaining steps in the cash flow cycle: After investing all that cash, the company finally sells something and begins the process of recovering that cash it's been investing. In the sales part of the cycle, it succeeds in selling products (on credit, of course) and sends out invoices that say "Net 30" on them. That means the customers will pay them 30 days after the date on the invoice, right? Not likely.

While collection may seem like a minor activity compared with production or sales, it's the critical step that makes all the rest pay off. Nolan Bushnell, founder of Atari and Chuck E. Cheese Restaurants, has told his employees and countless audiences of would-be entrepreneurs that "a sale is a gift to the customer until the money is in the bank." So the final step in the cycle is the one that turns the entire effort back into cash. At that point some key answers surface: Did the company make a profit on its business activities? Did the company plan adequately for the working capital it needs to finance the cash flow cycle in its entirety? As we've seen in the Wonder Widget example, one "yes" out of two isn't good enough.

Let's stop for a moment and consider the situation. The owners of Wonder Widget had a hit on their hands in terms of demand. There were lots of people eager to buy their widgets, and the company probably pushed productivity to the limit to meet as much of that demand as possible. So they ordered lots of materials, hired lots of workers, shipped lots of product, and then waited for lots of customers to pay them.

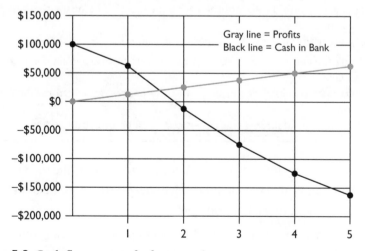

**Figure 5-2.** Cash flow curve of a fast-growing start-up company

The owners had to invest their cash up front to establish the company, make the widgets, ship the product, and invoice the customers. Meantime, since a new company often doesn't get much slack from its vendors, they probably had to pay their bills on time, often earlier than if they'd been in business for a while. And of course, if their customers thought that start-up Wonder Widget was glad for the business and would be patient about bill payment, some buyers may have delayed slightly in paying their invoices.

None of these activities by themselves would have rendered the company insolvent, yet together they did exactly that, because they all added up to critically delay the cash flow. Wonder Widget's situation might have looked much like Figure 5-2, with the available cash unable to sustain all the demands of growing the business.

---

**SMART**

**MANAGING**

### FAST GROWTH MEANS A BIG APPETITE FOR CASH

Fast-growing companies need more working capital than those growing more slowly or not at all. When incoming cash flow is delayed while fixed costs continue and paydays come every week, there's a limit to how long a company can operate comfortably, even if it is profitable. Remember the strong demand Wonder Widget was experiencing? Every month its sales grew from the month before, which meant that to fill larger orders from customers, they had to obtain more materials than they'd had to get a month earlier. Thus, the cost of production grew even before their customers began to pay. This kind of success can rapidly accelerate the cash squeeze on a company that's undercapitalized.

Managers in fast-growing businesses should follow these three rules:

1. Look for every opportunity to stretch your cash, especially for large purchases.
2. Forecast your cash needs as far into the future as you can reasonably see.
3. Arrange for additional sources of cash well before you need it.

---

Now, you may look at Wonder Widget and say that the owners could have done something to help themselves despite their failure to use some key management tools. For example:

■ The owners could have raised prices to produce more profit sooner. That would have helped eventually, but perhaps not in time. In fact, the company was profitable from the start. The problem wasn't in making a profit, but in converting that profit into cash.

- They could have gotten accounts receivable financing to help them get cash out of their receivables sooner. This might have also helped and perhaps it would be part of the ultimate solution. But history shows that most lenders are unwilling to lend to new companies until they've proven able to conduct business reliably, so that customers are less likely to raise complaints that would prevent prompt collection of the accounts that serve as the loan collateral.

- They could have raised more capital for their business from friends, family, or outside investors. We don't know if they tried this and were unsuccessful because their urgent need made potential investors wary. We do know that, although they ultimately survived, they didn't raise money in time to prevent the cash flow crisis.

But that's not the point of the story. Wonder Widget's owners had made serious management errors, in spite of having a great product, seemingly endless demand, and super profit margins. And those errors could have cost them their company. First, they didn't forecast their expected cash flow needs during their critical early months, a subject discussed in some depth in Chapter 12. Second, they didn't recognize the need to track cash flow results separately from profits. They looked at the income statement each month, saw that their efforts had produced a profit, and happily moved on.

## BUSINESS GOES WITH THE FLOW

The strength of a business depends on a healthy cash flow. More businesses fail due to the lack of cash than the lack of profits. Cash flow is not the same as profits; it's all a question of timing. It's essential, then, that cash flow be properly understood and managed as carefully as revenue, expenses, and profits.

Dave Berkus, a highly regarded (and highly successful) Southern California serial entrepreneur, investor, and author, has said:

Business plans that I see often show three to five years of projections, demonstrating profitability at the end of so many months of operation. Most every one of these uses an accrual basis for determining breakeven, never attempting to predict the cash impact of capital investment, slow collection times, large deposits upon leases, and other major items that consume cash.

If cash flow is so important, then why doesn't it show up somewhere in the books? And how can we make it easier to see and understand? Well, it does show up in the books, since every transaction involving cash is recorded somewhere. The challenge comes in putting it into an understandable format. (We discuss the Statement of Cash Flow in Chapter 6.)

## Cash Basis versus Accrual Basis

Financial reports can look different, depending on the accounting method used to keep the books. There are two basic choices of accounting method, as discussed briefly in Chapter 2—cash and accrual.

Some small businesses keep their books on the cash basis because it's simpler to understand—sort of like running the business out of your checkbook—and because it often coincides with the way they file their tax returns. As long as the owners don't care about the strict definition of profits, that works. An example might be a consultant who sells her time to clients. She's not very concerned about gross margins because her operating costs are relatively low. But she's very concerned about cash flow, because without it there's no paycheck for her.

On the other hand, most small businesses (and all large ones) keep their books on the accrual basis, usually for one or more of three reasons:

1. They're concerned about the profit margin on products they sell.
2. They want to know when they're making money and when they're not.
3. They're required by lenders, investors, or government authorities to report their activities in that way.

These are all good reasons to use accrual basis accounting, and most experts recommend that choice. But many of these same companies look only at their income statements, but don't prepare cash flow reports. Instead, they rely on good old rule-of-thumb methods to manage the cash so that they don't run short or let unused cash sit idle.

Our purpose here is not to tell you which accounting method is best for you—although, like most professional advisors, we prefer accrual accounting because it gives most business owners so much useful information. Rather, we want to help you understand the differences between accounting methods, so you can make the better choice. Some software packages, such as QuickBooks by Intuit, enable you to easily print reports using both the accrual and cash bases. Regardless of which method you use, keep in mind the importance of looking at the other method in some fashion so you can benefit from the management information that's available to you.

Let's take a closer look at some of the data that Wonder Widget management overlooked. In the process, you might see how your own company's management team might use its financial reports more effectively. For the sake of clarity, we assume your records are kept on the accrual basis of accounting, reflecting transactions when they happen, as discussed in Chapters 3 and 4.

# Net Profit versus Cash Flow in Your Financial Reports

How does bottom-line profit differ from cash flow, exactly? Or, more specifically, how do individual transactions affect your company's reported profits and cash flow differently? Anyone who has compared income statements and bank statements knows that profit never makes its way to the bank account in exactly the same amount that appears on the income statement. That difference is primarily the result of four kinds of transactions:

1. Transactions that increase profits but don't produce cash until later;
2. Transactions that decrease profits but don't reduce cash until later;
3. Transactions that put cash in the bank first but don't help your profits until later—if at all; and
4. Transactions that take cash but may or may not affect profits later.

Let's look at each of these in turn.

## Type 1. Transactions That Increase Profits But Don't Produce Cash Until Later

This is perhaps the largest and most obvious example of the difference we're talking about—and the most significant item in this group is accounts receivable. Consider this example.

If your business is a retail store, you typically sell something and get paid in cash. (For the moment we ignore the delays that come from credit card sales.) The result is an increase in sales and a corresponding increase in cash in the drawer. But if you're a supplier to that retailer—the whole-saler—you typically wait anywhere from 30–120 days or more to get paid, depending on the industry and time of year. You still record a sale when you ship your merchandise, but you don't receive payment at the same time. You issue an invoice with the payment terms of the sale, typically 30 days or longer. The retailer records the invoice into accounts payable when the merchandise is received and pays it weeks or months later, ide-ally in accordance with your terms. In the interim, you must acknowledge that although you have a sale and a resulting profit, you have no money to back it up. You must plan to have enough cash on hand or instantly available to pay operating expenses between the time you ship the mer-chandise and the time your customer pays the invoice, often including the cost of the merchandise itself.

For companies that sell on credit, waiting for customers to pay their bills is the largest single factor necessitating extra cash availability.

## Type 2. Transactions That Decrease Profits But Don't Reduce Cash Until Later

The other side of the coin is the situation that produces an expense or profit reduction first and a cash disbursement later. The most obvious example is accounts payable, liabilities that you incur when you pur-chase consumable supplies and services. The supplies and services are typically charged to expense (profits) when purchased, although the supplier's bill might not be paid until the following month.

Let's take our Wonder Widget example. The owners might have gained some cash flow advantage from purchasing their raw materials on credit, as most businesses do. In fact, given the demand for their prod-ucts, they might have even put some of those raw materials into produc-tion before they had to pay for them. If they did, they could potentially have shipped finished goods to customers before they had even paid their suppliers for the raw materials that went into the widgets. They would have recorded as expenses the costs of those goods, commonly called cost of goods sold, even though they had not yet written a check to pay for the materials. This would have postponed paying, but not delayed recording costs on their income statement. Thus, costs would appear on their income statement even though no cash had left their bank account.

## Type 3. Transactions That Put Cash in the Bank But Don't Help Your Profits Until Later—If at All

Cash flow means everything that affects your bank balance. That includes sources of cash that might never impact profits. Consider the effect of going to the bank to borrow money. You get the loan, deposit the money in your bank account, and thus, experience positive cash flow. Yet there is no change in your profits as a result of the loan—aside from the good things you might do with the money later that will improve profits. But you don't get to keep the money forever; sooner or later you must repay it. (We discuss this in the next section.)

Closely related, particularly for new companies, is the effect of having outsiders invest in their company. The investors write a check, then the company deposits the check and issues stock to its new investors. The company can use that money, but it never appears on the income statement. Wonder Widget started operations with money like that, and it was recorded directly on the balance sheet as capital stock, not in the income statement as sale of stock.

## Type 4. Transactions That Take Cash But May or May Not Affect Profits Later

Do you remember the loan that put cash in the bank without recording a profit increase? A loan repayment is the flip side—money is paid out but there's no reduction in profits. Of course, while you have the loan outstanding, you have to pay interest on it, which is recorded as interest expense on your income statement. But the principal reduction portion of your payment is simply returning the money to the bank, a transaction that affects both sides of your balance sheet but not your income statement.

Another example of a cash payment with a delayed impact on profit is the purchase of assets for a business—machinery, automobiles, etc.— that typically benefit the company for a number of years. A manufacturing company might pay cash for equipment that might last 5–10 years or more. Because the assets are purchased to benefit the business for years to come, accounting standards require that the cost of those assets be charged to income over the periods that receive the benefit, not the month in which the assets were purchased and paid for.

Of course, a manufacturer might choose to finance its purchases through installment contracts or leases and, thus, bring its cash payments and the periods benefited into closer alignment. It might finance a machine over five years and depreciate it over the same five years. This is helpful for many assets, but doesn't solve the problem entirely because financing periods often are shorter than the useful lives of the assets being financed. For example, a factory machine might last 7–10 years or more, yet few banks will finance such purchases for longer than 3–5 years. Thus, even in this seemingly ideal scenario, you still have a disparity between the cash disbursement and recording the depreciation expense.

Another example is prepaid expenses (discussed in Chapter 3), which are amortized, for instance, an insurance policy on which an annual premium is paid in advance. When you buy the insurance and pay the premium, that policy provides protection for a year. Proper accounting treatment says the premium benefits all 12 months and, therefore, should be charged to profits over the benefit period, not only to the month in which you paid the premium. So you write your check in January, but you record as expense only 1/12 of the check amount each month over the next 12 months, the period of coverage. Cash flow and expense are reflected totally differently in this example.

As you can see, some of these examples describe transactions in which the cash flow never affects profits, but most are cases where the expense and the cash flow happen at different times. Business managers often overlook these timing differences because they "know" the effects will pretty much equal each other over time. But they forget how significant such differences can be in the short term, when cash flow planning can be the most critical.

# Manager's Checklist for Chapter 5

☑ The cash flowing through every company is an endless process that converts cash to operating assets and expenditures and, ultimately, back to cash. The secret is to manage the process so there's more cash at the end than at the beginning. The management challenge is to know how well you're succeeding at that when a company is operating normally, with many cash cycles occurring simultaneously to create a net cash flow.

☑ Net cash flow is never the same as net profit; managers must track both to be well informed about their company's financial condition. The best way to do that is to prepare monthly financial reports that show both measures—cash flow and net profit.

☑ Managers in fast-growing companies always need more working capital to support growth. They should consider every opportunity to conserve cash for future growth by such means as financing large purchases and arranging backup lines of credit before they're needed.

☑ Businesses routinely take on obligations that require large amounts of cash, such as building inventories and extending credit to customers. Much of that investment is a necessary cost of doing business; however, keep in mind that every dollar invested in inventory and accounts receivable is at risk of loss until it again becomes cash.

☑ An estimated cash flow forecast that looks 6–12 months into the future is an excellent management tool. A forecast gives managers time to make decisions and arrange alternative sources of cash that can prevent surprise shortages.

# The Statement of Cash Flow: Tracking the King

I n the preceding chapters we examined the income statement in some detail. We noted its importance in measuring the organization's performance and its familiarity as the financial statement most readily recognized and understood by nonfinancial folks. We should also recognize three shortcomings of the income statement as the sole report card of financial operations:

1. It doesn't report on all transactions that occur in a company unless they have an immediate impact on profit or loss. Many transactions without such immediate profit and loss impact can be for big dollars, such as buying equipment for the plant or borrowing money from the bank.
2. It doesn't explain why the net profit never appears as an actual improvement to the company's bank balance.
3. It doesn't give growing companies a tool to manage their scarcest resource: cash to finance growth.

That's why we suggested in Chapter 4 that you resist voting for the income statement as the most important financial report until you hear from the unheralded, often unseen, frequently unread, but resoundingly relevant *Statement of Cash Flow.*

Most have heard that adage: Cash is king! Yet for many business professionals, that most often means making sure there's money in the bank or in the cash register or in their pockets. However, if there's one thing that consulting professionals, lenders, and turnaround experts all agree on, it's that the cash a company has on hand is a *trailing indicator* of its financial condition. In other words, by the time the status of a company's liquidity is reflected in the bank account, the cause of the problem is already history and there's not much managers can do about it. Company executives often focus on the symptom, fixing the immediate cash shortage, instead of finding and fixing the original cause of the problem— product pricing, operating efficiency, credit granting policy, or a host of other possible causes.

So the trick for every manager is to be continually aware of where the cash is coming from and where it's going, both for historical evaluation and for future planning. How best to do that? Well, there are two choices: They can pore over their cash journals and bank statements and prepare an exhaustive analysis of their bank account transactions each month *or* they can prepare an automated *financial report* that summarizes those transactions and identifies the general causes of increases and decreases. Hmm ... Which one should we choose?

Let's go for the financial report, shall we? And to make our job easier, let's pick one that shows us all the major reasons net profit didn't produce an identical amount of cash going into the bank. Huh? There couldn't possibly be a single report that contains that much information about something as critical as cash, could there? Wouldn't such a report be on the desk of every manager who has any kind of financial responsibility in his or her company?

Ladies and gentlemen, allow me to introduce to you the Statement of Cash Flow.

OK, maybe that's a bit dramatic. But the reality isn't too far afield from my playful musing. Most small businesses, for example, don't routinely prepare a statement of cash flow as part of their monthly financial reporting, even though almost all accounting software systems can produce one on demand. In larger companies with a well-staffed Accounting Department, the report is often produced but infrequently read, except by the accountants and the CFO, whose job it is to act on it (and perhaps tell others what it says).

# Beginning Where the Income Statement Ends

There are two basic formats for presenting the cash flow statement; in this book we use the indirect presentation method. It's the same format that appears in all published financial reports of public companies and that's readily produced by most accounting software. It's also the format that produces the most useful information with the least paper. And the good news is that it begins where the income statement ends—literally—because its intent is to answer that important question raised earlier: What's the difference between net profit and net cash flow?

Answering that question gets us into defining the differences and then presenting them in a way that nonfinancial readers can understand. A few words about format are helpful here before we take a look at a report.

Accountants have presented cash flow in two ways traditionally, the direct method and the indirect method.

The direct method is what you'd probably prepare if you were analyzing your checking account to see where the money came from and where it went. It would look something like Figure 6-1.

| Cash Receipts | |
|---|---|
| Amounts Collected from Customers | $372,500 |
| Advances from Bank Credit Line | 10,500 |
| Sale of Short-Term Investments | 24,000 |
| Total Cash Receipts | 407,000 |
| | |
| Cash Disbursements | |
| Paid to Creditors | 308,200 |
| Payroll and Payroll Taxes Paid | 122,600 |
| Purchase of New Equipment | 45,000 |
| Payments on Long-Term Debt | 4,000 |
| Dividend Payments | 5,000 |
| Total Cash Disbursements | 484,800 |
| Net Cash Flow (Drain) | (77,800) |
| Add Balance of Cash—Beginning of Period | 113,100 |
| Balance of Cash—End of Period | $35,300 |

**Figure 6-1.** Statement of cash receipts and disbursements

As you can see from Figure 6-1, the report shows cash coming in and cash going out. Well, isn't that what it's supposed to show? Yes. But it can and should show much more. Notice that there's no mention of net income on this report or an attempt to explain the difference between net income and net cash flow—a key difference for anyone managing a company. Nor does the report show inflows and outflows grouped by purpose or cause. There's more information that can be communicated as well. A variation of the statement of cash receipts and disbursements was once called the statement of sources and applications of funds, but it was only marginally more useful and is rarely seen these days.

That's why the indirect method was developed, why it's the standard report format used in published annual reports, and why it's the format that nearly all accounting software programs produce when you ask for a cash flow statement. It's a bit harder to understand initially, but the potential for meaningful analysis is far greater. That's why we discuss only the indirect method format in this chapter and what each line tells you. If you find you need to read over this section a few times to get the concepts working for you, it's time well spent.

**KEY TERMS**

**Direct method of presenting cash flow** Shows the major categories of cash receipts and cash payments, summarizing cash inflows and outflows. This method may be more understandable for people without accounting training; however, it lacks analysis value.

**Indirect method of presenting cash flow** Begins with net income and adjusts for changes in account balances that affect cash but are not included in the calculation of net income. Each adjustment either increases or decreases the net change in cash, which is the report's objective. This is today's standard method because it shows a line-by-line reconciliation between reported net income and net change in cash, and because that valuable information doesn't appear on other financial reports.

Let's look at the monthly statement of cash flow from the Wonder Widget Company's monthly statement of cash flow (Figure 6-2). Notice that the first entry on the page is net income, which tells us that this statement picks up where the income statement left off. The idea is that net income is presumed to equal the net cash flow, except for the adjustments that make up the details of this statement. Notice also that the entries are divided into three sections—Operations, Investing, and Financing—the three principal areas of cash activity for virtually all companies.

Let's explore Wonder Widget's activities and see what we can learn from its cash flow reporting. I've slipped in a couple transactions that our early-stage company might not be able to pull off yet, like long-term borrowing, but this gives us more opportunity to explain the kinds of entries we might see on a more fully developed company's report. I've also added a comment to each line on the report to help you understand the nature of the transactions that created the need for the adjustment. We comment on those further in the respective sections that follow.

| | | |
|---|---:|---:|
| **Net Income** | | $19,200 |
| **Adjustments from Operating Activities** | | |
| Add back depreciation—no cash paid for this | 7,500 | |
| Increase in accounts receivable—more sold than collected | (125,600) | |
| Decrease in prepaid expenses—amortized, but no cash paid | 1,500 | |
| Decrease in inventory—cash raised by lowering stock on hand | 10,600 | |
| Increase in accounts payable—cash borrowed from creditors | 28,500 | (77,500) |
| Cash flow provided by (used for) Operations | | (58,300) |
| | | |
| **Adjustments from Investing Activities** | | |
| Capital expenditures—cash invested in new equipment | (45,000) | |
| Short-term investments sold—net proceeds from sale | 24,000 | |
| Cash flow provided by (used for) Investments | | (21,000) |
| | | |
| **Adjustments from Financing Activities** | | |
| Increase in bank debt—new short-term borrowing from bank | 10,500 | |
| Net reduction in long-term debt—payments made on long-term loans | (4,000) | |
| Dividends paid to stockholders—cash paid out to owners | (5,000) | |
| Cash flow provided by (used for) Financing | | 1,500 |
| | | |
| Net Cash Flow (Drain) | | (77,800) |
| **Add balance of cash—beginning period** | | 113,100 |
| **Balance of cash—end of period** | | $35,300 |

**Figure 6-2.** Statement of cash flow (indirect method)

# Cash from Operations: Running the Business

*Operations* is the process of running the company, with all the related cash flows such as buying and selling goods and services, manufacturing, and paying employees. In the simplest situations involving only the day-to-day operations, this is the conversion of net income from operations into net cash flow from operations. You'll see how that happens as this chapter unfolds.

## Net Income

The first line is net income because, as we've noted, a prime objective of this report is to show the differences between net income and net cash flow. The net income number is the same amount that appears at the bottom of the income statement. Next we list as adjustments to net income all the operating items that increased or decreased cash in ways that were not included in the calculation of net income (e.g., loans).

## Add Back Depreciation

Do you remember the way equipment and other assets are charged to expense? Depreciation—the gradual charging of an item's cost to expense over its useful life, as discussed in Chapter 5—is recorded each month after the asset is put into use. No cash changes hands as a result of those depreciation entries, because the cash was all paid out when the asset was bought. So the monthly charge for depreciation expense must be removed from reported net income, in effect *increasing* income in Figure 6-2 by the $7,500 that had no effect on cash. (We call these *non-cash items.*) So depreciation expense is always added back to net income, usually as the first adjustment on this report.

## Increase in Accounts Receivable

Some of the customer balances (accounts receivable) that Wonder Widget had at the beginning of the month were collected during the month and some were not. Similarly, some of the sales made during the month were paid for by their customers, although typically payments for credit sales on 30-day terms would not have come in yet (retail cash businesses aside, of course). At the end of the month the company had some of the opening customer balances still outstanding, as well as some of the new balances.

Look at this another way. If all the customer balances at the beginning of the month and all sales during the month were collected in cash, there would be no ending accounts receivable, and the month's cash receipts from customers would equal their opening balances plus the month's sales. However, since there were outstanding balances at the end of the month, the amount of cash Wonder Widget took in must be reduced by those outstanding balances that will hopefully be paid later. Here it is as a formula:

Beginning accounts receivable + Sales − Ending accounts receivable =
Cash collections

But remember that the month's sales are included in net income. This line item on the report shows how much of the period's sales must be removed from the cash flow calculation because the cash for them hasn't yet been received. If we rearrange the formula, it now looks like this:

Sales + (Beginning accounts receivable − Ending accounts receivable) =
Cash collections

So the difference between sales (100 percent of which are included in net income) and cash collections is the difference between accounts receivable at the beginning of the month and accounts receivable at the end of the month. Since the company sold more to its customers during the month than it collected, this adjustment is a negative amount, showing less cash was collected than what was sold. In other words, Wonder Widget *loaned* its customers $125,600 in cash by not collecting as much as it sold, so cash was reduced as a result.

## Decrease in Prepaid Expenses

In our Chapter 3 discussion of Prepaid Expenses we talked about the up-front payment for items that have an extended period of value, such as insurance. We noted that such payments are expensed over the period for which they provide value by periodic charges to net income, *charges that do not require additional payment of cash*. Each monthly charge to income for a portion of prepaid expense is a noncash charge, just like depreciation, and the company would add it back to net income in the same fashion, getting one step closer to the actual cash flow for the month.

A NEGATIVE ADJUSTMENT FOR ACCOUNTS
RECEIVABLE IS A RED FLAG

**CAUTION**

This small gem of information (customer balances outstanding) is hugely important if cash management is important to the company, because the amount the company in effect loaned to customers means that cash has to come from somewhere—it will stay out of the company's cash balance until those accounts receivable balances are collected. If this increase in customer balances happens every month, the balance sheet could be growing and sales could be growing, but the company could be slowly slipping into insolvency, as Wonder Widget was in Chapter 5.

Now, having accounts receivable grow, i.e., lending more money to the company's customers, may be all right if sales grow as much or more, because a growing company that sells on credit—and does reasonable cash flow planning—should normally expect its accounts receivable to grow as its sales grow. But if sales are flat or down from the prior month and the company *still* loaned more money to its customers than it collected, that would mean its collection effort was inadequate. Its customers are using up the company's working capital by delaying payment. Remember: Any increase in receivable balances greater than the monthly increase in sales is an additional interest-free loan to your customers. That will sink a company that doesn't plan ahead.

Of course, the reverse is also true. In the same month the company might also pay an insurance premium for the coming year, thus making a big cash disbursement that would not be charged to expense—the opposite of the amortization adjustment above. In this case the adjustment would be negative, showing cash paid out that was not reported as an expense on the income statement.

This line on the statement of cash flow is the net of these two types of adjustments. The decrease of $1,500 in Figure 6-2 indicates that the non-cash expense for amortization was larger than any amounts paid out for new prepaid items. So we add back the $1,500 as additional cash generated by the month's activity.

## Decrease in Inventory

You may be able to visualize this one without too much effort. If Wonder Widget purchased only the merchandise it sold during the month—the way Dell traditionally has done it—it would need to keep essentially no inventory of goods on hand. It would buy only what it sold and sell everything it bought. Since that doesn't work for most companies—and even Dell has some inventory—the change in inventory balances works on the cash account just like accounts receivable.

Remember: The income statement includes the cost of all inventory sold during the month. The inventory adjustment on the statement of cash flow is needed *only* if the beginning inventory balance changed by the end of the month, indicating the company purchased inventory it didn't sell during the month or sold inventory it didn't have to purchase that month. As a formula, it would look like this:

Beginning inventory + Cost of inventory purchased − Cost of inventory sold = Ending inventory

Or, if we rearrange the pieces a bit:

(Cost of inventory sold − Cost of inventory purchased) = (Beginning inventory − Ending inventory)

And here's one more look to get us where we want to go:

(Beginning inventory − Ending inventory) = Increase in cash from liquidating inventory

The cash flow adjustment would be positive if the inventory balance was reduced during the month, indicating the company sold some goods out of beginning inventories and did not spend cash to replace them. This latter situation is what happened to Wonder Widget in the month shown. Conversely, the cash flow adjustment must *deduct* the cash cost of any inventory added to beginning inventory balances, meaning that

---

## INVENTORY UP, SALES NOT: ANOTHER RED FLAG FOR CASH!

**CAUTION**

A company adds inventory when it anticipates growing sales. Toy companies add inventory all year long for their big holiday selling season. But that costs cash—and inventory doesn't convert to cash for a long time. Inventory must first become sales and accounts receivable before it becomes cash again. If inventory is increasing and sales forecasts aren't growing accordingly, the company may be investing too much in goods that might never become cash. Liquidating old inventory is a poor way to raise cash—and it almost always results in a loss on the income statement.

the company bought more than it sold and inventory increased during the month, costing cash.

## Increase in Accounts Payable

The last operating item in the operating section of the report is accounts payable, amounts owed to creditors of all kinds. Since payment of liabilities requires the use of cash, any change in a company's accounts payable means it has either used cash to pay some trade obligations (reducing accounts payable) or it increased the amount owed to creditors, thus borrowing money from them for use in the company.

If a company raises cash by letting its creditor balances build, as Wonder Widget apparently did, thus increasing cash by $28,500, the result is a higher payables balance at the end of the month than at the beginning. The resulting cash flow adjustment is upward, showing cash coming in from creditors.

However, if the company had ended the month with lower accounts payable than at the beginning, it would have effectively paid more money to its creditors than it borrowed from them through new purchases; in that case the cash flow adjustment would have been a deduction, showing an outflow of cash. Again, the change in accounts payable from the beginning to the end of the month is a quick way to calculate the amount of this adjustment, whether it increased or decreased cash in the company's bank account.

# Cash for Investing: Building the Business

Investing in and growing the business involves plowing back some of the cash generated by the business or bringing in capital from outside the business. Growth investment can include buying equipment for expansion, buying or selling investment assets, and other activities that enable the company to increase its resources for doing more business.

## Capital Expenditures

The most common description of capital expenditures is the amount spent for equipment used in the business. Expenditures for such assets require cash, but are not charged to income. (Refer to the discussion of depreciation above and in Chapter 4.) Therefore the cash paid out for them is shown here as a reduction in cash. In our example, Wonder Widget paid $45,000 cash for equipment to use in its operations. Since the asset purchase is not an expense—that is, not included in the calculation of net income—its cash cost appears as a capital expenditure in the investing section of the report. Money spent for equipment is always considered an investment in the company, building its physical resources.

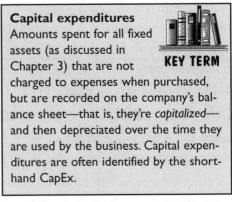

**Capital expenditures**
Amounts spent for all fixed assets (as discussed in Chapter 3) that are not **KEY TERM** charged to expenses when purchased, but are recorded on the company's balance sheet—that is, they're *capitalized*—and then depreciated over the time they are used by the business. Capital expenditures are often identified by the shorthand CapEx.

But maybe the company borrowed the money to pay for the equipment instead of writing a check. What then? Remember that purchasing equipment and borrowing money are two separate management decisions, so they're treated separately in the report details. Although the company may have obtained the purchase cash by borrowing it, the purchase is still a commitment of cash. So it appears here as a deduction. Had the company financed the purchase, an offsetting item would appear in the statement's Financing section, discussed below. Notice there's no comparable influx of cash in the Financing section, so it's unlikely that Wonder Widget borrowed money for this purchase. Rather, it used its available cash. Another example of management not paying attention to its cash needs.

## Investments Sold

Sometimes a company invests excess cash so that the money works for the company until needed in operations. Such investments are typically short-term commitments, such as bank certificates of deposit or marketable securities, which the company sells when it needs the cash. Emerging companies with successful public offerings of their stock (more on this in Chapter 14) often raise a lot of cash before they're ready to use it; short-term investments are a way to earn income from those otherwise idle cash balances. Since Wonder Widget had only long-term investments on its balance sheet (Figure 3-1), we assume management decided to sell some of them to raise cash.

When an investment is purchased, it appears as a cash expenditure in this section as a reduction in cash. When an investment is sold, as has apparently occurred in our example, the sale's net proceeds are an additional source of cash. Wonder Widget raised $24,000 in this fashion, perhaps to partially pay for its equipment purchase.

## Other Examples of Investment Items

There are other kinds of transactions that would appear on this statement if the company engaged in them. Notable examples include:

- Acquiring or selling off other companies, subsidiaries, or business segments;
- Purchasing real estate for future expansion or selling unneeded real estate; and
- Buying or selling long-term investment assets.

# Cash from Financing: Capitalizing the Business

*Financing* is an activity intended to raise money to pay for operations and investments when operations alone don't generate sufficient cash. When a company is expanding and needs more cash than it can raise through profitable operations and it lacks salable investments, outside financing is an option. Selling stock in the company to investors or borrowing money from banks or other lenders are ways to help finance the company that would appear in this section. Conversely, buying back the company's stock or repaying borrowed money are also financing activities, but they reduce cash by retiring the vehicles by which capital was brought in previously.

## Increase in Bank Debt

Wonder Widget has succeeded in borrowing $10,500 from a bank, perhaps all it could get to help with the equipment purchase. We can't tell the purpose of the loan by looking only at this report, but we can see that it resulted in an increase in cash during the month.

Of course, if we look further into the company books, we could see if the company actually borrowed more than $10,500 and used some of that cash increase to repay other loans, which would reduce cash. This line shows the net result of all such transactions, although the report might just as easily have shown two lines: one for new money borrowed (an increase in cash) and another line for loan repayments (a decrease in cash).

How do we find out what actually happened? A quick look at the Wonder Widget balance sheet (see Chapter 3) reveals it does have short-term bank loans on the books, so it likely made loan payments, which would appear in this section of the cash flow statement. If we were to prepare a longer form of this report, we might expand it to show both sides of these transactions on separate lines, thus providing additional information to readers.

## Net Reduction in Long-Term Debt

This item is similar to bank loans in the way it flows through the report; actually, it probably *is* bank loans. Additional borrowings increase cash; repayments reduce cash. The separate classification and different labels reflect the fact that long-term debt is shown on a different line of the balance sheet because of its different characteristics—long-term vs. short-term. This helps the reader associate the two statements when reading the company's financial report. In this particular month, Wonder Widget made a $4,000 payment on its long-term debt and apparently borrowed no more money in this category, so the net change is a cash reduction of $4,000. We can't be certain of this from the short format in our example, but logic tells us that a net change in cash of so modest a payment amount was unlikely to include anything other than a monthly payment. A quick look at the balance sheet in our example and the one from the prior month (if we had it) would likely confirm our notion that no new debt was incurred.

## Dividends Paid to Stockholders

A profitable company's board of directors often elects to pay a distribution of profits to its owners. A corporation makes that distribution in the form of a dividend on the shares of stock held by its stockholders, as in our example. Since such distributions are almost always in cash and they are not expenses that would appear on the income statement, this is the only report on which such payments are likely to appear.

**DIVIDENDS COME FROM PROFITS, NOT LOSSES!**
While Wonder Widget technically had enough profits to pay a dividend, you'd have to ask yourself why a new company without strong cash flow would do so—and that would be a good question to ask Wonder Widget's board of directors, in view of its modest cash position. Since the directors are probably also the owners, this could have been a self-serving act that wasn't in the company's best interests but in the interests of the owners personally.

Such questionable judgments are sometimes made in privately owned companies run by their owners, for whom personal cash flow problems often impact their companies. As we've seen in the past few years, even the largest companies can fall victim to the bad judgment of their top executives/stockholders. While this decision was not necessarily bad, you closely examine the reasons whenever dividends are not clearly coming from excess profits that the company doesn't need.

## Net Cash Flow (Drain)

*Net Cash Flow* is the sum of all the entries preceding it. It should always equal the actual change in the cash balance from the beginning to the end of the report. That's why the final step in this statement is to add this line to the beginning cash balance—which should have appeared on the prior month's balance sheet—to arrive at a grand total that's the new ending cash balance. That new balance should also appear on the balance sheet as of the same date, as it does in Figure 3-1. In this fashion the statement of cash flow is tied into the balance sheet just as it was tied into the income statement from the first line. This final step ensures that every transaction has been accounted for on one or the other of these reports.

## Using This Report Effectively

You've seen how each of a company's major activities can significantly affect cash flow. The statement of cash flow is intended to make those effects apparent, so that readers of a company's financial reports can identify and address negative impacts on cash and preserve positive impacts on cash. This report can be longer or shorter than the example used here, but it should include an adjustment for every balance sheet item that changed, except for cash itself.

You cannot understand a company's cash flow activities without this report or, alternatively, a substantial detailed analysis of its cash records. Sometimes this report indicates that even more detailed analysis is needed to answer questions that it raises, but it's better to raise those questions than to be unaware of them. In Chapter 7 we look at additional ways this information can be presented to give us an even better understanding of cash flow without the hard work.

## Manager's Checklist for Chapter 6

☑ The statement of cash flow fills a critical information need: It analyzes all the reasons net income didn't produce an equal increase in cash in the bank. The statement of cash flow is by far the easiest way to get that information.

☑ Cash is needed to finance customer purchases on credit. If accounts receivable grows faster than sales, it's a cash drain for the company. Accounts receivable is often the largest cash requirement a growing company faces, and cannot be ignored without risking impairment of essential working capital.

☑ Inventory is often the second-largest consumer of cash, and cash invested in inventory takes the longest time to be converted back into cash. If inventory grows faster than sales and expected future sales don't increase correspondingly, the company may be wasting its cash—and risking future losses when it's forced to liquidate old inventories.

☑ Investments in the company, purchases of assets, borrowing money, and other activities to finance company operations and growth usually involve significant amounts of cash. They are most easily seen and tracked in the statement of cash flow.

# Key Performance Indicators: Finding the "Hidden" Information

I n the first edition of this book, this chapter was entitled "Critical Performance Factors," a term I've used with clients and workshop audiences for many years. But in the ensuing years a more widely used label has gained acceptance, so I'm using the more commonly used label to avoid confusing readers, thus, Key Performance Indicators (KPIs).

Now that you're familiar with all the foundation financial statements that most companies use, you may feel pretty well prepared to understand how a company is doing financially. And you'd be right, compared with most folks. Since most companies don't prepare all those reports every month and people who read them often don't really understand how much information they contain, you are decidedly ahead of most of your peers in this area. And since you likely don't plan to become a financial analyst, you might feel comfortable with what you've learned so far. Why then would you even want to go digging for "hidden" information that isn't on the basic financial reports? Why KPIs?

The answer is ... It depends.

If you run the company or are in a senior management position, you do it because your banker will want to see the information. And your other lenders. And your investors. And your auditors. And the securities analysts who follow your stock. They all want to see them, because they want to see what's behind the basic financial statements, the strengths and weaknesses of your company that don't appear in bold type in your statements, or the accompanying footnotes. And if they go there, you want to be there first, to understand that information before they do.

If you're employed by the company, you do it because you may want to know how healthy it is beyond the rumors in the halls and the muffled comments in the washroom. If the company is in dire straits and needs to cut costs tomorrow, you might want to know that. If the company's foundation is as solid as the Rock of Gibraltar but it doesn't yet show up on the income statement, that might influence how much you put into your 401(k) or the company pension fund.

If you've invested in the company or are considering investing in it, you can look at KPIs because you can readily see how knowing things that other people don't know—good or bad—can make you look smart or keep you from being the last one out the door. Hidden information is what many insiders make their buy and sell decisions on—and what many people probably couldn't understand if they had it. But with the tools discussed here, you can.

OK, so the answer isn't "It depends." The real answer is that you *always* want to have this information, because it gives you insights, options, and alternatives that you aren't going to get elsewhere. It gives you information that gets to the root causes of problems only hinted at in the basic financial statements—information that can give you not only the sources of problems, but also important clues as to the solutions.

## What Are KPIs? Do They Mix with Water?

KPIs are the performance metrics that enable us to look at the relationships in a company's financial numbers in a new way. KPIs are best accompanied by a *benchmark*, a standard against which the metric is compared to see if the company is doing better or worse than was expected or hoped for. The result is an insight that we didn't have previously about an area that's important to us.

## Measures of Financial Condition and Net Worth

The measures of financial condition and net worth metrics relate to the company's balance sheet. They calculate the company's financial

## PRICE/EARNINGS RATIO

An investor follows a stock's price/earnings (P/E) ratio, which is a KPI of the stock's price performance.

If you've ever bought one of those investment newsletters—the ones that charge you to tell you how to invest what you have left after paying their subscription fees—you've seen the term P/E ratio many times. A *P/E ratio* is the relationship between the price of a share of stock and the slice of the company's earnings attributable to that same share of stock. (We talked about this in Chapter 4.) The P/E ratio is a favorite way to estimate if the price of the stock is too high in relation to the amount of money the company is earning. You might read that Walmart carries a P/E ratio of 32 and the analyst considers it overpriced at anything over 20. In this example, the metric is P/E ratio, the current reading is 32, and the benchmark is 20. You quickly have a lot of information about the company's earnings that didn't appear on its income statement. That's the power of a KPI.

strength at a point in time (remember the "pause" button in Chapter 2?) to give us a sense of how well the company has used its resources to build stockholder value. This section discusses some of the most common measures of financial condition and net worth you are likely to encounter.

## Current Ratio

This is perhaps the second most commonly used KPI in business today, after the price/earnings ratio. The purpose of the *current ratio* is to assess the liquidity of the enterprise—its ability to generate the cash needed to maintain operations. The current ratio is usually presented as two numbers separated by a colon. Using the data from Wonder Widget's balance sheet in Figure 3-1, the arithmetic to arrive at the numbers goes like this:

$$\frac{\text{Current assets}}{\text{Current liabilities}} = \frac{1,667,000}{819,000} = 2.1{:}1$$

This metric is the relationship between current assets (which are cash or will become cash within the next 12 months) and current liabilities (debts that must be paid within the same 12 months). (You'll recognize the terms "current assets" and "current liabilities" from the discussion of balance sheets in Chapter 3.)

**KEY TERM**

**Current ratio** A comparison of current assets and current liabilities, a commonly used measure of short-run solvency—the immediate ability of a company to pay its current debts as they come due. The current ratio is particularly important if a company is considering borrowing money or getting credit from suppliers.

Since current liabilities must be paid out of current assets, having a ratio of 1:1 should be OK, right? Wrong. That would seem logical on the surface, but let's look at this for a moment.

Current liabilities are bills with a firm due date and the requirement to pay them in full—all of them. Current assets probably consist of some accounts receivable and inventory. Do you recall the discussion about these assets in Chapter 3? They don't always deliver 100 cents on the dollar. Sometimes customers pay late and sometimes they don't pay at all. Sometimes inventory sells for full value and sometimes it becomes worthless or simply disappears. So a company needs *more* than $1 of current assets to cover $1 of current liabilities. Most banks want to see ratios of 2:1 or better to give them adequate reassurance that the business will have the cash needed when it's time to write checks. This standard varies by industry, of course, because different industries have different working capital risk characteristics.

## Quick Ratio

This is a variation of the current ratio, with a slight twist. The *quick ratio* removes inventory from the current ratio's calculation, on the assumption that inventory returns to cash more slowly and with more risk than other current assets. Do you remember the bad things that can happen to inventory while it's sitting around waiting to be sold? And that doesn't count the added time and cost that must be put into raw materials before they can become finished goods that can be sold. So removing inventory from the ratio results in a total for current assets that will more quickly become cash. The quick ratio thus becomes a more conservative version of the current ratio and is calculated this way:

$$\frac{\text{Current assets} - \text{Inventory}}{\text{Current liabilities}} = \frac{1,667,000 - 591,000}{819,000} = 1.3:1$$

Typically lenders look at the quick ratio rather than the current ratio if they believe a company's inventory carries a higher-than-normal risk or is a higher percentage of current assets than they consider wise. For the same reason as

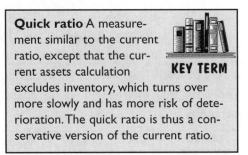

**Quick ratio** A measurement similar to the current ratio, except that the current assets calculation excludes inventory, which turns over more slowly and has more risk of deterioration. The quick ratio is thus a conservative version of the current ratio.

**KEY TERM**

the lenders, company management should keep an eye on this ratio if the company carries large inventories to ensure it's maintaining adequate liquidity regardless of inventory levels. If the current ratio should typically be 2:1 or better, the quick ratio might need only to be 1.3:1 or better, since it will become cash more readily, so less of a safety margin is required for prudent management.

## Days Sales Outstanding

We've emphasized prompt collection of accounts receivable numerous times in this book, not because we enjoy being redundant, but because it's vital to so many aspects of a successful business. Therefore, it's not too surprising that one key measure of liquidity deals squarely with that issue. *Days sales outstanding* (DSO) is the calculation of the number of days of average sales yet uncollected in accounts receivable.

The arithmetic looks like this, again using Wonder Widget's balance sheet on Figure 3-1 and its income statement in Figure 4-1:

$$\frac{\text{Monthly revenue}}{30} = \frac{\text{Accounts receivable}}{\text{Average revenue per day}} = \frac{940,000}{21,667} = 43 \text{ days}$$

The DSO calculation tells you how closely the company comes to adhering to the payment terms printed on its invoices. Ideally, a company sells its products or services with 30-day terms, and customers pay the invoices 30 days later, so the DSO would consistently be 30 days. Most companies offer 30-day credit terms, yet the average DSO for

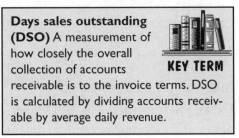

**Days sales outstanding (DSO)** A measurement of how closely the overall collection of accounts receivable is to the invoice terms. DSO is calculated by dividing accounts receivable by average daily revenue.

**KEY TERM**

companies nationwide is in the neighborhood of 45 days, with some companies experiencing even longer delays. With that in mind, a standard anywhere in the 40- to 50-day range is probably acceptable in most cases. By itself, DSO doesn't tell the whole story. To be certain there isn't a problem, this metric should be reviewed along with the age of the accounts.

---

**SMART**

**MANAGING**

### WHEN A DSO OF 43 IS BAD

A 43-day DSO isn't so hot if everything is late and getting later! Here are two examples of companies with accounts receivable, presented based on the length of time the accounts have been outstanding:

|                          | Company A   | Company B   |
|--------------------------|-------------|-------------|
| Average revenue per day  | 21,667      | 21,667      |
| Current, not yet past due | 600,000    | 600,000     |
| 0–30 days past due       | 250,000     | 40,000      |
| 31–60 days past due      | 70,000      | 0           |
| 61+ days past due        | 20,000      | 300,000     |
| Total outstanding        | 940,000     | 940,000     |
| DSO                      | 43 days     | 43 days     |

Company A shows a typical status of accounts receivable, as some customers pay on time, others take a while longer, and a few stretch out pretty far, a typical scenario. There's no problem with a DSO of 43 days. Company B's customers typically pay more promptly than Company A's, but nearly a quarter of Company B's accounts are way out at 61+, clearly indicating they don't intend to pay normally. The DSO is still 43 days, but there's a *big* problem!

Always look at both the DSO and the age distribution of the accounts, the detailed report showing how long customer balances have been outstanding, before concluding that everything is OK. That detailed report is called the *Aged Trial Balance of Accounts Receivable*.

---

## Inventory Turnover Ratio

For all the reasons mentioned earlier, the faster inventory is sold, the better for everyone watching the income statement and the bank account. If inventory is selling, it's usually not getting spoiled, broken, or lost. That's why companies try to keep their inventories as low as possible, consistent with an ability to promptly service customer orders. A key metric, therefore, is *inventory turnover*—how quickly inventory leaves the plant and is replaced by new inventory. The measurement looks like this for Wonder Widget:

$$\frac{\text{Annual cost of goods sold}}{\text{Average inventory}} = \frac{475,000 \times 12}{591,000} = 9.6$$

If Wonder Widget's inventory turnover ratio is 9.6, then inventory is being replaced on average 9.6 times a year, and there's a little more than one month's inventory on hand at all times (actually 1¼ months' worth, or 12 ÷ 9.6), on average. You'll note, incidentally, that we didn't give you enough history to compute average inventory or annual cost of sales, so we used what we had, one month's cost of goods sold multiplied by 12, and the inventory balance shown on our sole balance sheet. This calculation is subject to less misleading fluctuation if you use a broader period of time for this metric.

# Measures of Profitability

These metrics evaluate the company's earnings by calculating various relationships between elements of the income statement and other numbers. The intent is to measure the company's earnings performance, that is, how well its resources are working to produce profitable transactions.

## Gross Profit Margin

*Gross profit* is the amount of money earned from selling the product or service and paying the actual costs of making the product or providing the service, as discussed in Chapter 4. *Gross profit margin* (or simply *gross margin*) converts that amount into a percentage of gross revenue. We use the income statement from Figure 4-1 for illustration purposes:

$$\frac{\text{Gross profit}}{\text{Gross sales}} = \frac{175,000}{650,000} = 26.9\%$$

**KEY TERM**

**Gross profit margin**
Gross profit (net sales minus either cost of goods sold or cost of sales) as a percentage of gross sales or revenue. Also known as *gross margin*.

Gross margin is an important number because keeping Wonder Widget profitable requires that it make a profit on what it sells, before costs of engineering, marketing, and administration. Watching this metric over time is critical because there are so many components that typically affect it that cannot be controlled or managed easily. The amount of employee overtime spent to rush a past due order out the door affects gross margin, as does the cost of reworking a manufactured part because an inexperienced worker spoiled it.

## Net Profit Margin

*Net profit* is the amount of money the business has earned after selling its products and paying all the expenses of the business. This is the real "bottom line." *Net profit margin* converts the net profit amount into a percentage of gross revenue, which, referring again to the income statement in Figure 4-1, looks like this:

$$\frac{\text{Net profit}}{\text{Gross sales}} = \frac{19,200}{650,000} = 3.0\%$$

**KEY TERM**

**Net profit margin** Net profit as a percentage of gross revenue.

Net profit margin presents interesting analysis opportunities. By itself, it doesn't tell you much about the business' profit performance. A net profit margin of 3 percent in a mature software or drug manufacturing business would be pretty bad, but the same percentage in the supermarket business would be considered phenomenal. The value here, as with so many financial metrics, comes from comparison against a standard. In this case, the meaningful comparisons would be (1) with other companies in the same industry and (2) against a company's own historical profit margins. Both are valuable to different groups, but for different reasons.

If you're part of the management of a publicly owned corporation, you're probably very interested in the comparison with other companies. For such companies, net profit margin is published in the financial press

---

## THE GROWTH CURVE SIGNIFICANTLY AFFECTS PROFIT EXPECTATIONS

**CAUTION**

Note the reference in the text to a "mature" software or drug business. Now think back to the company lifecycle chart in Figure 2-1. It's important to remember that start-up or relatively new companies can't deliver the same kind of profit performance as successful, mature companies that have most of their infrastructure in place.

A new company must spend money to establish its initial market presence and its branding, to build production capacity, and to strengthen its management team. These costs often lower its profit margins below those of a more established company that may be inherently less profitable, but that has already absorbed those costs. This is why, to understand the real strength of a company, it's key to access historical trends that may show profit improvement and future business plans that may show the level of profits attainable after these costs have been incurred.

---

and, to some extent, it affects the price of the company's stock. If you hold stock or options in the company, of course, you may be affected personally as well as professionally.

By contrast, if your company is privately owned and you have a management role in delivering profit performance, you're probably most interested in current performance compared with past performance, because continuous improvement in this metric probably means management is doing a good job.

## Costs per Sales Dollar

Various ratios show costs per sales dollar, such as *sales and marketing costs per sales dollar* and *general and administrative (G&A) costs per sales dollar*. These are two examples of the kind of ratios that can be applied to any number of operating expense items for which company management wants to tie expense growth to revenue growth or to ensure that expenses don't erode profit margins. The arithmetic looks like this, if you use our income statement data for one of these calculations:

$$\frac{\text{Sales and marketing costs}}{\text{Gross sales}} = \frac{76,000}{650,000} = 11.7\%$$

This same ratio could be developed for G&A, R&D, or any other grouping of operating expenses. Many companies, once they're established and their infrastructure investment is behind them, associate growth in certain expense categories against planned revenue growth during the same period. This, then, becomes a useful way to track progress in those cost control areas.

# Measures of Financial Leverage

These metrics are related to the measures of financial condition above, in that they're based primarily on the balance sheet. However, these metrics fulfill a specific purpose: to determine how well the company is succeeding at using other people's money to improve the amount of resources it has working to produce profitable transactions.

## Debt to Equity Ratio

Recalling the discussion of ownership in Chapter 3, the assets used in a company are provided either by the owners through capital investment or by creditors through the money they lend to the company. The relationship between those two contributions is an important metric of a company's financial health. The ratio that tracks that relationship, this time using the balance sheet information in Figure 3-1, is computed like this:

$$\frac{\text{Total debt}}{\text{Total equity}} = \frac{1,267,000}{1,979,000} = 64\% = 0.64{:}1$$

**KEY TERM** **Debt to equity ratio** A measurement that compares assets provided by the owners through capital investment to assets provided by creditors through money loaned to the company. To calculate this ratio, divide total debt by total equity. A variation used by some banks uses only bank debt and long-term debt in this calculation, omitting trade credit.

If a company has too much debt, there's risk that a small reversal of fortunes may wipe out the owners' equity entirely or render the company unable to service its debt. While this by itself may not sink a company, it pressures management to return to profitability or invest more owners' capital in the business. Such pressure has often resulted in involuntary turnover in the management team, particularly at the CEO/CFO level.

By contrast, if the company has too little debt, management risks criticism that it doesn't have enough capital at work earning profits for the company. Do you remember our discussion of leverage in Chapter 3? While too little debt is definitely better than too much debt, it does limit somewhat a company's earning potential. We've seen how leverage can make a company more profitable and, therefore, more valuable.

As you can imagine, that there's no "right' number for this ratio. It depends on a number of factors, including:

- how effectively a company can use additional working capital and put it to work increasing profits by more than the cost of the additional resources;
- the amount of long-term vs. short-term debt, since long-term debt gives a company more time to put the money to work before having to deliver the added profits to repay the debt;
- interest rates that impact the cost of money, since long-term debt is typically borrowed under formal lending agreements that bear interest, as opposed to trade creditors' balances, which are generally interest-free; and
- how profitable the company can be in its industry, since a low-margin business can ill afford to pay high interest rates for additional capital, while a high-margin, high-growth business may be able to profit handsomely from every dollar it can get.

## Debt Service Coverage Ratio

This metric is useful primarily to bankers that lend money and to the companies that borrow it. *Debt service coverage* measures how well a company's cash flow will succeed in making the payments on its interest-bearing debt. The calculation uses EBITDA (discussed in Chapter 4) as a quick substitute for cash flow, and actual debt service (principal plus interest) for the same period of time to determine how well debt service is covered by approximate cash earnings for the same period. Here's a computation of debt service coverage:

$$\frac{\text{EBITDA}}{\text{Debt service}} = \frac{50,000}{40,500} = 1.23 \text{ times}$$

The value of this ratio to lenders should be obvious. They usually have a minimum acceptable ratio, or at least closely watch trends because it's important to them. They want to know they have a safe mar-

**Debt service coverage ratio** A measurement of a company's ability to make the payments on its interest-bearing debt through its cash flow (as approximated by its *earnings before interest, taxes, depreciation, and amortization*—EBITDA). To calculate debt service coverage, divide EBITDA by the loan payments (principal and interest) on its bank debt. The lower the ratio, the greater the debt burden on the company. Most banks require a ratio of at least 1.2, often building that requirement into loan agreements. Variations occur here as well, with some banks using pretax income instead of EBITDA in their calculation.

**KEY TERM**

gin to ensure they won't have a nonperforming loan on their hands in the event of a reversal in their borrower's fortunes, however temporary. The borrower probably doesn't look closely at this number, except when its lenders are looking at it and who would get upset if the ratio gets too low compared with expectations or if it falls below a loan requirement. If you're the borrower and cash flow is tight, you want to watch this one closely, so you're aware of it before your lender calls you. If you have invested in a company with bank debt and a troubling metric here, be prepared for the possibility of an announcement about debt restructuring or other lender intervention unless this turns around quickly.

### FIND ANOTHER BANK

**FOR EXAMPLE** One of my firm's clients was in the midst of a turnaround when the megabank holding the mortgage on their building notified them that a penalty interest rate would be assessed with their next payment because they had for some time been out of compliance with the debt service coverage ratio. The penalty interest rate in the fine print of their mortgage loan agreement effectively doubled their already above-market interest rate. This was a clear message from their bank to find another lender, and do it quickly. Needless to say, they did.

## Return on Equity

The last metric in the financial leverage series is one that is most meaningful when evaluating publicly owned companies. *Return on equity* measures the rate of return on the stockholders' investment in the company. Referring this time to both Wonder Widget's balance sheet *and* its income statement, we come up with this calculation:

$$\frac{\text{Net income (annualized)}}{\text{Stockholders' equity}} = \frac{19,200 \times 12}{1,979,000} = 11.6\%$$

Unlike some of the other measures, ROE is a bit artificial for two reasons. First, owners' equity bears no relation to what the owners actually paid for their stake in the company. Second, owners' equity bears no relation to what they could sell it for. Other than that, no problem!

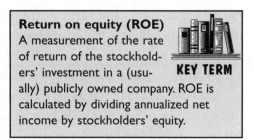

**Return on equity (ROE)**
A measurement of the rate of return of the stockholders' investment in a (usually) publicly owned company. ROE is calculated by dividing annualized net income by stockholders' equity.

**KEY TERM**

So is the ROE useless? Not at all. It serves us well as a measure of a company's earning power, even if only a theoretical comparison is possible. Since the same limitations apply to all companies, the calculation enables a company-to-company comparison, which is useful when selecting stocks to purchase. Often investment advisors look at this metric to demonstrate the superior earning power of one growth company over another. As with any of these metrics, the pattern of change over time—see "Trend Reporting" below—enables us to see a company's progress against its own history.

# Measures of Productivity Metrics

These metrics are a little different in that calculating them often requires numbers that don't appear on the financial statements. They're operationally oriented, intended to measure the performance of particular resources within the organization, e.g., its employees, to see if these resources are delivering the kind of results that contribute to improved numbers on the income statement and balance sheet.

## Backlog of Firm Orders

In my mind, this is the most important metric that doesn't come out of the company's general ledger. It tells us how much business the company has sold that it has yet to deliver to its customers. There isn't much arithmetic to this one. It comes from the company's order entry system, it's represented in the sales value of those orders, and it's computed like this:

Backlog of orders = All orders received – All orders shipped and invoiced

For companies that ship orders that take some time to fulfill, such as most manufacturers and many distributors, this is a crucial measure of their immediate future. It's also an indicator of the sales team's success at keeping the production capacity of the company humming. Like any good metric, it comes with good news and bad news.

If the backlog falls over time, it can mean the company isn't bringing in new orders as fast as it's filling prior orders. A trend like that cannot continue indefinitely or the company will eventually have no orders to fill. It means either the production department is very efficient or the sales department isn't. It would be important to find out which it is and fix it because in the long run it's not healthy.

If backlog increases over time, that could be equally undesirable. If the sales staff is bringing in orders so fast that the production department can't fill them, customers will be unhappy and may take their business to a competitor. This will hamper the sales department's continued success and dampen salespeople's enthusiasm. Of course, in a rapidly growing company, this may simply indicate an urgent need to put more production capacity into place.

The objective of the Sales Department should be to continue to build the backlog, while the objective of the production department—and this includes salespeople and drivers in a distributor's office and service providers in a service business—should be to deliver on orders faster than salespeople can bring more in. Management's role, then, is to beef up whichever side is falling behind, so that backlog is where management wants it to be. Where should that be? It depends. You could say that the backlog should be measured by how long, on average, it takes to bring in an order and fulfill it, relative to the customer's expectations.

In reality, I can't recall ever hearing a company say its backlog was too high. Too old, maybe. Too difficult to fulfill, sure. Too unprofitable to fret over, unfortunately, yes. But too high? Nope, never. Companies use backlog to measure the success of their sales efforts. I recommend to clients they build a measurement of backlog into the incentive plans of their top sales and marketing executives, and that they track it regularly and visibly.

## Late Backlog

This subset of the backlog is a ratio that companies have found useful in spotting upcoming problems with customer satisfaction. It's the percentage of backlog that's behind the customer's desired delivery schedule. This ratio it is most useful when it's calculated customer by customer. Calculated in sales dollars but presented as a percentage, it looks like this:

$$\frac{\text{Backlog of Customer A's orders behind schedule}}{\text{Total backlog of Customer A's orders}}$$

It doesn't take much thinking to realize that customers expect their goods to be delivered when they asked for them and when you promised to deliver. An aerospace manufacturer that doesn't get parts on time from a supplier can't deliver airplanes to its customer on time. A retailer who has advertised a big sales event will be unhappy if the goods don't arrive in time for the sale. While those examples may seem extreme, they happen frequently, particularly in our increasingly just-in-time-focused economy. What this metric tells you is the volume of a given customer's orders that have not been shipped when promised. If that number grows, you're at risk of having a shipment rejected and returned, and possibly losing a customer.

## Order Processing Time

Another metric that doesn't require complex calculations but can impact a company's success is the time to process an order. This one isn't for everyone, but when it fits, it's a great way to build and measure customer satisfaction. Once a customer has placed an order, they have an expectation of when it will be fulfilled. As the seller, you have an obligation to accept orders that fit within your ability to process them and to meet expectations. As noted above in the discussion of backlog, if you don't meet your customers' delivery expectations, you'd better be the only source in town—or your customers will soon be shopping for another supplier.

While this metric is most obviously suited to distribution companies with a short production process, it can also apply to manufacturers with a firm enough handle on their production times—e.g., standard stock items rather than custom manufacturing processes—to be able to make reliable estimates of delivery dates.

This measurement is usually presented in terms of days elapsed from the time a company representative receives the order until the order ships to the customer. It can be adversely affected by a number of functions within the company—sales, order entry, credit, production, quality control, and shipping, not to mention the delivery service you use. Management's goal is to coordinate all these activities so employees work together toward the mutual objective of satisfying the customer, rather than trying to avoid blame if the order is late.

## Sales per Customer, Sales per Employee, and Sales per Square Foot of Floor Space Metrics

Each of these three metrics measures the productivity of the sales effort—how well a company spends its sales dollars. They're important measures and easy enough to calculate, although often hard to change. Each metric is used when appropriate, based on the sales model. All can be useful in a retail environment. Some are only useful for a retail business. Let's look at each metric briefly.

*Sales per customer* is useful when a company finds its cost to process an order is fixed or at least controllable. In that case the company can increase profits significantly if it can increase the average amount a customer buys, because there may be little or no increase in the costs of making the sale (beyond the actual cost of the merchandise, of course).

*Sales per employee* is most useful when the department or company is strongly sales-driven. Retail sales organizations often fall into this category. In some companies, the entire organization is encouraged to think in terms of sales, while in other companies the sales department is the prime mover. However this metric is used, it helps when assessing the effect on sales of adding another employee or when comparing one branch office or division with another. When applying this measure, CEOs need to recognize the differences and similarities among departments or divisions. Some business models are different enough that they cannot efficiently be compared on a sales-per-employee basis, and to do so would inhibit one business model or the other from operating most effectively in its market.

The *sales per square foot* metric is used almost exclusively in retail stores and restaurants, where stores must use every foot of space productively, space is limited, and the contribution of a product display can be measured by how many sales it produces per foot of space it occupies.

This is commonly used by chain store management to compare the productivity of one store with another. This metric often accounts for your favorite food product disappearing from your supermarket's shelves; it didn't generate enough sales volume to justify a place on the shelf. Again, absolutes may not be possible because of the different locations and the demographics of their areas (higher or lower income, younger or older, blue collar vs. white collar, and so on).

# Trend Reporting: Using History to Predict the Future

Most people who read financial statements look only at the monthly or annual reports, and most of those reports present their period data in comparison with the period immediately prior or the same period a year ago. The more enlightening reports compare results against a budget, which is a carefully considered benchmark in its own right. (See Chapter 12 for more on budgets.)

But in all these cases there's a flaw in the lone comparison that can prove dangerous over time: It overlooks the fact that a small flaw, a minor deterioration from the prior period, a tolerable budget variance, if repeated over a series of past and future periods, can become a major surprise when taken cumulatively. When the surprise is pleasant, everyone can laugh and say, "How weird we didn't see that earlier!" When the surprise is unpleasant, however, the tendency is to begin a frantic search for answers. "How did this happen?" "When did this happen?" "Why didn't we know it was happening?"

## What We Learn from Trends

The most important things we learn from studying trends are clues to the future. In high school physics, many of us learned the principles of Newton's first law (the law of inertia): An object in motion tends to continue in motion in the same direction at constant speed unless acted upon by another force. (That may not be exactly what your teacher said, but it's close enough for our purposes.) Of course, the object your teacher used to make this point wasn't being bumped around by market forces, interest rates, recessions, and human intervention and emotions, or its path would have been a lot more erratic. So, too, the paths of many of our economic indicators are often erratic, but that doesn't change the validity of studying their trends so we can try to estimate where they might go in the future.

As it turns out, a strong sales effort that brings in good sales numbers tends to continue to do so, given no radical changes in its environment. A company whose costs are rising slowly and steadily because it doesn't effectively control them will likely continue to see its costs rise until it takes some action to disrupt the trend. Human nature being what it is, costs without controls are more likely to rise than to fall, so studying cost trends is useful to enable management to identify those trends soon enough to keep the cumulative effect within acceptable limits.

## LESSONS LEARNED FROM THE STOCK MARKET— OR MAYBE NOT LEARNED

Much stock market analysis and commentary are based on the premise that what happened in the past may be projected to some degree into the future—with all the usual caveats that the analysts don't guarantee that any of this is true or predictable or even relevant. We've learned how inaccurate they can be in predicting the future from the past, but there are ample stacks of evidence to suggest the premise is true, even if the application in specific instances is decidedly imperfect. Anyone who has studied technical stock market analysis can point to countless examples of stocks acting pretty much like they did before, given similar market influences. The trick is to judge with acceptable accuracy the variation between past experience and future expectations.

## The 6 to 12 Rule

I've found that the most effective way to follow a company's trends is to use an easy-to-read format that shows a series of months or weeks of metrics on a single page as part of a regularly published, monthly or weekly management report. How much should you pack onto that one page? If there's too much information on the page, it's overwhelming to those uncomfortable with financial reports and is likely unread. If there's too little information, it raises more questions than it answers, with resulting delays in taking action.

The ideal combination, in our experience, is a page with 6–12 metrics presented over the past 6–12 periods where the metric is represented by numbers, or up to a year's data if represented in graphic form, along with the benchmark or standard most appropriate for each metric. That could be the budgeted result at year-end or the ratio set out in the company's lending agreements or the amount needed to take the company to the next growth level. Figure 7-1 (page 116) shows a representative KPI trend report for a manufacturing company.

In addition to KPIs, certain financial statements should always be prepared in a 12- or 13-month trend format, in addition to the standard formats produced by most accounting systems. At a minimum, because of their importance in reviewing operating results, an abbreviated income statement (shortened to one page) and a statement of cash flow (also only one page) should be a part of every monthly financial package the accounting department produces. These two reports provide so much insight with a quick scan that they are often reviewed instead of the static current month reports typically produced by accounting software.

## Which Metrics to Track? Where Do You Want to Go This Year?

Which metrics are most meaningful to a company depends on a series of factors, including management goals and objectives, problem areas that bear watching, and improvement projects under way. A sales-driven company may be heavy on sales-related indicators, while a company deeply into research and development of leading-edge products might have metrics related to development timetables and costs. Since KPIs are short-term metrics, they primarily relate to improvements desired and controls needed in the current year. Longer-term goals are best set forth in a company's business plan (see Chapter 9) and built into KPIs only for the current year of the long-range plan. However, the name really says it all. KPIs should be key factors for the business and they should relate to *performance*. Here are some areas to consider for such a report:

■ **Sales trends.** Number of orders received, dollar volume of orders received, backlog changes, RFPs responded to, sales per whatever (customer, employee, square foot of floor space, and so forth), sales staff in the field, volume of orders shipped, etc.

| Metric | Actual Results for the Week Ending: | | | | | | | | | | | |
|---|---|---|---|---|---|---|---|---|---|---|---|---|
| | 8/16/13 | 8/23/13 | 8/30/13 | 9/6/13 | 9/13/13 | 9/20/13 | 9/27/13 | 10/4/13 | 10/11/13 | 10/18/13 | 10/25/13 | 11/01/13 |
| **Operations** | | | | | | | | | | | | |
| Orders Shipped (Net Sales) | 12,430 | 189,577 | 59,002 | 27,748 | 38,393 | 131,752 | 24,645 | 57,606 | 71,078 | 42,012 | 99,228 | 11,384 |
| Orders Shipped on Time | 800 | 19,040 | 3,402 | 27,748 | 741 | 9,983 | 17,377 | 57,326 | 44,985 | 13,362 | 6,594 | 1,024 |
| Past Due Orders in House | 1,345,920 | 1,181,612 | 1,128,172 | 1,135,331 | 1,120,594 | 1,084,906 | 1,088,125 | 1,104,272 | 1,081,075 | 1,056,700 | 956,455 | 949,763 |
| **Sales and Marketing** | | | | | | | | | | | | |
| New Quotes Issued | 1,709,010 | 524,583 | 921,760 | 2,130,817 | 3,802,839 | 864,870 | 3,283,517 | 2,201,621 | 3,464,634 | 2,823,921 | 712,581 | 945,168 |
| Beginning Backlog | 1,900,000 | 1,926,479 | 1,783,311 | 1,743,528 | 1,724,176 | 1,828,440 | 1,718,797 | 1,737,229 | 1,689,532 | 1,641,768 | 2,367,713 | 2,333,101 |
| + New Orders Booked | 38,909 | 46,409 | 19,219 | 8,396 | 142,657 | 22,109 | 43,077 | 9,909 | 23,314 | 767,957 | 64,616 | — |
| – Shipments to Customers (Net Sales) | (12,430) | (189,577) | (59,002) | (27,748) | (38,393) | (131,752) | (24,645) | (57,606) | (71,078) | (42,012) | (99,228) | (11,384) |
| Ending Backlog | 1,926,479 | 1,783,311 | 1,743,528 | 1,724,176 | 1,828,440 | 1,718,797 | 1,737,229 | 1,689,532 | 1,641,768 | 2,367,713 | 2,333,101 | 2,321,717 |
| **Finances and Administration** | | | | | | | | | | | | |
| Percent of A/R Beyond 90 Days Past Due | 20% | 20% | 14% | 16% | 14% | 23% | 18% | 17% | 17% | 8% | 10% | 16% |
| Percent of A/P Beyond 45 Days Past Due | 12% | 15% | 19% | 19% | 18% | 21% | 19% | 22% | 21% | 18% | 15% | 14% |
| Notes Payable—Basic Loan Balance | 500,000 | 499,445 | 534,445 | 484,445 | 560,000 | 640,000 | 705,000 | 705,000 | 305,000 | 375,000 | 425,000 | 425,000 |
| Beginning Cash Balance | 35,000 | 50,324 | 67,120 | 130,629 | 53,791 | 79,443 | 1,944 | 58,118 | 204,225 | 60,727 | 45,941 | 49,216 |
| + Receipts | 79,827 | 23,704 | 90,664 | 22,542 | 60,060 | 32,199 | 17,066 | 207,790 | 374,557 | 3,720 | 11,892 | 13,382 |
| + – Bank Credit Line Advances | 35,000 | (555) | 35,000 | (50,000) | 75,555 | 80,000 | 65,000 | — | (400,000) | 70,000 | 50,000 | — |
| – Disbursements | (99,503) | (6,353) | (62,155) | (49,380) | (109,964) | (189,698) | (25,892) | (61,683) | (118,055) | (88,506) | (58,617) | (55,459) |
| Ending Cash Balance | 50,324 | 67,120 | 130,629 | 53,791 | 79,443 | 1,944 | 58,118 | 204,225 | 60,727 | 45,941 | 49,216 | 7,139 |

**Figure 7-1.** Financial metrics trend report

- **Operations trends.** Average days to ship an order, overtime or premium hours paid (manufacturers), percent of jobs proceeding on time (job shops), number of orders shipped on time or late, backlog in dollars, etc.
- **Financial trends.** DSO for receivables, average payout period for payables, cash balances, bank credit line status, invoicing timeliness, financial reporting timeliness, purchase discounts taken vs. discounts offered, etc.

While trend reports are most compact if presented in a tabular format, they are often easier for nonfinancial managers to read if presented in a graphic format—charts, curves, and lines convey powerful visual images of trends in ways that tables of numbers typically can't. To keep such reports to the recommended single-page length, management may need to choose between a longer list of KPIs to track in tabular format and a shorter list in graphic format.

# Manager's Checklist for Chapter 7

☑ Key performance indicators (KPIs) are tools for tracking a business' key indicators of success. KPIs are best accompanied by a benchmark or standard against which they're measured. They must be computed separately, because in most cases they don't appear in the basic financial statements.

☑ KPIs are most effectively used when a company identifies its most sensitive areas in sales, operations, and finance and establishes goals or standards for each area to be improved. Common financial KPIs include measures of financial strength, profitability, liquidity, and leverage. Key operational KPIs include relevant productivity indicators. Sales KPIs should include sales backlog and sales force performance.

☑ Trends tell us what a single piece of data can never tell us: what the future might look like. The trick is to capture the right KPIs and present them in 6–12 periodic readings, so it becomes easier to see where the trends are going and whether action should be taken to encourage or counter observed trends.

# Cost Accounting: A Really Short Course in Manufacturing Productivity

"Cost accounting" sounds redundant, doesn't it? After all, isn't all accounting about cost? Well, yes and no. To folks in the business of accounting and those most familiar with accounting practices, *cost accounting* is a special branch of the field that deals exclusively with the cost of making or buying a product or service that the company then sells to its customers. Costs that are the purview of the cost accounting specialists (known affectionately as cost accountants) are all the costs on the income statement between the Revenue line and the Gross Profit line, referred to in Chapter 4 as Cost of Sales.

While this area is considerably more complex in a company that conducts manufacturing operations, every company—manufacturing, distribution, retail, or service—needs to understand and manage its gross profit. Remember: *Gross profit* pays for all the operating costs of running the company, as well as providing a net profit to the owners. If gross profit isn't managed well, it's difficult for other areas of the company to make up the difference. Underlying the whole idea of cost accounting is the need of every business to protect and grow its gross profit, while maintaining the quality of its product or service at acceptable levels.

This chapter explains some of the unique attributes of cost of sales and the efforts that go into understanding and controlling them. You'll notice as you read this chapter that we talk primarily about manufactur-

**KEY TERM**

**Cost accounting** An area of management accounting that deals with projecting and monitoring the detailed costs of individual production units to help managers identify, measure, and control gross profit margins that are the key to the business' overall profitability.

ing companies, because those are businesses for which cost accounting is most challenging, yet most valuable. If you work for or run a distribution company, a retailer, or a service business, some of the tools and terms we discuss here may seem less important to you. Keep in mind that the principles are universal for every business enterprise.

**SMART**

**MANAGING**

## Cost Accounting in Context

Don't let the seeming complexity of this topic deter you—in principle, it's really common sense. The concepts are not complicated; it's just the application that can be confusing if you're applying them to a many-faceted manufacturing operation. I suggest you apply the examples here to your own company, your own employer, or your own department. I think you'll find they make more sense when you relate them to a company you already know well.

# The Purpose of Cost Accounting— Strictly for Insiders

Amazing as it may seem, many companies don't know whether they're making a gross profit on many of the products they sell. But it's a simple matter for a company with even the most fundamental bookkeeping to determine if it's making a gross profit over all of its product sales. But if a company makes a number of products, each with different cost structures and levels of complexity, the managers often don't know how much each product contributes to—or subtracts from—the overall gross profit. And as you'll see, that can be dangerous.

Cost accounting is the classic example of what a company's outside observers don't want to or need to see. Cost accounting is a detailed, often time-consuming process of counting small amounts of money, materials, and labor. Yet these small elements of cost, when multiplied by the number of units a company makes and sells over a month or a year, become the foundation for the profit that outsiders *are* anxious to see from companies they follow. *Cost accounting*, then, is the ultimate example of internal management reporting: It's information presented in a form designed for managers to use in running the company, and frankly, it's not user friendly to those unfamiliar with the company or the business.

## Are You Making a Profit or Just Building Sales Volume?

You may know the adage "We're losing money on every piece, but we're making it up on volume!" That clever shtick makes everyone laugh, but it's not so funny in many of today's companies, particularly those that don't have a strong cost accounting analysis function. Among the most difficult areas of finance to manage is accounting for all the variety and complexity of costs that go into manufacturing a product. One reason is that information about cost of sales requires additional levels of data collection, some of it from company employees most removed from the financial recordkeeping function: the factory worker. It's on the shop floor that costs are incurred, fabrication decisions are made, and hours are spent productively or wastefully—and it's the factory worker who ultimately determines if the company has a comfortable gross profit or none at all.

## Profit Management Begins with a Timecard and a Bill of Materials

Key to gross profit management, then, is collecting the right information at the right level of detail. One of the most challenging aspects of this is capturing the time that workers spend on each job or part that they work on—job costing or process costing.

---

**Job costing** Collecting costs for a manufacturing process that's geared to producing products in individual lots, or jobs, and assigning costs to those jobs. Jobs may be customized to the customer's requirements, as in a machine shop, or small lots of products for selling later from stock.

**KEY TERMS**

**Process costing** Collecting all costs incurred in a continuous process or processing department, then averaging these costs over all units produced in that department. This is a mass production kind of operation, such as might be used in making chemicals, gasoline, or textiles. It's different because the nature of the product is different. Instead of specifically identified production lots, there's a continuous flow; the final output is complete only when the process is stopped, rather than when the order for X units is filled.

## How to Make More Money by Making Less Product!

Wonder Widget makes two home products, each with identical unit sales. The WW-1000 sells for $425; the custom-made WW-Super 1000 sells for $575. The combined sales of $1 million produces a gross profit of $250,000 each month, or 25 percent. But the company doesn't know how much each unit costs. They just know that the WW-Super 1000 sells better and because it's more difficult to make, they're charging more for it. They believe the resulting gross profit shows that their strategy is sound. But at the urging of their bank, they engage a consultant to analyze the data and validate their assumption.

The financial consultant divides all their costs of sales into two buckets, including the added labor it takes to make the luxury model.

| | WW-1000 | WW-Super 1000 | WW-Super 1000 |
|---|---|---|---|
| Selling Price per Unit ($) | 425 | 575 | |
| No. Units Sold | 1,000 | 1,000 | |
| Total Sales ($) | 425,000 | 575,000 | 1,000,000 |
| Cost per Unit | | | |
|   Materials ($) | 25 | 25 | |
|   Labor ($) | 40 | 240 | |
|   Overhead (150% of Labor [$]) | 60 | 360 | |
| Total Cost per Unit ($) | 125 | 625 | |
| Total Cost of Sales ($) | 125,000 | 625,000 | 750,000 |
| Gross Profit ($) | 300,000 | (50,000) | 250,000 |

**Figure 8-1. Gross profit contribution from multiple products**

To their surprise, Wonder Widget owners learned that their best revenue producer was actually losing money due to the high cost of labor. The real surprise: They would make $50,000 a month more—increase their current gross profit by 20 percent—if they stopped making the deluxe model!

The data collection challenge comes in several forms:

■ Convincing workers to accurately measure time on a job and the raw materials they use—tasks that are not often to their liking and not always in the skill sets for which they were hired.

- Convincing workers that the purpose of the detailed timekeeping is to cost out the products, not to keep track of how much downtime they have on the job.

- Convincing supervisors that the time their workers spend reporting time and materials data instead of working on another job is productive.

- Teaching accounting departments how to collect the information accurately and use it properly to calculate the labor cost component of the company's products, then produce meaningful reports for management.

Here are the fundamental data collection tools of job cost accounting:

- A bill of materials that enables the company to identify the materials required to manufacture a particular unit.

- Timecards or timesheets for manufacturing employees who work directly on products, broken down by product or stages of a product.

- A materials requisition form on which workers record all the materials issued to the job, including materials that might have been put into production and then damaged or scrapped and the materials issued to replace them. These details may be later transferred to a job cost sheet.

- The job cost sheet, either paper or electronic, that follows a job through the factory and on which actual production costs are recorded as they are incurred. This may include labor details, providing an audit check that all hours paid for were charged to jobs or otherwise accounted for appropriately.

Individual companies may have their own versions of these tools, but the objective is the same: to accumulate, on the one hand, the labor and materials that are intended to be consumed to complete the job and, on the other hand, the labor and materials that were

> **Bill of materials** A list of all the parts and components that go into manufacturing a product, including how many of each item of raw material. This document is the basis for purchasing and assembling the parts and subassemblies needed to produce a given quantity of finished products.
>
>
> **KEY TERM**

actually consumed to complete the job. The differences are later analyzed to help managers understand why the actual costs incurred differed from the expected costs. (See "Manufacturing Cost Variances" later in this chapter for more insight into this kind of analysis.)

*Process costing* is simpler than job costing, due to the *continuous* nature of the manufacturing process. The Accounting Department collects all the costs incurred by a particular manufacturing department for each manufacturing process carried out in that department and groups the costs into essentially two categories: direct materials and conversion cost.

> **KEY TERM** **Direct materials** The raw materials that go directly into making a product. The direct materials to manufacture a chair, for example, would include wood, fabric, screws, and glue. (For ease of accounting, some minor costs may not be assigned directly, but rather may be grouped into manufacturing overhead and allocated to all production rather than specific jobs or parts.)

*Conversion cost* is the sum of all the direct labor and manufacturing overhead costs that belong to that department and that process. Dividing the total costs charged to that manufacturing department by the total number of units the department's efforts produced gives us the unit cost of all units produced during the period being measured. The final unit cost is equivalent to the unit cost arrived at in a *job costing* environment. The difference is that a continuous process does not permit the individual collection of costs by unit during the process, a factor that could limit the analysis potential later on.

# Fixed and Variable Expenses in the Factory

In any department of every company, including the manufacturer's shop floor, there are costs that don't change from day to day and there are costs that change constantly, depending on the company's level of activity. Understanding costs that do and don't change is important to the manager's ability to manage the costs for which he or she is responsible.

Costs that essentially remain unchanged even though the business increases its volume of sales are called *fixed costs*. Such costs may be more easily predicted and managed because they rarely change. An

**KEY TERMS**

**Conversion cost** The sum of all the direct labor and manufacturing overhead costs that belong to that department and that process.

**Direct labor** The cost of wages paid to workers directly employed in manufacturing products or in providing the services for customers. On the shop floor, it's the labor of the machinist or the welder. In a consulting firm, it's the time of the consultant who's working with the client. In a distribution company, there may be little or no direct labor, as products are generally purchased in finished form, which is to say, the direct labor was incurred by the original manufacturer and included in the purchase price paid by the distribution company.

**Manufacturing overhead** All the costs necessary to operate the business not classified as direct labor or direct materials. Often referred to as *indirect costs*, these may include rent, insurance, utilities, janitorial service, and the supervisors who oversee the direct labor workers but who do not work on jobs directly themselves. All these indirect costs are necessary for the manufacturing process, but they are not charged directly to specific jobs. Instead, they're grouped and then allocated to all the jobs or products in some manageable way. *Allocation* is most often based on a factor directly related to the work produced, such as direct labor hours worked on the job or direct labor dollars charged to the job.

example is the rent on a building occupied under a long-term lease. For the most part, that monthly lease payment remains unchanged for the life of the lease, predefined increases aside. Another example is depreciation expense on an asset, which remains constant until the asset is removed from service, assuming it lasts as long as intended.

Costs that increase in direct relation to sales volume are called *variable costs*. For example, a 10 percent increase in sales results in a 10 percent increase in variable costs. You can see that direct materials and direct labor would be variable—the more units you make, the more of those costs you would incur. Packaging materials used in shipping the finished goods would also vary with production levels.

Costs that increase in relation to sales but at a slower pace, for example, 5 percent for each 10 percent increase in sales, are said to be *semifixed costs*, meaning they have aspects of both variable and fixed costs. For example, a manufacturing scrap pickup service might accept larger amounts of scrap without raising its pickup prices until it needs to send a larger truck and two operators. Then it might increase the price and keep

**KEY TERMS**

**Fixed costs** Those costs that essentially remain unchanged even though the business increases its sales volume.

**Variable costs** Those costs that increase in direct relation to sales volume.

**Semi-fixed costs** Those costs that increase in relation to sales but at a slower pace. Semi-fixed costs have aspects of both variable and fixed costs.

it fixed until the larger truck can no longer haul more scrap away. The cost over time becomes semi-fixed as sales, and therefore manufacturing scrap, increase.

In the interest of avoiding unnecessary complexity, we ignore the semi-fixed attributes of costs and, instead, label every cost element as either fixed or variable because we're trying to understand how costs behave in certain circumstances. For example:

- If variable costs increase faster than sales, there's inefficiency in the process that management needs to identify and correct, because variable costs should never grow faster than sales under normal conditions.
- If costs identified as fixed rise unexpectedly, it's good to know this shouldn't be caused by a change in sales volume, and the cause should therefore be investigated.
- If costs identified as variable are not moving up or down proportionately with sales, the cause should be investigated, because there may be unrecorded expenses that distort reporting in the month being reviewed (costs too low) and in the month when they finally get recorded (costs too high).

Knowing these characteristics enables us to budget more accurately, particularly if we're planning for the possibility of different levels of sales and we must be prepared for several possibilities. (See Chapter 12 for a discussion of flexible budgets.)

It's wise to keep this simple principle in mind: *All costs are fixed in the short term and all costs are variable in the long term.*

In other words, regardless of the label you put on it, any cost can be reduced by effective management, given sufficient time. In the case of a company's building lease payments, "sufficient time" may mean at the

---

> ### Don't Get Stuck on Labels
> An effective manager thinks outside the categories of fixed costs and variable costs. Don't assume that you can't reduce fixed costs, or that variable costs are easy to reduce. Sometimes it's possible to reduce costs by converting fixed costs to variable costs by outsourcing services or renting equipment only as needed. Or you may try to reduce the time it takes to assemble a unit, only to find that you're spending more time inspecting and correcting.

---

expiration of the lease. Most costs can be modified in a much shorter timeframe, even those we call fixed.

By contrast, even the most variable of costs, such as the labor that goes directly into making a product that will be sold immediately (like the amazing Wonder Widget), cannot be changed instantly. Labor reductions—often the result of technological advances—typically require giving employees reasonable notice, providing termination pay, overcoming resistance to losing skilled workers, and other factors that effectively stretch out the time it takes to reduce the net cost to the company.

So, the terms fixed costs and variable costs are not entirely accurate. However, financial managers and the users of their information, as well as production planners and managers, adopted the terms to create a framework for approximating how these costs are likely to act. Why? To enable them to predict future cost relationships and thereby manage the bottom-line outcomes of management actions at various sales volumes. As with so many management decisions, this often becomes a choice between greater accuracy at higher cost and lesser (but still acceptable) accuracy at lower cost.

## Controllable and Uncontrollable Expenses

Now let's look at costs from another angle: our ability to control their movement up and down.

Costs that responsible managers can readily control are called, logically enough, *controllable costs*. Some examples are travel expenses, non-production labor costs, most marketing expenses, office supplies, and long-distance telephone charges. Notice I didn't say that these costs are controllable without consequences, only that they're controllable, which means a manager can make and implement a conscious decision to reduce expenditures in these areas. Even though the company may lose the benefits to be gained from incurring these costs, they're still controllable because managers *can* lower or eliminate them.

*Uncontrollable costs*, by contrast, cannot in general be controlled. Examples that readily come to mind include income taxes, depreciation, and rental or lease payments.

Let me repeat what I stated earlier: *All costs are uncontrollable in the short term; all costs are controllable in the long term.*

This is a conceptual truth that is, by and large, useless in the Accounting Department or in budget preparation. But in concept, it's important to realize that you're not captive to any costs charged to your department or unit, as long as you're prepared to manage these costs actively and as long as you can accept or ameliorate the consequences of removing those costs, which may include loss of their attendant benefits.

In a company's Production Department, controllable costs are those for which managers are appropriately held accountable. Cost estimates should be built around the realization that some costs just are what they are, regardless of management efforts. If your department has a large drill press on its floor, you're likely to be charged for the depreciation of that machine as long as you're using it. You can't control that cost if you need the drill press to do your job. But by proper preventive maintenance, you can control the repair costs and downtime of that machine—and that's your responsibility if you're running the department.

Stepping outside the Production Department for a moment, the concept of controllable and uncontrollable costs applies equally throughout a company's organization structure. Lease payments on property are

---

**SMART**

**DESIGN INCENTIVES TO MATCH THE RESULTS YOU WANT**
It's not uncommon for managers to incent their workers to achieve more with less cost. That's called increasing productivity.

**MANAGING** But the most successful management performance reward programs recognize the distinction between the costs that employees can control and those they cannot. Avoid challenging an employee or a supervisor to meet bottom-line goals that he or she cannot really control or significantly influence.

uncontrollable for the duration of the lease. Once the lease runs out, those costs are again controllable, until you sign another lease, after which they again become uncontrollable. Labor costs are always controllable to a degree, but not totally. You cannot run an organization without people, but you probably can run it with fewer people than it normally employs, if you're willing to redistribute the essential work and forgo the less essential work that people do.

Consider the possibilities. What if you were able to distinguish between the essential work and the less essential work every day? What if you could focus on minimizing the unessential and expediting the essential? Would your department be more successful? The power of financial analysis lies in its ability to help identify the financial ramifications of doing just that and to quantify the benefits in dollars and cents. It's a wonderful tool for helping to make decisions from a place of knowledge, rather than estimating, or worse, guessing.

That's why I wrote this book.

## Standard Costs—Little Things Mean a Lot

One of the challenges in using financial reporting for cost accounting purposes is to determine the actual cost of a unit of finished goods that was produced during the month, in time to issue a financial statement reasonably soon after the month-end. Accounting departments are sometimes criticized for issuing financial reports too long after the accounting month is over, when the reports are of little value in managing the succeeding month (or two, in some cases). Financial statements that take several weeks or more to prepare may not be available soon enough to help managers adjust their performance in the next month. Lessons learned from January reports issued at the end of February cannot be put into use until March, meaning it's likely that January's mistakes were repeated in February. In a fast-moving or highly competitive or slim-margin business, that should be unacceptable to an alert management team. This is why in recent years technology advances have fostered the growth of *real-time accounting*—systems that collect accounting information continuously and provide selected management reports on demand, without the need to formally "close the books."

In the manufacturing environment, the short-term answer to this need has traditionally been *standard costing*, a term that means using standard costs in lieu of actual costs to account for individual manufacturing steps. Standard costing is a way to estimate the actual unit cost for purposes of prompt financial reporting, while still leaving a way to return later for more detailed analysis. Standard costing takes the budgeting process down to the components of unit cost so a company can budget direct labor and raw materials for each unit of finished goods that it plans to produce.

**Standard costing** A management tool that estimates the overall cost of production, assuming normal operations.

**KEY TERM** Standard cost methodology enables a company to more quickly produce production reports and thus react more quickly to what those reports say and close the books more quickly at month-end. Standard costs, rather than actual costs, are used in accounting for materials, labor, and even overhead, assuming an efficient plant operating at normal capacity. The standard costs and actual costs are compared periodically to see if actual costs have gotten out of control or standard costs are no longer relevant. Unavoidable or permanent variances in price or quantity, e.g., price increases, may result in revised standard costs for those items.

## Manufacturing Cost Variances: Analysis for Action

Using standard costing enables a manufacturer to budget the unit costs of production and to compare actual costs with standard costs in its financial reporting. The benefit of such reporting is not seeing whether the two agree, or even by how much they disagree. The benefit of standard costing is in analyzing those differences and using that information to enable managers to change what they're doing and make the business optimally profitable. This process is called *variance analysis*, meaning the analysis of differences, to enable managers to see where to minimize or eliminate those variances.

**Variance analysis** The process of identifying, measuring, and investigating the causes of significant differences (variances) between budgeted plans and actual results. Variances can be calculated according to time, volume, cost, efficiency, or price.

The advantages of standard costing include:

- Helping to more easily estimate inventory value and product cost;
- Enabling efficient price setting and contract bidding based on realistic costs;
- Permitting performance measurement and evaluation based on standards;
- Quickly identifying problem areas through the principles of management by exception; and
- Identifying causes of unsatisfactory performance so corrections can be made.

We discuss variance analysis in some detail in Chapter 12 because variance analysis is the principal tool for getting the most value from budgets in general. Variance analysis has particular application in manufacturing when standard costs are used, and so it belongs in this chapter as well.

> **Management by exception** A management practice by which standards are set for operating activities, actual results are compared with those standards, and significant differences are brought to the attention of the managers, along with the reasons for the differences and recommended corrective action, if appropriate.
>
> **KEY TERM**

In *standard costing* there are two basic kinds of variances, or differences, from established standards: price variances and usage variances. *Price variances* occur when materials or labor used in production cost the company more or less per unit than was projected when the standards were set. *Usage variances* occur when the production run consumes more or less of the materials or labor than planned.

For example, consider this example from Wonder Widget's weekly manufacturing variance report (Figure 8-2).

| Component | No. Units Produced | Standard per Unit (1) | Actual per Unit (2) | Variance (2 – 1) |
|---|---|---|---|---|
| Super Widget Model 4000 Power Switch | 1,000 | | | |
| Labor Hours per Unit Produced (A) | | 1.2 hours | 1.5 hours | .3 hours |
| Labor Cost per Hour (B) | | $25.00 | $28.00 | $3.00 |
| Labor Cost per Unit Produced (A×B) | | $30.00 | $42.00 | $12.00 |

**Figure 8-2.** Report of manufacturing cost variances

In this example, actual labor cost per unit was $42 (1.5 hours at $28/hour). The standard per unit for this switch was $30 (1.2 hours at $25/hour). The total unfavorable variance for 1,000 units was $12,000 (($42 – $30) x 1,000 units). That information by itself is interesting, but not particularly useful. It might be difficult to give a plant supervisor that information and expect an informed plan to eliminate the variance. But let's look at what happens when we analyze the components of the variances (Figure 8-3).

| Nature of the Variance for the 1,000 Units Produced | Unit Variance (1) | Standard per Unit (2) | Amount per Unit (1x2) | Total Variance Amount |
|---|---|---|---|---|
| Time—Unexpected Rework Caused Extra Time | 0.3 per unit | $25.00 | $7.50 | $7,500 |
| Price—Workers Being Paid Higher than Standard | $3 per hour | 1.5 hours | $4.50 | $4,500 |
| Total Variance Accounted for | | | | $12,000 |

**Figure 8-3.** Analysis of cost variances

Now we know the causes of the variances, and we know what each kind of variance is costing us. We can approach the supervisor about getting the time back to the standard of 1.2 hours per unit of labor, or finding out if the standard should be increased because more time is required to make these switches correctly. And we can approach the Human Resources manager to find out why we paid more than standard wages for our labor. For example: Did we hire overqualified people? Has the market gotten tight for workers with the skills we need? Did we do a thorough enough search for workers within our price range?

This same analysis can be carried out for the materials variances.

Now we have a plan of action, and we know which managers we should talk to about carrying out the plan. That's what standards can do for a manufacturing company, *if* the managers know what each unit costs and *if* they know what each should cost. Variance analysis now becomes a powerful management tool for controlling the unit cost of the switch, which contributes directly to the gross profit line on Wonder Widget's income statement.

And that's a good thing.

# Manager's Checklist for Chapter 8

☑ Cost accounting is about protecting and growing gross profit by understanding and managing the details of the cost of sales, i.e., the costs incurred in producing revenue.

☑ Knowing the costs and gross profit margins on each product a company sells is a critical tool for managing overall gross profit. This is true for all kinds of businesses, but it's more challenging for a manufacturing company because of the complexity of the business.

☑ Cost accounting is possible only when detailed production costs are collected at the source, on the shop floor.

☑ Understanding how costs behave is key to controlling them. Tools such as standards, budgets, and classifications such as "controllable," "variable," and "direct" help us to do that.

☑ Variance analysis is the way managers use standards and management by exception to reduce variation from predicted outcomes.

# Good Investment or Bad? How Do You Decide?

Whether the business is a roadside ice cream vendor or a spacecraft manufacturer, management must at some point invest in the equipment it needs to run the enterprise. Wonder Widget's business falls somewhere in the middle. We all know how valuable its widgets are to its customers, but they don't give much thought to the capital decisions that management must make to ensure its products are

**Figure 9-1.** Investment issues

the best they can be for the price. In this chapter we review the tools management uses to make investment decisions. You'll see how the same tools can be used by any company, including yours. The trick is knowing which tool to use and when to use it.

## Capital Investment: A Game of Choices, Risks, and Hoped-For Outcomes

Probably the most challenging choices most companies must make are those that involve capital investment—allocating cash to R&D, manufacturing, sales and marketing, and administration. Since no organization has unlimited resources (except perhaps the U.S. government), the choices that Wonder Widget's management must make about how to best allocate its resources will determine its success or failure in the long run. You only have to recall the rise of Google or the decline of Research in Motion/BlackBerry to realize that those decisions can make or break a company's future and impact its ultimate survival.

Here's the basic idea. We make an investment. We buy a machine or a building or a truck or whatever. We measure how that purchase will enhance the company's profitability while we use it. If we're a well-managed company, we do a front-end estimate of those calculations before we write the check. As with most business decisions, allocating capital among competing alternatives is about making the best choices. Since we can't always control the outcomes of our decisions, we look for ways to estimate the cost, minimize the risk, and maximize the return before we make the investment. The general term for such analysis is *return on investment (ROI)*, but in reality there are several ways to calculate expected returns, some with widely varying

**KEY TERMS** **Return on investment (ROI)** The amount of money earned on an investment compared to the amount of money invested to gain that return, most often presented as a percentage of the amount invested.

**Payback period** The time it takes, usually presented in terms of months or years, to earn back the total amount of money invested, without regard for any opportunity cost or the cost of money. An investment of $10,000 that earns $5,000 a year would be said to have a payback period of two years.

results. That's why choosing the tool, understanding its strengths and limitations, and assessing the risk inherent in each tool require forethought. Let's get started with the simplest of the tools, the generic ROI.

# Return on Investment: The Concept and the Purpose

In its simplest form, ROI involves comparing the total cost of an investment with the total amount that it earned for the company during its useful life, expressed as a percent. Let's look at an example taken from an operating experience of Wonder Widget. Assume that Wonder Widget's plant management was considering buying a widget stamping machine for the factory. Automating this operation instead of doing it the old way would save them $10,000 a year in operating costs (maybe because the machine doesn't take coffee breaks or sick leave). It will last for 10 years and Wonder Widget will pay $50,000 for it.

| Upfront Cost | Lifetime Return | The Formula | Calculated ROI |
|---|---|---|---|
| $50,000 | $100,000 | 100,000 ÷ 50,000 | 200% |

The total return over 10 years is expected to be $100,000. Comparing the cost to the savings gives us an ROI of 200 percent. Sounds like a pretty good deal. The VP of manufacturing brought the proposal to a management meeting for discussion and approval, and he added confidently that there weren't many ways to make that much money on that small an investment. Someone suggested that maybe they should buy a dozen of them.

Or maybe not. At that point the CFO had two questions:

1. How do we install it?
2. What other upfront costs will we incur to get it up and running?

The CFO said the simple ROI calculation that the manufacturing VP did, while accurate, was not enough information on which to base a decision; the missing information could significantly alter the proposed savings and the actual benefit of the purchase. So the manufacturing VP went back to his staff to answer the questions and find a better way to make the case. They decided that a different analysis tool would add impact and be just as easy to calculate. They chose the payback period method.

# Payback Period: A Quick and Easy Way to Understand the Approach

*Payback period* is just that, the length of time it takes to earn back the original investment through the cumulative cost savings or additional earnings generated by that investment, expressed in months or years. After recognizing the CFO's concerns, the factory analysts dug into the numbers and determined that there would indeed be setup costs they had not included. Out-of-pocket setup costs were estimated at $5,000. Their calculations then took that into account as well as the payback period, and their proposal looked slightly different at the next management meeting:

| Upfront Cost | Lifetime Return | The Formula | ROI | Payback Period |
|:---:|:---:|:---:|:---:|:---:|
| $55,000 | $100,000 | 100,000 ÷ 55,000 | 182% | 1.5 Years |

After hearing the revised presentation, the CFO noted that the ROI was still very good, and the payback period was a good way to determine how soon they would earn back their investment. After reaching the payback period, everything the machine earned would be profit—well, almost. She had a couple of new questions.

1. What other costs will we incur to keep it working—maintenance, repairs, downtime, etc.?
2. When are those costs likely to occur—every year or later, as the machine ages?

The CFO noted that those costs might be incurred years down the road, but they would still impact the net return on the investment, and repair costs may not be easy to estimate for the later years when those costs typically climb. Further, she added, interest rates were expected to rise over the next few years, and the time value of money had to be considered. Now the calculations were more complex, but the information gained was more valuable.

Going back to the vendor, the analysts learned they could buy an annual maintenance contract that would spread the maintenance costs evenly over the life of the machine, avoiding the painful climb in maintenance and repair costs as the machine aged. The annual maintenance contract would cost $1,500 a year and would cover all parts and labor for the life of the machine.

## The Time Value of Money: Today and in the Future

It's easy to see that having a dollar today is worth more than having a dollar a year from now. We know that we can invest a dollar we have, but we can't invest a dollar we don't yet have. And the longer it takes for us to get that dollar, the less it's worth because we have to wait longer to get the benefit from having it. Whether it's money being paid out or money being received, *when* it happens makes it worth more or less to the company in terms of today's dollars. This is the concept of *present value* and *future value*.

**Present value** The value of a sum of money in today's terms, when received or paid either today or at a future date. A sum of money received today has a present value of its face amount, whereas a sum of money received a year from now **KEY TERMS** has less value today because of the delay in receiving it and the lost earning opportunity that such a delay represents, based on a defined interest rate assumption.

**Future value** The value at some future date of a sum of money invested today, to be returned at a future date, together with its earnings at some assumed rate of return.

Consider this example: A dollar in your pocket today has a value of $1. That is its present value. If you invest that dollar at 10 percent interest for one year, it will be worth $1.10 at the end of that year.

$1 + ($1 x 10%) = $1.10

So your dollar's future value is $1.10. (Of course, if you invested that dollar at 4 percent, its future value in one year would only be $1.04.) And when you consider the time element, you get the benefit of *compound interest*, because the interest itself earns interest. So that dollar invested for two years at 10 percent, assuming the interest earned is applied—compounded—annually, the future value of your $1 at the end of the second year would be $1.21. Its growth would look like this:

Year 1: $1 + ($1 x 10%) = $1.10
Year 2: $1.10 + ($1.10 x 10%) = $1.21

Key Fact: Notice that future value is a function of time, rate, and the *compounding period*, that is, how often the bank applies interest to your account so the interest can earn interest along with the principal. If your $1 were invested in an account that applied the interest earned—compounded—quarterly instead of annually, your money would grow a bit faster, like this:

End of Quarter 1: $1 + ($1 x 10% x 3/12) = $1.025
End of Quarter 2: $1.025 + ($1.025 x 10% x 3/12) = $1.050625
End of Quarter 3: $1.050625 + ($1.050625 x 10% x 3/12) = $1.076890625
End of Quarter 4: $1.076890625 + ($1.076890625 x 10% x 3/12) = $1.103812890625

Your $1 would now have a future value of $1.1038 instead of $1.10. Doesn't sound like much, does it? But let's remove all the decimal places to make it more meaningful. Let's take $1,000 and compound interest daily instead of annually. Without showing you the 365 daily calculations, trust me—you do, don't you?—when I tell you that $1,000 in present value would have a future value of $1,105.16. That's a 5 percent growth in earnings by compounding daily instead of annually.

Keep in mind that this works both ways. If you promise to lend money to someone, say your itinerant brother, who will need $1,105 in a year to pay for a new paint job for his car—yes, he checked the price, and it's $1,000 plus sales tax of 10.5 percent—you would need to put away $1,000 today and earn 5 percent compounded daily to be ready to honor your promise in a year.

Let's get back to Wonder Widget's investment decision. Without waiting for the next meeting, the CFO sat down with the manufacturing VP to describe in more detail her concerns about the time value of money. She posed the question that the CEO was likely to ask her, "What else could we do with those funds that would earn even more money? We're either going to take the purchase price out of the company savings (earning a paltry return today, but almost certainly more later) or borrow the money and pay interest on a loan." Those were additional costs the factory analysts had not taken into consideration because they didn't impact the factory. But they would impact the company's overall performance, and

Wonder Widget's CEO would likely ask what other way could they evaluate this opportunity and compare it with the other investment opportunities they had.

So the CFO and the VP discussed the timing of the payment. Suppose they took the $50,000 purchase price from company cash and paid for the machine up front. That would eliminate the need to borrow money and pay interest on a loan, but it would also drain the company's cash reserves. An equipment loan would preserve the company's cash and spread the payments over time, perhaps enabling the company to save enough on using the machine to cover the interest cost on the loan in addition to a reasonable ROI. If the company had other worthwhile opportunities or critical needs to consider, this might be an issue for discussion. It only took a moment for the CFO to scotch the idea of using company cash reserves to make the purchase, since the cash would be needed to build inventories for the upcoming selling season. So if the machine was going to be purchased, it would have to be with a bank loan at about 5 percent interest.

So far, so good. They knew the simple ROI and the payback period, but still didn't know the effective ROI after considering the time value of the money invested vs. the money saved. The CFO explained to the manufacturing VP the concept of discounted cash flow, the next level of analysis she wanted to see.

# Discounted Cash Flow: Evaluating Long-Term Investments

The purpose of a *discounted cash flow* calculation is to fine-tune the basic ROI analysis by adjusting for the time value of money. This is especially valuable when the cash inflows and/or outflows happen at different times during the life of the investment. In the case of the proposed stamping machine, the outflows include the

> **Discounted cash flow** A more sophisticated way to look at ROI. Discounted cash flow takes into **KEY TERM** account the cost of money employed and the amount of time it has been committed, as well as the timing of the earnings on that investment, all at an assumed interest rate.

upfront purchase price and the annual payments for the ongoing maintenance contract. The inflows, while subject to operating volumes, are generally believed to be $10,000 a year, earned at the assumed rate of $833.33 a month. The maintenance contract of $1,500 is paid annually, presumably at the beginning of each year. Ready for the next step?

We next have to decide what interest rate to apply to those amounts. The CFO opted for 5 percent as their average borrowing cost. This is a judgment call among the methods that she might have used to select a rate, and we discuss that a bit more in the next section. For now, assume that every dollar saved earns Wonder Widget a 5 percent return. So, the questions are: What is the present value of the stream of savings, less the present value of the stream of payments? How does that compare to the present value of the upfront investment, which we already know is $55,000?

At this point, some books on this topic insert a page or two full of excerpts from a statistical table used to calculate the present value. Others walk you through an elaborate formula that does the same thing more easily. Both seem to want to make accountants of their readers, but that's not why I wrote this book. I want you to understand the concepts so you can get someone else to do the heavy lifting.

Think this through for a moment. You know from our discussion of present value that money that comes in the future—like our annual cost savings—is worth less than its face amount because we have to wait for it, while the cost of the machine purchase is upfront. As it happens, the present value of savings of $833.33 a month for 10 years, with a face value amount of $100,000, at a 5 percent assumed rate of return, is $78,567 because of the waiting time for the money. Similarly, the maintenance contract payments, which total $15,000, will also have a smaller present value because we pay them out over time, and that present value at the same 5 percent yield is $11,583. As for the bank loan on the purchase price, our 5 percent equipment loan will have 60 monthly payments, but since the loan interest rate is the same 5 percent and we plan to finance the installation costs as well, the present value of our machine purchase is still $55,000. Here's the resulting tally:

| Present value of the machine purchase | -$55,000 |
|---|---|
| Present value of the factory cost savings | $78,567 |
| Present value of the maintenance contract | -$11,583 |
| Net present value | $11,984 |

So our net present value is the sum of the combined numbers above, or $11,984. That's the value in today's dollars of making the proposed investment of $55,000, and it represents a 21.8 percent return in today's dollars (11,984 ÷ 55,000 = 21.8%).

The VP of manufacturing leaps out of his chair, pumps the air, and yells, "Yes!" He thinks he's got the sale, and maybe he does. But you know how CFOs are. The good ones are thorough to a fault. There's always one more question, or two. In this case the CFO wants to go through the mental checklist she uses to evaluate all investments, whether they look instantly good or instantly bad, so that every opportunity is given the same degree of scrutiny. Now back to class for some more theory.

# Weighted Average Cost of Capital: Enhancing the Return to Shareholders

When the company has well-informed investors, as Wonder Widget does, management must keep an eye on the overall return the company pays for the capital it has attracted, including the cost of its debt (typically interest expense) and the cost of its equity (usually through dividends). All that adds up to a material consideration in assessing the company's overall value, as company valuation is critical to strategic initiatives like raising investor capital for growth, negotiating new credit lines, mergers and acquisitions, and ultimately, the exit strategy of the company's current owners. The higher a company's weighted average cost of capital, the lower its valuation, the higher

**Weighted average cost of capital (WACC)** The calculated cost of all the capital employed by the business, including capital obtained from trade credit, all other liabilities, and stockholder investment (via dividends paid). This calculation helps management evaluate the value to the company of some investment with a given return by comparing it to the overall cost the company pays for the capital it employs before making the investment.

**KEY TERM**

the perceived risk of its business, and the higher cost it must typically pay for additional capital.

How does the arithmetic work? Think of the money borrowed from a bank. The Wonder Widget balance sheet in Chapter 3 shows short-term notes payable to banks of $150,000. If the interest rate on those borrowings is 6 percent, then $9,000 (150,000 x 6%) is the cost of capital for the short-term debt. For accounts payable incurred on normal interest-free trade terms, the cost of capital is typically zero, a big plus. For capital stock, it's the dividends paid to stockholders. The *weighted average cost of capital (WACC)* is the combination of all those elements across the company. For Wonder Widget, the calculation would look like Figure 9-2, based on the balance sheet in Figure 3-1:

| Category | Rate (%) | Amount ($) | Annual Cost ($) |
|---|---|---|---|
| Current Liabilities, Except Bank Debt | 0% | 617,000 | 0 |
| Notes Payable to Banks, Short-Term | 6% | 150,000 | 9,000 |
| Long-Term Debt | 5% | 300,000 | 17,600 |
| Lease Contracts | 10% | 125,000 | 12,500 |
| Loans from Stockholders | 4% | 75,000 | 3,000 |
| Stockholders' Equity* | | 1,979,000 | 5,000 |
| **Totals** | | **3,246,000** | **47,100** |
| **WACC** | | | **1.45%** |

*Dividends paid annually to stockholders, shown on Figure 6-1. Income tax effect omitted.

**Figure 9-2.** Weighted average cost of capital

As you can see, Wonder Widget's WACC is favorable, typical of a well-run company, and well below the rate of return expected for the new machine, another arrow in the VP's quiver when management next meets. The new machine, if it achieves the projected returns, will increase profits, raise stockholders' equity, and further lower the WACC. Everybody wins.

# Internal Rate of Return: Deciding What Return Is Good Enough

The last commonly used measure of the value of an investment return is internal rate of return (IRR). I've noticed that managers often confuse IRR with ROI, and they label an ROI calculation as an IRR, when they've never actually calculated their IRR. For most companies this last calculation is an extra level of sophistication, but for the completeness of this chapter I want you to understand what IRR really is. So here goes.

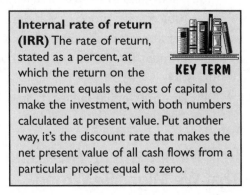

**Internal rate of return (IRR)** The rate of return, stated as a percent, at which the return on the investment equals the cost of capital to make the investment, with both numbers calculated at present value. Put another way, it's the discount rate that makes the net present value of all cash flows from a particular project equal to zero.

**KEY TERM**

The purpose of an *internal rate of return* (*IRR*) calculation is to find that rate of return, stated as a percent, at which the return on the investment equals the cost of capital to make the investment, with both amounts calculated at present value. Put another way, it's the discount rate that makes the net present value of all cash flows from a particular project equal to zero. Generally speaking, the higher a project's IRR, the more desirable it is to undertake the project. As such, you could use IRR to rank several prospective projects. Assuming all other factors are equal among the various projects, the project with the highest IRR would probably be considered the best and undertaken first. Recall the net present value of Wonder Widget's machine investment was $11,984, or 22 percent, well above its WACC of 1.45 percent. Had the projected savings been less over the 10-year period, the net present value of the investment would have shrunk, and at some point it would neither add to nor subtract from the company's WACC. You can get a big insight here: *Never invest in a project with a net present value or an IRR of less than zero.* Of course, to reach that decision you must do the math.

What's left to talk about? As noted at the beginning of this chapter, the role of these investment analysis tools is to help management estimate the cost, minimize the risk, and maximize the return. Having estimated the cost and calculated the return, the last item on the CFO's mental checklist is minimizing the risk, and her final questions before a decision is made fall into that area. She asks:

- What are the chances that the stamping work this machine does won't be needed in 10 years as a result of technology advances, product obsolescence, process evolution, etc.?
- How certain can we be that the vendor can honor the maintenance commitment for the entire period without significantly increasing the price?
- How sure are we that the machine will consistently produce the projected savings?

## Risk Management: Assessing the Probability That We Might Be Wrong

In every business decision dealing with the future, after all the estimates have been made and the numbers crunched, there's one element of the decision that can't be forecast accurately: the risk that the company's assumptions may be wrong. The possibility always exists that something can happen down the road that we couldn't forecast or that we could forecast but couldn't protect against. Management's role in addressing that risk is called *risk management*. In its simplest terms it means management must consider the options and take appropriate action to:

- Remove the risk entirely, thus avoiding the consequences;
- Mitigate some of the risks and accept those that can't be removed;
- Pass on the risk to others, e.g., through insurance, thus avoiding it entirely; or
- Knowingly accept the risk that the event may occur and bear the cost if it does.

I can't tell you how the CFO satisfied herself and the CEO that their risks in making this investment were reasonably under control, but they did move ahead with the purchase, and the machine did perform pretty much as projected. You can't ask for more than that.

# Manager's Checklist for Chapter 9

☑ The goal of ROI analysis is to estimate the cost, the risk, and the return when considering a capital investment.

☑ Return on investment (ROI) is the percentage of gain or profit that comes from an investment over the investment's projected life, before considering the time value of money or risk management. It's the fundamental tool for assessing the worthiness of a given capital investment.

☑ Payback period is the number of time periods it takes for a given investment to return enough gain (profit) to fully return the investment's original cost, again before considering the time value of money or risks.

☑ Discounted cash flow (DCF) is the ROI calculation that takes into account the time value of money, using either present value or future value calculations, to place the comparison of cash inflows and cash outflows on an equal footing.

☑ Weighted average cost of capital (WACC) is the percentage that demonstrates the overall cost to a company of all the capital it employs in its business, both debt and equity.

☑ Internal rate of return (IRR) is the determination of that point, expressed as a percentage, where the cost of capital invested in a project equals the return of capital from that project, both measured in present value terms.

☑ Uncertainties are present in any forecast, and management must decide how to deal with those uncertainties to minimize the risk of making a decision that harms the company.

# Get to Breakeven First!

Just so we're on the same page, here are two definitions of *breakeven point.*

First, for a product or service, *breakeven point* is the level of sales volume that, when reached, has effectively earned enough sales dollars to pay for all the costs of developing, producing, and delivering the product or service being sold. Put another way, it's that point at which the seller is neither ahead nor behind on the income statement as a result of selling the product or service.

Next, for an enterprise or company as a whole, *breakeven point* is the level of sales volume of all products and services sold by the company that, when reached, has effectively earned enough sales dollars to pay for all the costs of developing, producing, and delivering the products or services being sold *and* the fixed costs of operating the business that's producing those products or services. Notice the key difference between breakeven of a single product and breakeven for the company as a whole. While a single product can't be expected to pay the light bill and the rent, everything the business sells must do exactly that if the business is to survive.

Notice that neither definition speaks to profit, the objective of running a for-profit business. Not yet anyway. This chapter's discussion is about getting to the point where you're ready to earn a profit. Put another way, you can't make a profit until you get past breakeven. So let's under-

**KEY TERM**

**Breakeven point** The sales volume of a product or service at which the sales dollars earned are exactly equal to all the costs incurred to make or buy, and deliver to the customer, the product or service, resulting at that point in neither a profit nor loss to the company.

stand what breakeven is all about first.

## What Does "Breakeven Point" Really Mean?

Breakeven point is one of those terms that people toss around to make a point, often without knowing what it is. Conceptually we can understand without straining too many brain cells that it's selling enough of something to cover its cost. Make a widget for $10 and sell it for $10 and you've broken even. But of course it's not that simple, because making and selling a widget typically involves far more than just the cost to make one.

Here's an example: A publishing company client of my firm buys the rights to an academic journal written by a learned professor in some highly technical area. Then the publisher sells subscriptions to that journal, pays the author a royalty on those sales, and keeps what's left as profit. What is the cost of each subscription the publisher sells that needs to be recovered to reach breakeven? The paper, ink, and printing cost of the journal? Postage? Royalty paid? Yep, all those things. Oh, and then there's the commission paid to the person who sold the subscription. And what about the front-end cost to purchase the rights in the first place? That front-end payment must be recovered as well, or any breakeven point is wrong.

That brings up a calculation dilemma: Does that front-end cost, akin to a development investment, get thrown into the cost of the first subscription sold or the first one hundred subscriptions or the first one thousand? Or is it some period of time—one year, 5 years, 10 years? You'll recognize this as similar to the depreciation discussion in Chapter 4, i.e., over what period are these costs to be recovered? When R&D is involved—think biotech industry—that can dramatically alter the conclusion. Our client, incidentally, chose a 5-year window for their analysis, believing that the journal's useful life was in the range of 10 years, and they wanted to have fully recovered their costs soon enough in the product lifecycle to have a reasonable run time of high returns to justify the commitment of their front-end investment.

So while the cost to print a single copy of the journal may be pennies, that is by no means the total cost to be considered in reaching the journal's breakeven point. Remember the key line in the definition that opened this chapter: that point at which

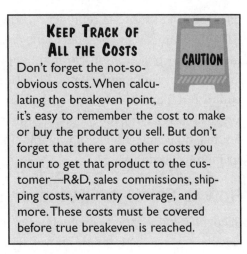

**KEEP TRACK OF ALL THE COSTS**

**CAUTION**

Don't forget the not-so-obvious costs. When calculating the breakeven point, it's easy to remember the cost to make or buy the product you sell. But don't forget that there are other costs you incur to get that product to the customer—R&D, sales commissions, shipping costs, warranty coverage, and more. These costs must be covered before true breakeven is reached.

the seller is neither ahead nor behind on the income statement as a result of selling the product or service.

## Why Is This a Critical Factor in Profitability?

Far too many companies, which is to say the CEOs and owners who operate those companies, make decisions to launch a new product or service based on the belief that the product is in demand and will be well received in the marketplace. Solid thinking as far as it goes. As a general rule, you can't sell something that nobody wants. But the corollary to that is you shouldn't sell something you can't sell profitably, and you can't sell it profitably unless you can sell it for more than it costs you. OK, what does it cost you? Sounds like a no-brainer question, but it's not, because new products are often rolled out, especially by smaller companies, without any of the analyses that we discuss here. Product launch decisions based on back-of-the-envelope cost estimates are frequently inaccurate because they are invariably too low, a detail only learned after the fact. By then pricing has been announced, orders solicited and filled, and the realization that a price increase is needed comes far too late.

The moral of this chapter: Every new product offering must have a realistic analysis—in writing—of the total cost of researching, developing, producing or buying, marketing and selling, delivering, and if appropriate, after-sale servicing of the product before the decision is made to offer the product. My entrepreneur readers may object at this point, realizing that some of the best decisions are made without all the facts and more than a little intuition. No argument there. And any analysis of future expectations is inherently based on estimates, and thus inherently inaccurate. But that's no reason to make less than your best effort to use this key decision-making tool. A good estimate, carefully thought out, is better than no estimate and is a valuable supplement to even the most prescient intuitive thinking.

## How to Calculate Breakeven for a New Product

Recognizing the varied considerations that might enter into the actual calculation (see the example above), let's see how Wonder Widget might use this analysis technique in making a product launch decision for the proposed WW-Super 2000, a product filled with so much new technology that the Marketing Department can't wait to start promoting it to the legions of loyal customers. Let's look at the steps that would be needed—and their related cost estimates—in the Accounting Department's analysis after gathering data from Engineering, Marketing, and Sales. See Figure 10-1.

Wonder Widget now has the information it needs. Dividing the net cost incurred by the potential selling price tells management the number of units the company needs to sell at that price to cover all its costs. Management likely assumes that the lower the selling price, the more units they're likely to sell, provided there's adequate demand. At the same time, the lower the selling price, the more units they *must* sell to achieve breakeven. At this point management must decide which price will succeed in selling at least the number of units needed to break even and whether the sales potential at that price will produce sufficient profit to warrant a full-scale introduction of the new product.

Note that only incremental or variable costs are considered in the calculation. We don't include the cost of internal staff whose jobs involve the new product in some way unless they were specifically hired to support it. As an example, a food manufacturing client of our firm acquired a new product line from a major brand company. As part of the deal our client had to add two employees to the kitchen testing staff because of the addi-

| Steps in Process | Cost | Sales | Nature of Cost |
|---|---|---|---|
| Purchase marketing study | 10,000 | | One-time cost |
| Purchase license to key technology | 25,000 | | One-time cost |
| Materials & labor to build prototype | 2,000 | | One-time cost |
| Focus group to test prototype | 3,000 | | One-time cost |
| Redesign prototype | — | | No incremental cost |
| Build initial production run:<br>    Materials and direct labor | 3,000 | | One-time cost |
| Marketing campaign in test market | 10,000 | | One-time cost |
| Sales launch in test market | | 20,000 | One-time cost |
| Royalties paid to technology licensor | 1,000 | | Variable cost of product |
| Costs incurred for first year sales:<br>    Production costs, 1st production<br>    run—1,000 units | 80,000 | | Variable costs for this product |
|     Sales commissions and selling<br>    expenses | (20,000) | | Variable costs for this product |
|     Marketing launch campaign | 55,000 | | Product-specific cost |
| Total costs incurred | 199,000 | 20,000 | |
| Less sales earned during test market campaign | 20,000 | | |
| NET COST INCURRED | 179,000 | | |
| Potential selling price per unit sold | $250 | $200 | $150 |
| Unit sales needed to breakeven | 716 | 895 | 1,193 |

Note: No incremental costs for using company staff already on the payroll, however, we assume that direct labor cost is only incurred for actual production, so those costs count.

**Figure 10-1.** Breakeven analysis: the calculation

tional demands of the new product line, even though they had staff already in place in that department. Thus, even though other members of the kitchen testing staff might spend time on the new product, only the new hires who specifically and exclusively worked on the new product were included in the breakeven calculation, because they were truly an incremental cost, rather than a reallocation of existing costs.

If yours is a service company rather than a manufacturer, the process and the logic are the same even though the individual elements will vary. And in both cases, when adding employees to support the new product or service, don't forget to budget for payroll taxes. These, too, are part of the cost of adding staff.

# What About the Entire Company's Breakeven Point?

From the definitions that opened this chapter, you know that the arithmetic is different when you're evaluating the breakeven point for an entire company. While I believe it's important to understand the breakeven point for all your products, or at least all the major ones, that doesn't necessarily give you the information you need to assess the sales volumes needed to produce a profit for the overall enterprise. The reason becomes pretty clear if you look again at the calculation in Figure 10-1. You'll see that it includes only incremental costs of the new product. No overhead, no administration, no vacation pay for the owner, etc.—none of that. Yet all of those costs need to be covered if the company is to be successful as a whole.

How do you make that calculation? Well, it's simpler to do now because we're dealing with overall costs and not trying to split hairs for a single product. And it takes into account all those other costs that aren't part of a single product evaluation. In its simplest form, then, the companywide breakeven point looks like Figure 10-2 in chart form:

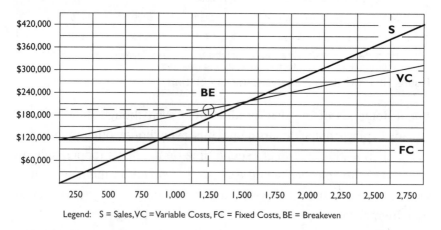

Legend:  S = Sales, VC = Variable Costs, FC = Fixed Costs, BE = Breakeven

**Figures 10-2.** Breakeven analysis: the classic chart

For the sake of simplicity, we assume that all costs are either fixed or variable (see Chapter 8 for a review of these terms). In reality some costs have characteristics of both—they're largely fixed but over time can have some of the attributes of variable costs. For now, for our purposes, costs are either fixed or variable.

Figure 10-2 shows a horizontal line representing Fixed Costs, meaning those costs that are always present. The figure also shows a rising line beginning at zero that represents Sales. Every activity period starts with zero sales and rises as sales build, as our chart shows. The third line, labeled Variable Costs, represents the costs Wonder Widget incurred only because of its production of the products it sells. They are the costs to make or buy what it sells, to deliver to the customer, and to pay other costs directly related to those sales, such as sales commissions. Without sales these costs would not be incurred and, in general, their magnitude is directly related to those sales.

Notice that the Variable Cost line begins not at zero but at the top of the Fixed Costs line, because variable costs are incurred in addition to the fixed costs that were already in place. So we chart the Variable Cost line to effectively represent on the vertical scale *the total of fixed and variable costs*. Now the picture becomes clear. Where that Total Cost line crosses the Sales line is the point at which total sales have paid for the total costs of the business. That's the business' breakeven point, and all sales beyond that level should result in a positive bottom line. That, as they say, is a good thing.

One valuable use of the companywide analysis is in helping determine if a company can operate profitably as currently configured, a critical piece of information if you're the CEO or a turnaround consultant to a troubled company. If the breakeven point is too far into the upper right corner of the chart, the first question to ask is: How can fixed costs be lowered? The second question, which usually takes more study, is: How can variable costs be lowered, or sales volume or pricing increased?

## What to Do If You Don't Like the Answer

While a breakeven analysis in advance of a product decision is an excellent management practice, there's no guarantee that you'll like the answer or that the estimates will prove accurate or that the marketplace will buy all the products you need to sell at the price you want to sell them. Sometimes this analysis will tell you the whole thing isn't going to work. Either you have to sell your product for much more than the competing product or you have to sell more units than the marketplace can absorb. At that point smart managers will stop and reevaluate their options. Those options are basically three:

1. Disbelieve the whole analysis and proceed on the basis that your intuition is more accurate (not recommended).

2. Scrap the whole idea and look for a better product, or sell more of what you've already got.

3. Modify the product plans in ways that will also modify the analysis in a positive way; for example, add features that will increase the market appeal—and the resulting unit volume or selling price, or both—by more than the added features will cost.

The key take-away from this discussion is that a breakeven analysis is an important risk assessment tool. It enables you to test your assumptions before you spend money, with the dual objective of getting the best possible result from any launch while avoiding wasting money on a half-baked idea.

**SMART**

**MANAGING**

### MAKE BREAKEVEN A REQUIREMENT

Breakeven analysis should be a requirement for any new product decision, even those that will require research and/or development. While estimates may be challenging to develop, a good estimate is better than a bad surprise after the product is in the warehouse. And if you don't like the answer you get the first time around, don't explain it away by arbitrarily changing your assumptions. Reevaluate the product from start to finish. If your assumptions are valid, however they may be estimated, seriously consider if this is the right product, the right time, the right market, the right pricing, and so on.

## Manager's Checklist for Chapter 10

☑ The breakeven point is the level of sales volume that, when reached, has effectively earned enough sales dollars to pay for all the costs of developing, producing, and delivering the product or service being sold. Put another way, breakeven is that point at which the seller is neither ahead nor behind on the income statement as a result of selling the product or service.

☑ Every new product offering should have a realistic analysis—in writing—of the total cost of researching, developing, producing or buying, marketing and selling, delivering, and if appropriate, after-sale servicing of the product before the decision is made to offer the product.

☑ Breakeven analysis is also valuable on a companywide basis, helping to determine if a company can operate profitably as it's currently configured, a valuable piece of information if you're the CEO or a turnaround consultant to a troubled company. If the breakeven point is too far into the upper right corner of the breakeven chart, the first question to ask is: How can fixed costs be lowered? The second question, usually taking more study, is: How can variable costs be lowered, or sales volume or pricing increased?

☑ While a breakeven analysis in advance of a product decision is an excellent management practice, there's no guarantee that you'll like the answer or that the estimates will prove accurate or that the marketplace will buy all the products you need to sell at the price you want to sell them. Sometimes the analysis will tell you it won't work. At that point it's wise to stop and reevaluate your options.

**Chapter 11**

# Business Planning: Creating the Future You Want, Step-by-Step

I n my consulting business I speak to a lot of managers, from for-profit businesses to nonprofit organizations. They are busier today than ever before, it seems, and we find more frequent use of planning. Yet despite the apparent trend toward greater use of business planning methods, a common refrain from some harried business managers is: "We're too busy running our company to do formal business planning." Even start-up CEOs, who are creating a whole new company, are prone to add: "If potential investors want to look at something, we'll do a plan for them, but we certainly don't need one ourselves. We're clear about where we're going, and we don't have the interest or the spare time to write it out on paper."

Thus begins still another chapter in the myths of business planning. Figure 11-1 includes some of my personal favorites.

## Why Take Time to Plan?

Every organization with a goal in mind develops a plan to get there. Every manager with a job to do develops a plan to get his or her daily work done. Yet, for the most part, these plans are informal. Often people only carry them around in their minds and detail them as needed, improvising and modifying along the way.

Most people don't think of themselves as planners, yet they plan every day, formally or informally. We plan pretty much for the best rea-

| The Myth | The Reality |
|---|---|
| Planning is a lot of work; busy managers don't have time for still another task. | Planning actually saves work and time by helping managers to avoid doing more work than is necessary to reach their goals. |
| Plans are obsolete as soon as they're done. | Plans are dynamic and change as the business evolves. The best ones get reviewed and modified regularly. |
| Plans must always be long and detailed to be of any value. | Plans need not be any more detailed than the company needs to guide its activities. Some very focused plans for small businesses will fit on a single page. |
| Business moves too fast to be held back by a plan. | The speed of business is a big reason why plans are important, because we can find ourselves far off the mark in a short time. Plans don't hold managers back; rather, they guide managers' forward movement. |
| Planning is not as important or valuable as doing something productive. | Planning makes what we do more productive by enabling us to avoid doing things that don't contribute to our productivity as measured by end results. |
| We should leave the planning to the planners and let the managers do their work. | Plans done without the substantial involvement of the managers who are making the decisions are largely useless because they don't reflect reality. |

**Figure 11-1.** Myths of business planning debunked

sons: because planning helps us to reach goals, whether the goals relate to getting our daily work done, laying out the family vacation, or financing our retirement. *We plan when we don't know how to get where we want to go.*

People who regularly plan in their personal lives sometimes resist planning when their company announces the annual budget or the quarterly business plan review. And yet the plans serve the same purpose: to reach desired goals. The company version is different, of course. For one thing, it's usually more formal and more detailed, for several reasons, all related to executing the plan:

- Execution requires the coordinated efforts of many people.

■ Execution consumes substantial, expensive resources.

■ The plan involves multiple, often interlocking and related goals and tasks that must be achieved.

For much the same reasons, a business plan should be a *written* plan. Putting a plan in writing enables us to gain several important benefits for our planning efforts:

■ **Clarity.** What must be done and the steps to get there are clarified. We're less likely to forget something or to have to hastily redirect our efforts to include a missing task if we've written down the tasks ahead of time. When we carry plans in our heads, funny things sometimes happen. We can change the plan in mid-thought in case it looks more difficult to reach than we originally thought and no one will know. We can rationalize with ourselves that 75 percent is as good as 100 percent, and no one will hold us accountable for our questionable adjustment of the metric. When a plan is written, it's crystal clear what the goal was—75 percent or 100 percent or whatever—because it's there on the page in black and white.

■ **Roadmap.** If you can remember the last time you tried to find a new street address without a map, you may recall making a few wrong turns, stopping to ask directions, retracing your steps, and generally proceeding more slowly because you weren't sure where you were going. A plan tells you which turns to take and which ones to avoid, and you know the route ahead of time because you've thought it through before the journey began. Fewer wrong turns means less time wasted, less money spent, and better results with the same resources.

■ **Communication.** We have a means to communicate consistently and easily the goals we want to achieve to everyone who we believe helps us meet those goals, such as staff, bosses, customers, and suppliers. Clearly communicated goals—without ambiguity or confusion or the distraction of today's emergencies—are more likely to receive support from all those who can help us get there.

■ **Empowerment.** In any challenging endeavor, we face goals that seem difficult if not impossible to reach. They may not be impossible, but the idea of getting that far beyond where we are today can seem that way—and when something seems impossible, that can be a self-ful-filling prophecy. By writing down our plans, along with all the critical steps to get there, we effectively break the goals into small steps. We can then look at each step and clearly see the possibility—even the probability—of achieving it. Thus we give ourselves permission to believe the goal is achievable. That permission does powerful things in our minds, shifting what is often the most significant obstacle to success: our own belief systems.

## Strategic Planning versus Operational Planning

There are business plans—and then there are business plans. Let's begin by distinguishing between the two principal types of business plans: strategic plans and operational (or operating) plans. The two look differ-ent and are written in a different style, because they are intended for dif-ferent audiences. Every marketing manager knows that a brochure, to be effective, must be customized to its audience. The same holds true for a business plan, whichever type it is. It should always be written for its

---

**KEY TERMS**

**Business plan** The generic name for a plan written for a busi-ness. It generally includes a statement of the plan's objective, the period it covers, and the goals to be achieved by the new business. How those ideas are expressed depends on the type of plan.

**Strategic plan** A type of business plan designed to define the vision and mission of a business, its strategy and long-term objectives, and the key details important to the strategic reader. The plan is typically intended to drive the company's strategy for several years, and serves as the basis for the company's operating plan.

**Operating plan** A detailed description of what the company will do to pursue the objectives of its strategic plan for the next operating period, usu-ally one year. The operating plan contains enough detail that the company's operating managers can use it to guide their daily and monthly activities.

**Financing plan** A special version of a strategic plan written to attract out-side financial resources to the company, usually intended for equity investors, but sometimes written for lenders as well. This version emphasizes the amount of money needed, how it will be used, and how the investors will receive a return on their money. The plan may also discuss, or at least touch on, the plans for an exit strategy (more on this in Chapter 14).

intended purpose and directed to its intended reader.

A *strategic plan* is usually more than a statement of goals. It's a statement of corporate purpose, a request for support, and a call to action. In other words, the plan's purpose usually includes an emotional appeal of some kind. Therefore, the form as well as the content should be aimed at capturing that support.

The purpose of a strategic plan is to guide the organization's direction: to define its grand purpose, what it wants to achieve, and the general strategies it will use to get there. The plan might include the definition of the company's market, its product categories, and the ways in which it will change the buyers' lives in its intended market. The plan might also define the organization's long-range goals and provide a segue to the shorter-term and more detailed activities that are laid out in the operational plans.

The strategic plan typically doesn't contain a lot of details about implementation. Rather, it talks in global terms about the business the company is engaged in, the strategies the company will pursue, the benefits that will be achieved when the implementation is complete and how that will enable the company to move closer to achieving its fundamental purpose.

The *operating plan*, by contrast, is primarily intended as a short-term playbook (usually one year) for the executive managers and staff who have responsibility for carrying out the plan. It contains details they need to do their work—milestones, action steps, detailed budgets, timetables, and so on. Such a plan would make dull reading for the analyst who's studying the company's strategic direction. But its contents are essential to the manager charged with delivering the assigned sales goal, upgrading the computer network to the next software version, or finding out how much money is budgeted to build the new trade show booth or hire the new engineer.

Let's look at the principal elements of a business plan, and examine how each would be treated in a strategic plan vs. an operating plan.

# Vision and Mission: The Starting Point

The vision and mission are intended to express the organization's grand purpose, the point from which everything else should emerge. There are a thousand definitions for these terms—and at least that many opinions about whether either, or both, or a "purpose statement" instead, should be the foundation for a plan. Rather than add my opinion to the pack, let me tell you what they bring to a plan. Then you decide whether a plan has adequately included them.

## Vision of the Future

Any organization starts with some sort of grand purpose. Typically that arises when the founder looks around and sees that a worthwhile need is going unfilled. Abraham Lincoln had the vision of a great nation undivided by slavery. Henry Ford had the vision of a world in which almost any family could afford to own and drive an automobile. Bill Gates had the vision of a computer in every home. Steve Jobs had a vision of technology products that were both attractive and easy to use. In each case, the vision was of the world as they thought it should be, not as it was then. I suspect their visions seemed beyond the imagination of those around them at the time. But then, their visions *were* beyond the imagination of normal people of their time. Their fervor—and probably more than a few carefully laid plans—may explain why they were able to convert those visions into reality. So, let's look at my definition of *vision* as I've just described it: *Vision is the world as you define it, rearranged as you would like to see it.*

## Mission: The Path to the Holy Grail

Once you understand the definition of vision, the definition of mission is easier to grasp: *Mission is the role of the organization in achieving the vision.*

If the vision is grand enough, it may not be something one organization can achieve by itself (although it may be able to, as the organizations led by the visionaries above did). As a rule, first the vision is defined, then the organization does what it can to get there.

---

### Vision and Mission in Action: A Case Study

I had a client some years ago who defined his world as the dental industry in Southern California. His company's vision was for a world (the aforementioned industry) in which hazardous waste materials from dental work would not contribute to environmental pollution. For a variety of reasons, that world didn't exist when his company was formed. Novocain, mercury, and other byproducts of dental services did not have the regulatory controls and enforcement that more visibly hazardous materials did. It was a worthwhile purpose that was not being effectively addressed.

He went about building a company and a service that brought cost-effective hazardous materials collection and proper disposal within reach of every dentist in his world. Within a few years his company was the dominant provider of this service throughout Southern California. He may not have achieved his mission completely, but he made great progress in that direction and ultimately sold his company to a larger company that wanted to use his methodology to expand its own presence in that market. The buyer, in effect, took over the mission the founder had envisioned. And, yes, he was an excellent planner as well as a visionary entrepreneur. Today he helps other entrepreneurs achieve their visions.

## Strategy: Setting Direction

Once a company has decided its mission, the questions likely arise: Now what? How do we start? What direction do we move in? In most situations these questions require a deeper look at the organization before management can develop effective answers. That deeper look often takes the form of examining the organization's internal strengths and weaknesses, as well as the external opportunities and threats that exist in its world or its marketplace. The analysis technique for this exploration is called a *SWOT analysis*, SWOT being the acronym for Strengths, Weaknesses, Opportunities, Threats (Figure 11-2). By looking at each of these objectively, the company can learn a great deal about its likelihood of success and what it must build on or, alternatively, overcome to enhance that likelihood.

**SWOT analysis** The analytical process of determining the significant internal and external advantages an organization possesses, and the internal and external obstacles it must overcome to develop an effective strategy for achieving its goals.

**KEY TERM**

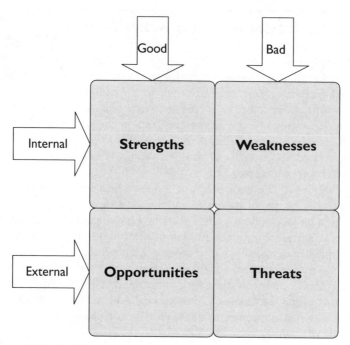

**Figure 11-2.** SWOT analysis matrix

*Strategy* is essentially deciding what direction the decision makers take as they begin to pursue their mission, and strategy is decided when the decision makers make an assumption about what it will take to overcome the vision's most significant obstacles and what assets the organization has at its disposal. Abraham Lincoln had to react to the creation of the Confederate States of America; he decided the best strategy was military force because he felt the Confederate states wouldn't be convinced to rejoin the United States otherwise. Henry Ford saw how few people could afford the luxury cars that were the only ones being built at the time; he decided he had to find a way to build a car that could be sold for $400 to average income earners. Bill Gates perceived that people's learning curve and resistance to technology were the prime obstacles to adopting personal computers; his strategy was to develop software that had a consistent look and feel and that would enable people to more easily use those computers. Steve Jobs saw the same obstacles Bill Gates saw, but his strategy went well beyond the Microsoft concept by emphasizing consumer appeal and ease of use while maintaining tight control of the hardware platform on which Apple's software ran. Together Gates and Jobs transformed the global concept of personal computing in a wave of technology enhancement that's still unfolding today.

In each case, the decision maker assessed the market, identified the obstacles, and crafted a strategy to address those obstacles. That sets the pattern for setting specific goals and objectives, which is a primary purpose of a business plan.

## Long-Term Goals: The Path to the Mission

The business plan elements we've discussed up to now have been global, intangible, and largely nonspecific. Once we move into setting goals, specificity is essential to success. In fact, setting effective goals requires attention to both the goal's content and structure. This is best demonstrated by an acronym that many of us have heard in one form or another at planning seminars and workshops. The acronym is SMART, and we use it to arrive at SMART goals, the kind that get results. Here are the characteristics of SMART goals:

**Specific.** The goal is identified clearly, by how much and when. How much of the desired result constitutes success—$50,000 or five offices or 15 new employees? By when will the goal be achieved—a specific date or a specific length of time after beginning? This specificity is needed to ensure everyone knows whether the goal has been achieved. I suggest to workshop audiences that the goal is specific enough if your 16-year-old son or daughter would recognize it.

**Measurable.** You must be able to measure the success with available data. Setting a goal to capture 20 percent of the market by year-end is specific enough, but if there is no industry data available to measure who has what share of market, it's a meaningless goal. Set goals for which you can get reasonably reliable information. Bonus: It precludes your staffers dismissing the goal as smoke because they know it can't be measured.

**Achievable.** The goal must be challenging but still achievable. More to the point, it must be perceived as achievable. If the staff believes the goal is unattainable, they'll give up on it from Day 1, and any efforts to reach the goal will be wasted. Goals should be set so they are a stretch beyond what exists, so people recognize the need to exert effort to get there. Yet people should have a reasonable belief that if they shoot for it, they can get there.

**Relevant.** The goal should be relevant to the organization's vision, mission, and strategy. That's the whole point, after all: to get to the vision. Occasionally a manager gets excited about an opportunity that doesn't relate to the mission and devotes resources to achieve what sounds like a great idea. The problem? It takes resources and focus away from the job of the organization—fulfilling the mission.

**Trackable.** This adds substance to our goal-setting methodology. A goal is trackable if you can establish milestones to track progress toward the goal. This enables you to monitor progress and avoid unpleasant surprises at the 11th hour, when your staff "discovers" they won't make it by tomorrow, as was committed. A trackable goal might be an annual sales goal of $120,000. Seasonal adjustments aside, you should expect to bring in $10,000 a month and ask questions if any month falls much short of that. Thus you will know how the team is doing well before the fourth quarter, and can take action to redirect resources, if necessary, to ensure that the goal is met.

**SMART GOALS**

At any level in any organization, smart managers know that they get the best results by setting goals that are SMART: Specific, Measurable, Achievable, Relevant, Trackable.

# Short-Term Goals and Milestones: The Operating Plan

Once the grand design of the strategic plan has been laid out, the company needs a detailed plan for its managers and employees to follow. While the strategic plan typically covers a period of three to five years, its implementation is usually thought of in terms of one-year periods, each of which is guided by an annual operating plan.

The year covered by an operating plan is typically the company's operating or fiscal year. The plan lays out the company's goals for the coming year, and the support those tasked with individual goals and action items will need for the company to meet its overall goals. Further, for a plan to be effective, it must be trusted, meaning that employees must believe that the plan was drafted with reasonable foresight, knowledge, awareness, and thoroughness. Otherwise it will be second-guessed at every step, with the likely result that every step will cost more in resources than planned, and some more challenging goals won't be met because people don't trust they can get to where the plan says they can.

The operating plan and the related budget (discussed in Chapter 12) constitute the playbook for action during a company's operating year. The operating plan is usually the joint effort of every department, coordinated by the Finance and/or Planning Department. Each department head will have participated in the planning process by writing the goals his or her department will achieve during the plan year. The operating plan may outline the goals and targets of each major unit within the company, the P&L budget for the year, and a budget of planned capital expenditures. In addition, subsections of the plan may be devoted to individual departments, so that each has its own roadmap to follow. Information included in the departmental subsections, in addition to goals, might include staffing, existing and planned additions, and the department's budget for the year. A suggested outline for an operating plan appears in Figure 11-3. This is the document that goal-driven incentive plans typically use as a measuring stick.

---

**Overview**
 Vision, mission, strategy
 One-year summary of company goals
 Companywide challenges and opportunities
**Production Department Plan**
 Goals
 Milestones
 Organization and staffing
 Facilities
 Challenges and opportunities
 Budget
**Marketing and Sales Department Plan**
 Goals
 Milestones

---

**Figure 11-3.** Outline of an operating plan for a business (continued on next page)

Organization and staffing
Facilities
Challenges and opportunities
Budget
**R&D/Product Development Department Plan**
Goals
Milestones
Organization and staffing
Facilities
Challenges and opportunities
Budget
**Financial Department Plan/Budget**
Goals
Milestones
Organization and staffing
Facilities
Challenges and opportunities
Budget
**Companywide Budget**
Summary of projected basic financial statements
Departmental budgets
Departmental staffing plans
Capital expenditures plan

**Figure 11-3.** Outline of an operating plan for a business (continued)

The layout of this outline and the order of its contents aren't as important as having all the bases covered. In other words, the plan should cover all these topic areas in a way that's logical to everyone in the organization, regardless of where in the plan each topic appears. I have found that organizing the plan by department makes it easier for each department to incorporate its contribution, as well as to refer to its part of the plan during implementation or assessment of progress. The following sections will help you to understand what should be covered in each part of the plan.

## Overview

It helps to begin by reminding readers of the operating plan's relationship to the grand design—the overriding purpose of the company—and the direction the company is moving to fulfill that grand design. Knowing that Wonder Widget's stated purpose was to become the dominant provider of high-quality widgets in the western United States puts in perspective the specific goals that the company wants to achieve during the coming year and enables every manager to buy in anew to that strategy as he or she begins work on the current year's goals. Whether a company decides to recite the entire vision, mission, and strategy at the beginning of the document or simply give a summary, as suggested here, is less important than the effort to reinforce the grand purpose in a way that generates renewed enthusiasm for the long-term plan.

The overview should also contain the company's key goals for the year and the key challenges and opportunities it faces, to keep everyone focused on the company's direction and to keep them from getting too wrapped up in their own department's agenda at the expense of the team objectives.

## The Production Plan: Getting the Product Ready to Sell

Whether the company makes or buys its products or provides a service, some activities must be initiated and satisfactorily completed to have something to sell. Goals might include reaching monthly production or service levels that support sales forecasts, improving machine output or maintenance downtime or setup times, or moving to just-in-time ordering to lower average inventory levels. The plan should lay out these goals, along with the timetable, staffing, and financial resources needed to achieve them.

The plan should also identify the production challenges that must be met to reach the goals, and the steps the organization plans to take to meet those challenges. This information will have been identified during the SWOT analysis mentioned earlier. These challenges might include heavy recent turnover of several skilled supervisors, the age or condition of the machines in the plant, pricing pressures from suppliers who demand price adjustments to provide just-in-time shipping, and so on. If the plan doesn't specify the challenges and deal with them effectively, it will quickly be seen as irrelevant by employees who find their paths blocked by obstacles they can't control.

## Marketing and Sales Plan: Generating Interest and Making the Sale

Given the availability of the product or service, the company's marketing and sales organization (or organizations, if they are separately managed) must determine how it will interest the company's potential customers and then sell enough products to reach the sales goals. Representative goals here might include hiring and training more salespeople, launching a targeted marketing campaign to raise brand awareness, introducing five new products during the year, opening and staffing three sales offices, or reducing customer complaints about product delivered vs. promised.

Challenges to be addressed might include a large competitor with a similar product, an aging product that hasn't kept up with changing market demands, strong competition for quality salespeople that keeps compensation high and candidate quality low, or pricing pressures caused by a bad economy. These challenges might be addressed by simply lowering the revenue forecast, but that indirect approach sidesteps the more effective method of approaching each obstacle directly and identifying the steps to mitigate the potential damage.

## R&D/Product Development Plan: Bringing New Ideas to Market

Some companies provide services that drive their sales, and continuing sales depend on delivering reliable levels of service at reasonable prices. Other companies sell products they buy from others (usually based on the desires of their customers) and don't create or manufacture any products. But many other companies sell proprietary products, that is, products they have developed and that they make or over which they maintain manufacturing control.

Such products have typically been developed by these companies at some cost in time and money. That cost must be identified and reflected in their planning, along with the expected fruits of that effort in terms of new research advances, technological breakthroughs, new products developed and brought to market, and so on. For these companies, an R&D section of the operating plan is essential to ensure resources are

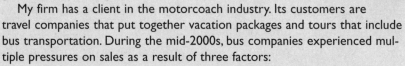

## THE DILEMMA OF THE TOUR BUS INDUSTRY

While this example is a few years old, its unique circumstances make it an excellent case study for exploring the value to be gained from planning.

My firm has a client in the motorcoach industry. Its customers are travel companies that put together vacation packages and tours that include bus transportation. During the mid-2000s, bus companies experienced multiple pressures on sales as a result of three factors:

- Pricing pressures from customers in a market where vacation travel was 25 percent below normal in the aftermath of September 11, 2001;
- High replacement costs for new buses combined with falling trade-in prices for older buses, causing greater demands on their cash to periodically upgrade equipment; and
- Dramatically rising insurance costs from insurers looking to replace loss reserves reduced by 9-11 claims.

Any bus company at that time had to address these challenges in its operating plan to have any chance of achieving its stated goals for revenue and gross margin. For example, a company might have offered its customers extra services that delivered high value in the customers' eyes without raising costs too much, thus lowering price resistance from customers. A company might also sharpen its search for better financing and hold buses a few months longer than normal, thus lowering bus replacement cost pressures. Or, a company might shop for insurance coverage more aggressively and raise deductibles to lower insurance premiums. Perhaps the best solution would be a combination of all these options. Clearly industry-wide pressures of this magnitude tend to squeeze out the weaker players, typically those with less able management teams.

How well did the industry do? While it's hard to associate outcomes with specific actions or inactions over the years, the American Bus Association reported that the number of motorcoach companies in the United States and Canada shrank by 30 percent between 2007–2010—another difficult economic period.

allocated to these activities and to clearly set forth the expected results from use of those resources.

Plans might identify the new products they intend to bring to market during the coming year, based on projected outcome of development efforts. For a drug company, results might include a key drug moving from basic testing to first clinical trials. While the company is still years from marketing this product, it can still plan for and measure results in terms of progress along the development path and through the lengthy regulatory process.

A company engaged in R&D faces numerous and substantial challenges. For one thing, it's often impossible to know how long it will take to reach a given research goal or how much money it will cost. Unknown events or testing failures or breakthroughs can dramatically affect the process. Most drug company research projects never produce a product that can be marketed and sold profitably, an outcome that cannot be known when the research on a specific product begins. These companies must find a way to allocate resources, manage expectations against results, and be prepared for good news and bad news along the way.

### Financial Plan: The Budget

The *financial plan* is the financial report card, the section of the plan that shows the financial results of all the work outlined in the plan. It shows the revenues the company expects to achieve if the sales goals are met and the expenses to be incurred to support the sales and other goals, if everything goes according to plan. This key document is covered in depth in Chapter 12.

# Manager's Checklist for Chapter 11

☑ The term *business plan* is a generic label. It's important to determine the purpose of the plan, its intended readership, and what's expected of its readers in order to know the kind and depth of material it should contain.

☑ We all plan some of our activities, but the more complex the business activities we must manage, the more important it is to have a plan to guide us. A plan needed to manage a business activity should be in writing to ensure it provides clarity, a roadmap to the desired result, consistent communication of what is to be done, and the means to empower those who will carry it out.

☑ Goals must be crafted with care to be effective in driving performance. SMART goals encompass the key characteristics that make them most likely to succeed—or at least most likely to produce a clear, organization-wide understanding of what was expected and what was delivered.

☑ Strategic plans are typically long-term (three to five years) and broad in their description of the goals to be achieved. Operating plans are usually short-term (one year) and more detailed in their description of the work. Strategic plans guide the operating plans. Operating plans guide the day-to-day activities that get work done.

☑ A realistic operating plan should define the goals the company wants each department to achieve. The plan should also identify the challenges the company must overcome to reach the goals and how they will be met if the plan is to be both believable and achievable.

# The Annual Budget: Financing Your Plans

Once management has decided on a business plan that sets company goals for the next year, they need to determine (a) if they can afford to achieve those goals, (b) if the plan will make a profit for the company, and (c) if the plan will meet the goals set by management. Those questions are best answered by converting the operating plan's goals and actions into dollars and cents, then breaking down the plans into chunks that can be evaluated and managed during daily operations. That's the purpose of the annual budget. The *annual budget* is the estimate of the financial resources that will be needed and the anticipated financial outcome of all the actions the managers will take during the budget period. The budget is also the *financial benchmark*, the report card against which their success in managing their financial resources will be measured.

The format of a typical annual budget includes a detailed, department-by-department, line-by-line, month-by-month estimate of the income and expenses that will occur if the operating plan is carried out as intended. The budget contains sufficient detail to enable department managers to allocate and manage the resources assigned to them: employees, production equipment, advertising dollars, office supplies, and so forth.

A well-prepared budget is as detailed as necessary to track all material sources of revenue, all significant planned expenses, and the cash flow effects of that activity. The budget should also include expected changes in the balance sheet as a result of the flow of money, because balance sheets are the basis for many performance measurements (as you learned in Chapter 7) and because they are also the tools lenders use to measure compliance with loan covenants. The annual budget is the focus of this chapter because it's the most useful and most used of the financial estimating tools. However, it's not the only technique for estimating the company's financial future.

## Tools for Telling the Future: Budgets, Forecasts, Projections, and Tea Leaves

There are lots of labels you may hear for financial plans. Some folks will tell you this or that is the "correct" name for the plan. But it matters less what you call it and more what you intend to do with it. Whether you call your plan a budget, a forecast, or a projection—it doesn't matter to the company owners as long as you hit it on the money. (Of course, if you call your plan "tea leaves," you may have a credibility problem, even if you achieve great results.) Most of these words differ principally in the level of detail they contain, the depth of work that went into their preparation, and the period of time they cover. Still, it's worthwhile to know the most common usage, if for no other reason than because they are the definitions we use in this book.

**KEY TERMS**

**Financial plan** The generic label for any kind of future estimate in financial terms. Budgets, forecasts, and projections are all financial plans. Aside from the generic usage, *financial plan* is most often used for a long-term business plan that identifies the financial effects of all the plan's activities. In Chapter 11 we referred to the dollars-and-cents representation of our long-range plan as a financial plan. The resulting definition: an integrated, multiyear plan of income, expenses, cash flow, and balance sheet changes.

**Projection** An estimate that's less detailed than a financial plan and usually covers a shorter period. Typically a projection is prepared to demonstrate expected financial results over a few months or a year, perhaps for a special purpose such as a bank loan or to test the continuing validity of a budget or long-range plan. A projection may not include an integrated balance sheet, but it almost always includes a P&L projection or a cash flow projection, depending on the focus.

> **Forecast** Typically a short-term view of the next few weeks or months, perhaps to test the validity of the operating budget under a set of conditions that might not have existed when the annual budget was created. Short-term cash forecasts are typically not very detailed. A forecast might also be used as the starting point in budgeting, such as producing a sales forecast that forms the basis for the sales budget.

### FORECASTING RATHER THAN PLANNING

Forecasts are often prepared by companies that don't use annual budgets, often employed when management finds they need a tool to help them see into the immediate future. This might be the case in a company with short-term cash flow problems. Small businesses may use forecasting when executives don't appreciate the value of a formal planning system (a risky situation), yet recognize from time to time that they can't mentally assimilate all the factors that will influence their immediate financial future.

## How to Budget for Revenues: The "Unpredictable" Starting Point

For valid reasons, every budget preparation cycle should begin with a revenue forecast. Revenue typically drives the business and determines the level of growth and the degree of success that the business may anticipate. The level of revenue determines the magnitude of investment that management can make in the business, as well as the resources they may need to purchase to run the business.

For many managers, preparing a budget is a frustrating activity. Not only must they take the time to prepare a budget, but they have to start with the one thing they can neither control nor accurately predict: the amount of products and services their customers will buy from them during the budget period. Still, that's how it's done, except in the smallest of companies or companies with aging owners who have become highly risk-averse or some professional service firms where the primary focus is on covering fixed costs. Such narrowly focused thinking is inconsistent with building a successful, forward-looking company, but for owners these limited approaches represent protecting what they have, a primary concern.

SMART

MANAGING

**THE SALESPEOPLE KNOW BEST!**

Whatever the company's structure, the sales forecast should come from the people directly responsible for bringing in the sales, the company's sales force. Salespeople typically know the market better than anyone else. While senior management may feel it's important to announce their sales desires, hopes, and expectations, building those goals into the company budget without validation from the people who sell the goods or services is risky. They know what customers want and don't want, even if they don't always communicate it effectively to management. Besides, the salespeople must buy into the sales budget, just as any employees should take personal responsibility for any goal assigned to them. Otherwise, they may well consider it "management's budget" and not theirs, with the likely result being failure to achieve the plan.

This approach does have some risks, however. Salespeople may want to set less aggressive sales goals because they don't want to be evaluated against a target they're not sure they can hit or because they want to be assigned a target they are certain they can meet or exceed. Also, if your salespeople are primarily outside sales representatives rather than employees, their sense of your market and their commitment to the company may influence the care with which they prepare their estimates. However, these risks don't lessen the importance of having the salespeople adopt the sales forecast as their own.

If we accept the value of beginning with a sales forecast, the next question is usually: How do we do it? How to budget for revenues depends in large measure on the nature of the business, its history, and customer buying patterns. Figure 12-1 shows some ideas and the kinds of businesses for which they might make sense.

The completed sales estimate is then presented to management, who evaluates its viability in terms of:

- A reasonable balance between aggressiveness and conservatism. Did the sales manager push for more than was easily attainable without creating expectations that no one can reasonably meet?
- The likely acceptance of the estimate by the salespeople, balanced against the company's ability to make an acceptable profit if the estimate is adopted and met.
- The abilities and resources available to the production side of the company to deliver the goods and services outlined in the estimate.

| Sales Scenario | Ideas for Estimating Annual Revenues |
|---|---|
| The company sells its products to an identifiable list of customers and there are good relationships between Sales and its customers. | Identify the top 50 (or X) customers representing 60% or more of the company's business and contact them for their buying intentions for the coming year. Include an estimate for the remainder, based on the trends seen in the first group. |
| The historical sales pattern has closely followed some indicator of growth that's still available and still reasonably valid, e.g., airline passenger miles, housing starts, auto sales, defense spending, personal income statistics, etc. | Obtain the most valid forecast of that indicator for the coming year and base the sales estimate on the same relationship that has existed in the past year. If the relationship has changed over the years, weigh the most recent periods most heavily in your estimates. |
| The company has been able to sell all it can make in a strong market and it's feeling the pinch of reaching its productive capacity. | Project sales as a percent of maximum capacity to produce, recognizing that 100% is not attainable, but that capacity will strongly affect a company's ability to deliver. In this case, the production managers should also be part of the estimating team. |
| Your customers perform work under long-term contracts with their customers, so they must line up supplier commitments to enable them to project profitability on their performance. | Similar to the first example above, except that the estimates are likely to be more reliable. Still, history tells us even these are uncertain, as delays by others can cause postponement or even cancellation. This is, after all, just an estimate. |
| Sales have grown at a rate that has been reasonably consistent from year to year and nothing in the market is expected to change. | This is the no-brainer estimate, providing nothing is expected to change in the coming year. Use the same growth rate, perhaps increased by whatever the company's managers think they can do to boost results further. |

**Figure 12-1.** Estimating revenues

If the sales estimate is deemed acceptable, it becomes the company's sales budget. All other budgets will then have to take into account the resources they'll need to support the sales budget. If the sales budget is not yet acceptable, it likely means a back-and-forth process of questions, additional research, and negotiations between management and the sales organization until an acceptable revenue budget is adopted. If this process is normal, it should be considered in developing the timetable for budget preparation.

# Budgeting Costs: Understanding Relationships That Affect Costs

*Budgeting*, in its simplest form, is an attempt to estimate what will happen to a company's financial condition if it sells a certain quantity of goods and services and runs its business in support of that sales result. Managers want to know what they will have to spend in the coming year to sell the quantities they have budgeted and exactly what they will spend it for. This sounds simple enough—except for this principle, perhaps an obscure extension of Parkinson's Law: There is always a good reason to spend money. (Parkinson's Law [Wikipedia]: "Work expands so as to fill the time available for its completion.")

As Parkinson might have said it, the need for money expands to consume all available funds. In other words, there's always a logical reason to approve a given expenditure. Every department needs more resources to do its job—or at least that case can always be made and apparently supported. Most companies today try to get by with lower costs than previously, as a hedge against the possibility that sales or profits will be lower than planned. Whether an expenditure will deliver the expected benefit is a big question, of course, but a manager can't know the answer with certainty until he or she makes the expenditure, so it's hard to disapprove an expenditure in advance unless it violates some predetermined standard, like the budget.

Given that premise, managers can choose to accept every rationale put forward by an employee that seems logical, or they can spend time and resources to audit the validity of every request to spend money, or they can simply make arbitrary choices until they run out of money. Since none of those options is wise in today's business environment, senior managers must find a way to relate the need to spend money to what's really needed to support their sales goals, their R&D goals, their expansion goals, or whatever their operating plan calls for as the measure of success for the coming year.

Enter the budget: a planning and analysis tool that enables management to estimate the expenditures needed to support a given level of sales and to set spending limits based on those estimates. Remember that some expenses are variable with sales, some are fixed, and some are somewhere between variable and fixed (semi-fixed). You can begin to see the possibility that we can create a budget that documents those relationships, thus setting limits on reasonable spending for potentially every item in the company's chart of accounts.

We already know that variable costs grow or shrink in direct relation to sales levels. If you think about it, though, many other cost items in a budget have identifiable relationships to other cost items, not only to sales. Those relationships enable a company to base its spending decisions on its own operating history.

For example, assume that last year's group medical insurance cost the company 2 percent of wages paid, and the insurer has announced a 10 percent rate increase for the coming year. It makes sense to build a budget that includes health insurance at 2.2 percent of budgeted labor costs for next year (10 percent more than last year's 2 percent), comfortable in the knowledge that the relationship will hold at almost any labor level. Now the company doesn't have to reconsider healthcare costs with every budget revision. It can allow budgeted health insurance costs to follow budgeted wages, which are controllable.

Figure 12-2 shows a few relationships that may help a company develop a budget with built-in cost controls that might otherwise be difficult to estimate, based on their relationship to other, more visible costs.

You can probably think of more of these relationships that would apply to your company's budget, but this gives you an idea of the possibilities. Keep in mind that a budgeted line item based on a percent of sales—when the activity bears no direct relation to sales—is a waste of time as a control tool. That becomes a calculation without accuracy and without value, other than to fill a space in the budget file. Look for the relationships that have meaning, even if the basis for a predominantly fixed cost is only last year's actual expense plus an inflation factor (as it might be, for example, when budgeting for building rent).

| This line item to be budgeted ... | and may be assumed to change in relation to ... |
|---|---|
| Sales commissions | Sales volume, especially if segmented by products commissioned at differing rates |
| Payroll taxes, health insurance, and workers' compensation insurance | Wages and salaries |
| Auto expenses | Number of employees reimbursed for such expenses |
| Selling expenses | Sales volume (in units, if available) |
| Telephone expense | Number of employees with offices and phones |
| Plant supervision wages | Number of employees with that job title |
| Factory janitorial services, outsourced | Square feet of factory space serviced |
| Profit-sharing expense | Wages and salaries of eligible employees |
| Travel expense | Number of employee travel days planned* |
| Sales taxes | Taxable sales |
| Utilities | Square feet of space occupied (plant vs. office) |
| Property taxes | Square feet of space occupied |
| Building repairs and maintenance | Square feet of space occupied |
| Machine repairs and maintenance | Machine hours in use or available |
| Telephone expense in the sales department | Number of full-time equivalent salespeople |

*This can be further refined by intrastate, national, and international travel days.

**Figure 12-2.** Cost relationships that facilitate sound budgeting

# The Budgeting Process: Trial and Error

You've exerted diligent effort, honestly given your department's budget your best sense of accuracy, and provided for every cost you think might be incurred to meet the goals you've been assigned. You feel confident as you send your budget to your boss. (You're the first of her direct reports to get yours in—another feather in your cap.) You wait for the feedback

## SOFTWARE TO EASE THE WORKLOAD AND MINIMIZE MISTAKES

**TOOLS**

For many years companies have used spreadsheet software, such as Microsoft Excel®, to build their budgets, manipulate the numbers for presentation, develop alternative versions, and insert the countless changes that come out of the negotiations inherent in the process. Two problems that users face with these traditional tools are the lack of flexibility of such models and the high risk of error caused by the need to make multiple entries for each change, requiring the data entry person to remember everywhere in the model a given change has impact. Since most such models are built by the company's Finance Department staff, the strength of the design to overcome these challenges varies widely. While large companies could purchase high-powered software with built-in safeguards, until recently few affordable options were available for small and midsized companies.

In the past few years a range of software products has arisen to fill that gap. The Excel spreadsheet format is quickly being replaced by more sophisticated interfaces that are better able to make real-time use of external databases and general ledger information, the mainstays of today's midlevel and enterprise organizations. In addition, the move to Software as a Service and other cloud-based platforms means updates to these products can be made continuously, collaboration and error-checking are easier, and security is substantially enhanced. Small and midsized companies can usually get solid recommendations from their CPA or a number of Web-based review sites for such products.

after all the other departments submit their budgets and all the departments, divisions, and cost center budgets are combined into a total company draft plan.

Imagine how you'd feel if the next thing you heard was your manager telling you that you need to cut 10 percent from your budget, without any reduction in the goals for which you will be held accountable. If you've been in the corporate world for any time, you know this is common. But why? If everyone else did his or her part as diligently as you, this wouldn't happen, would it?

Well, actually, it might.

The process of producing a companywide budget involves various departments estimating the resources they feel they will need to meet their goals—sales targets, customer service response rates, launch of new products or services, Marketing Department development of new collateral materials for trade shows, etc. No one knows what the total of all those cost budgets will be until they're merged. Only then can management get the first sense of whether their sales and profit goals are likely to be met by the combined budget submissions. If they do, approval is all that's necessary to make the draft the new, official budget. But more often they don't, at least not at first.

In fulfilling their responsibilities to the owners or stockholders, management must ask everyone to take another look at his or her proposal and find ways to raise revenues (again) or reduce expenses (again) to improve the budgeted bottom line. This is exactly the back-and-forth process that occurred earlier with the revenue budget. The objective is to achieve a happy medium in which management is satisfied with the sales and profit commitments of the organization, and managers with budget responsibility are comfortable that they can achieve the assigned goals with the budgeted resources.

During such reassessment, managers might look to ideas such as these to reevaluate their cost requests:

- Operate with the minimum number of employees that can handle the work.
- Train workers better to improve productivity and reduce turnover.
- Reduce operating costs, such as by using automation to save on labor costs.
- Perform a lease vs. buy analysis before acquiring new equipment (note that this also has cash flow implications, another consideration for growing companies).
- Negotiate better prices and terms with suppliers and develop alternate suppliers.
- Plan more use of overtime to reduce the need to hire more permanent workers (although the cost in terms of overtime premium somewhat reduces the savings from this option).
- Modify planned sales and marketing campaigns where results are not reasonably assured.
- Change distribution methods, combine delivery routes, reduce the number of smaller orders, and so on.

---

### HARD LESSONS LEARNED THE EASY WAY

Senior management, by mandating a cut of a certain percentage across all departments, may do more than create a furor; they can also cause serious, lasting damage. What does a savvy manager do who anticipates an order to reduce by 5 percent across the board? He or she raises all figures by 5 percent. So management gains nothing—unless it orders a 10 percent reduction. And a savvy manager who is unsure about the percentage to be applied would likely pad the budget for a worst-case scenario.

The result is that the managers are playing cat-and-mouse "negotiation" games with the figures, wasting a lot of time and effort simply because senior management prefers making budget cuts the easy way. Good managers make hard, individual budget decisions for the good of the company.

---

In a company where budget decisions are controlled by senior management, the negotiation process may be simply an edict to every department to "cut 10 percent." In 1967, when Ronald Reagan became governor of California, he created a furor when he did exactly that in trying to balance the state's budget. He soon had to relent and find a more nuanced way to reduce costs. But the lesson Reagan learned was lost on many corporate managers, perhaps because an across-the-board cut avoids making hard, individual decisions.

In a more empowering management environment, senior management asks subordinates to remove more money from less critical functions and less from the more critical departments. This process takes longer and involves more back-and-forth, trial-and-error manipulation of the numbers. But it usually results in a more credible budget that's easier for subordinates to buy into, rather than the alternative—acceptance of the edict from above, all the while holding the quiet belief that "it will take a lot of luck to make these numbers."

## Flexible Budgets: Whatever Happens, We've Got a Budget for It

One of the most useful tools in the manufacturing environment, and in many other kinds of companies as well, is the *flexible budget*. This tool is an extension of the classic budgeting methodology that is most valuable when these two statements are both true:

■ The company expects or may experience wide variations in activity levels within some area of the company, such as sales.

■ Many significant costs vary directly with those levels of activity, e.g., they are direct costs tied to sales, and the budget controls for these costs would be nearly useless if activity levels were significantly different from those in the budget.

In this situation, it's wise to develop a flexible budget, in which directly related costs are budgeted for various activity levels, and the budget used for comparison with actual results is the budget that's based on the actual activity levels achieved.

---

**KEY TERM**

**Flexible budget** A set of revenue and expense projections at various production or sales levels. Because the projections are based on different levels of activity, a flexible budget is useful in specifying the resources needed for various production levels (e.g., to manufacture product to respond to an unexpected 20 percent favorable variance in sales) without having to revise the budget or incur needed budget variances to support the new sales level. A series of budgets can be readily developed to fit any activity level.

---

How does a flexible budget work? Let's assume the Wonder Widget Company projects sales and production of its WW-1000 at 500 units a month. With a strong sales effort on the one hand, or inefficiency or production problems on the other, volume could be anywhere from 300–600 units, a big variation for which to plan. Such fluctuations could significantly impair budget analysis.

Looking at the internal reports, we see that production numbers for July came out as shown in Figure 12-3.

---

**FOR EXAMPLE**

**BUDGETS AND EXPECTATIONS**

Suppose the company sold 600 units in June, but couldn't make more than 400 with the existing budget and resources. Unhappy customers might be inclined to cancel their unfilled orders, resulting in lost sales and unhappiness all around. By contrast, if the company sold only 400 units when the plant was budgeted to make 500, production could be inefficient yet not exceed the budget, with a negative impact on profits even though expenditures could still be under budget.

| Item | Budget | Actual |
|------|--------|--------|
| Units Produced | 500 units | 400 units |
| Direct Labor | $32,500 | $28,500 |
| Variable Overhead | $75,000 | $64,000 |
| Total Variable Costs | $107,500 | $92,500 |

**Figure 12-3.** Wonder Widget production statistics for July 2013

Production in this example fell well short of the amount budgeted, with the result that variable costs, which fluctuate based on the amount produced, were lower than planned. A budget variance report using a static budget—one based solely on a single, planned level of activity—might look like Figure 12-4.

|  | Actual Cost per Unit Produced | Budget Cost per Unit Produced | Actual | Static Budget | Variance: Favorable (Unfavorable) |
|---|---|---|---|---|---|
| Production in Units |  |  | 400 | 500 | (100) |
| Direct Labor | $71.25 | $65.00 | $28,500 | $32,500 | $4,000 |
| Variable Overhead | $160.00 | $150.00 | 64,000 | 75,000 | 11,000 |
| Total Variable Costs |  |  | $92,500 | $107,500 | $15,000 |

**Figure 12-4.** Wonder Widget budget variance report using a static budget

On this basis, the Production Department looks like it did pretty well because it beat budget by $15,000. However, it was only 80 percent successful at meeting production expectations. So, how efficient was it?

If we look at the same facts under a flexible budget system, we get a different, more accurate picture of its success in meeting company goals. In this case, we use a budget based on the volume of activity and a cost-volume formula that enables us to produce a budget tailored to the level of activity. Figure 12-5 shows the result.

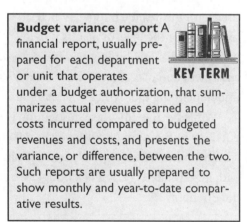

**Budget variance report** A financial report, usually prepared for each department or unit that operates **KEY TERM** under a budget authorization, that summarizes actual revenues earned and costs incurred compared to budgeted revenues and costs, and presents the variance, or difference, between the two. Such reports are usually prepared to show monthly and year-to-date comparative results.

| | Actual Cost per Unit Produced | Budget Cost per Unit Produced | Actual | Flexible Budget | Variance: Favorable (Unfavorable) |
|---|---|---|---|---|---|
| Production in Units | | | 400 | 400 | — |
| Direct Labor | $71.25 | $65.00 | $28,500 | $26,000 | $(2,500) |
| Variable Overhead | $160.00 | $150.00 | 64,000 | 60,000 | (4,000) |
| *Total Variable Costs* | | | *$92,500* | *$86,000* | *$(6,500)* |

**Figure 12-5.** Wonder Widget budget variance report using a flexible budget

---

**TRICKS OF THE TRADE**

## INEFFICIENCY COSTS MONEY IN MANY WAYS

If you look closely at Figure 12-4, and in particular the unit costs for budgeted vs. actual production, you'll notice that the budgeted unit labor cost was $65 per unit ($32,500 ÷ 500) but the actual labor cost came out to $71.25 per unit ($28,500 ÷ 400). How can that be when the costs vary with production quantities? The answer is that labor is inefficient when it doesn't function at the levels for which the workforce was designed. The labor force in this case didn't use its time efficiently, but still got paid for the time spent. The result: The actual direct labor cost incurred was more per unit than budgeted.

Looking at the variable overhead, a similar situation exists. Budgeted overhead per unit was $150, but actual overhead was $160. Since overhead allocation typically follows labor cost, this increase resulted from allocating overhead to the inefficient labor that was charged but produced nothing.

---

The combination of the underproduction and the use of a flexible budget convey a very different and more informative picture.

As you can see, the Production Department's efficiency is better measured with the flexible budget, which shows it actually exceeded the budget by $6,500 for the level of results it delivered. That information would have been lost if a static budget had been used. That's why flexible budgets are smart when management wants to create a budget that doesn't reward the underspending that typically accompanies underproduction.

While flexible (or "flex") budgeting is more effort to prepare, it's more effective in the right circumstances. Of course, the reverse is also true. If conditions don't vary greatly, such as in an administrative department with largely fixed costs, a flex budget would simply be a lot more work for little benefit.

# How to Live Within Your Budget

As noted earlier, when lacking a budget, there's always a good reason to spend money. However, once you have a budget, that argument is invalid and your spending level is always within the budget—not! Having a budget is the first step. Managing to it is the second and more critical step. This concept is right up there with the idea that a plan is worthless unless you actually use it. Later in this chapter we cover what to do when spending differs from the budget, but here I want to offer some thoughts about avoiding that discussion entirely. Here are five proven ideas for living within that budget so you don't have to explain later why you didn't.

1. "Oops!" is not a good explanation for overspending. The easiest way to live within your budget is to look at it before you reach for your credit card or purchase order. The objective is to see how much money is actually planned for whatever you want to buy and in which time period the purchase was planned. If you know you've budgeted $500 for office supplies in May, you should think twice before spending $1,000 for office supplies that month. You may still decide to proceed, but you'll have a reason for doing so other than "Oh, I didn't know that."

2. If you must spend money for something that's not in the budget, remove or postpone a like amount of money from something else in the budget. In other words, make a trade-off with something you planned for that can be postponed, so your bottom line comes out even. Spend more here, spend less there, because almost never does every dollar have to be spent when you planned it.

3. Negotiate a price with vendors whenever their current price is more than you budgeted. A perfectly reasonable defense in negotiation is the truthful statement "That's all I have in my budget this month." That strategy is neither unfair nor illegal; it's a negotiating strategy. A supplier who wants the business may be flexible on price to get the order, and if not and you must have it now—and you're authorized to exceed budget if necessary—you have a reason to go ahead with the purchase.

4. If company revenue doesn't develop as planned, compensate by underspending accordingly. The budget is ultimately about the bottom line. If revenue is less than planned, you likely don't need as much expense to support it. So find what was planned to support the revenue that didn't come in and don't spend it.

5. Timing is not trivial. Don't spend ahead of schedule. It can wreak havoc with the cash flow budget that may have been carefully laid out to avoid a cash squeeze. If you must spend before you planned to, postpone something else in the same time period until you can catch up. This is another trade-off that keeps the bottom line on track and you out of the penalty box.

# Variance Reporting and Taking Action

In Chapter 8 we explored variances from standard manufacturing cost and how they help us identify and correct production inefficiencies. When standard costing methodology is used in the manufacturing environment, standard cost is, in effect, the budget for making a single unit of product. Nonmanufacturing companies and the other departments in a manufacturing company don't use standard costs per se, but they all use budgets, and for them, variance analysis serves the same purpose.

Variance reporting is a variant of the traditional management concept of *management by exception* (see Chapter 8). Variance reporting enables managers to more rapidly and efficiently locate and correct problems by creating reports that focus primarily on the problems, or exceptions. The report is formatted to calculate and highlight differences between actual and budgeted costs. Figure 12-6 shows an example of such a report for Wonder Widget's Sales & Marketing Department.

Unfavorable numbers in variance columns appear in parentheses. The format facilitates quick review and recognition of the numbers that are out of bounds or over budget. Some reports might also include columns for variance percent, to show each variance as a percentage of the budget for that line item. Again, the idea is to easily identify the significant differences, so management can move immediately to take corrective action. A report such as this should be prepared monthly for every department and for the company as a whole to help everyone manage to the profit goals.

The Wonder Widget Company
Budget Variance Report, Sales, July 2013

| | Current Month | | | Year to Date | | |
|---|---|---|---|---|---|---|
| | Actual | Budget | Variance | Actual | Budget | Variance |
| Salaries | $42,050 | $40,920 | $(1,130) | $294,500 | $287,000 | $(7,500) |
| Payroll Taxes | 4,420 | 4,092 | (328) | 29,920 | 28,700 | (1,220) |
| Workers' Comp | 575 | 409 | (166) | 3,010 | 2,870 | (140) |
| Group Insurance | 1,550 | 1,200 | (350) | 15,200 | 8,500 | (6,700) |
| Advertising | 3,250 | 1,976 | (1,274) | 42,005 | 45,000 | 2,995 |
| Automobile | 800 | 650 | (150) | 5,520 | 4,800 | (720) |
| Business Promotion | 950 | 1,050 | 100 | 7,260 | 7,500 | 240 |
| Commissions | 1,520 | 1,478 | (42) | 11,650 | 10,500 | (1,150) |
| Meals and Entertainment | 475 | 560 | 85 | 4,250 | 3,600 | (650) |
| Insurance | 675 | 642 | (33) | 2,650 | 4,300 | 1,650 |
| Office Supplies | 250 | 200 | (50) | 1,675 | 1,400 | (275) |
| Outside Services | 810 | 1,000 | 190 | 8,210 | 7,200 | (1,010) |
| Postage | 275 | 300 | 25 | 2,246 | 2,500 | 254 |
| Rent | 11,500 | 11,500 | — | 80,500 | 80,500 | — |
| Telephone | 400 | 450 | 50 | 3,350 | 3,200 | (150) |
| Trade Shows | 5,450 | 5,000 | (450) | 18,450 | 25,000 | 6,550 |
| Travel and Lodging | 3,695 | 3,500 | (195) | 17,320 | 18,000 | 680 |
| Total Sales/Marketing | $78,645 | $74,927 | $(3,718) | $547,716 | $540,570 | $(7,146) |

Note: Variance column data are formatted to show that (parentheses) are unfavorable variances, while numbers without parentheses are favorable variances.

Figure 12-6. Wonder Widget departmental budget variance report

# The Capital Expenditure Budget

While not exactly the same kind of budget this chapter has focused on so far, capital expenditure is another area that needs an approved budget but that doesn't appear in the operating budget we've been discussing. That's because capital expenditures aren't income or expense items. As noted in Chapters 3 and 6, capital assets aren't expensed when purchased; rather, they're capitalized and depreciated over time. While that depreciation is normally included in the operating budget, the amounts intended to be spent on new capital assets during the year are not.

For proper management control of planned expenditures, the capital assets the company plans to buy must be built into a separate, capital asset budget that indicates the kind of asset, its estimated cost, and when during the year it will be purchased. This enables the company to fully control its cash expenditure plans, both expense and capital, through the budget process. In this way, cash (or borrowing capacity) is available when needed and management has the opportunity to review and approve capital asset purchases just as it does the budget for income and expenses.

# The Cash Flow Budget

The point has been made often in this book that everything ultimately boils down to cash. If you have more cash coming to you than you had when you started—and you don't have less of something else offsetting the cash gain—you've won the game, so to speak. But our budget at this point has been about budgeting income and expenses using the accrual method of accounting, not the cash method. In other words, our income and expense budget shows income when it's earned (not when customers pay for their purchases) and expenses when they are incurred (not when they're paid for). Careful readers will recognize that the profit or loss Wonder Widget's income and expense budget produces won't manifest itself in its bank account due to the differences between cash and accrual accounting discussed in Chapter 5.

If "cash is king," our budget isn't complete without including a plan for cash flow as well as income and expenses. The cash flow budget should include all the elements in the income and expense budget, all the capital transactions outlined in the capital expenditures budget, and all other transactions not appearing in either budget, such as borrowing or loan repayments, dividend payments to stockholders, etc. The cash flow budget should incorporate those elements into a cohesive plan for cash that covers the entire period of the budget.

The most useful format for a cash budget is the format of the cash flow statement described in Chapter 6. Referring to Figure 6-2, recall that the cash flow statement begins where the income statement ends, at the net income line. Following the logic of the cash flow statement, each element of the overall plan that increases or decreases cash should appear in the cash flow budget, concluding at the bottom of the budget with two key numbers: the budgeted change in cash and the resulting budgeted ending cash balance.

It's easy to see why these are critical numbers to calculate and react to. A budget that shows any month-end with a negative cash balance presents an immediate call to action for management. Because the company can't operate without cash, something has to change to eliminate negative cash balances or cash balances that are too low to sustain normal operations before the critical moment arrives. The income and expense budget may produce acceptable results, but if the overall plan results in an unacceptable cash balance during the year, management can't approve that budget until the cash shortfall has been resolved. Resolution can come in the form of:

- Revising the income and expense budget to lower or adjust the timing of expenses, or perhaps changing the timing of a sales campaign to bring in revenue sooner;
- Adjusting the timing or payment source of capital expenditures, e.g., borrowing instead of paying cash; or
- Ensuring adequate borrowing capacity to provide a source of cash to carry the company through the low point until cash is restored to an appropriate level.

When the net income projection and the cash projection are acceptable, the budget is ready for management approval. Well, almost. The next and final step is integrating the budgets with the balance sheet.

## Integrating the Entire Operating Budget

Referring to Figure 2-3, recall the interrelationship of the income statement, the cash flow statement, and the balance sheet. It's not too much of a reach to see that same relationship in the annual budget as well. In fact that's the final step in building the operating plan: integrating all the elements we've now completed into the balance sheet so we can see their impact on the overall value of the business.

You might ask why we would care. We have our income and expense budget, our cash flow budget, and our capital expenditure budget. Isn't that all we need to move the company toward its operating plan objectives for the year? If you're asking that, take another look at Chapter 7, "Key Performance Indicators." In the first few pages of that chapter, I discussed the reasons for KPIs and all the constituencies who are interested in them. If you review that chapter, you'll note that many of the metrics outlined there come from the balance sheet and others come from merging data from the income statement and the balance sheet. So if we don't have an integrated budget balance sheet, how will we know if our budget is going to produce positive or not-so-positive KPIs? The answer, of course, is we won't.

The beauty of this requirement to calculate KPIs for your budget is that you've already developed virtually all the pieces needed for this last step. If your company is using either an integrated Excel budgeting model, as our smaller clients do, or any of the more sophisticated budget-building applications, the design of the model does this last step automatically.

---

### THREE MAGIC QUESTIONS FOR VARIANCE CONTROL

A department manager should look at his or her variance report each month and ask these questions:

**TOOLS**

- Why did this variance occur? What happened that caused the amount we spent to be materially different from what we intended to spend? "We bought more office supplies." Wrong. "We bought more office supplies to avoid a large, just announced price increase." Right.
- What action must I take now, immediately, to keep a negative variance from continuing or to keep a positive variance from skipping away?
- What am I learning from the answers to the first two questions that will make my budget next year a more effective management tool?

These short questions are very powerful and useful for two important reasons:

1. They help the manager to move quickly from analysis to action.
2. The manager's boss is likely to ask the same questions, one way or another, and it's useful to have the answers in advance, if the manager is career-minded—or just interested in surviving.

---

## Manager's Checklist for Chapter 12

☑ Every budget development cycle should begin with an estimate of the revenues the company expects to earn. While this may first be announced as a management goal, it's critical for the Sales Department to accept as its own whatever sales budget is adopted. That usually occurs when it's directly involved in the revenue budget development process.

☑ There's always a seemingly good reason to spend money. Budget developers and approvers must always keep in mind the company's operating goals for the period under review and not allow a "good reason" to permit a budgeted expenditure that's not in the best interests of meeting those goals.

☑ Budget preparation is a trial-and-error process, because we're bringing together information from diverse sources to work toward a company goal. The chances of hitting that target on the first try are slim, so managers should expect to rework the budget at least once and accept the frustration of repeating their efforts because a good budget is worth the work.

☑ Flexible budgets are an excellent tool for organizations, with outcomes and costs that can vary widely. Management uses a flex budget when it wants to create a budget that doesn't reward the underspending that typically accompanies underproduction. A flex budget enables adjustment of cost budgets to align with various levels of productivity, thus letting management measure efficiency at the actual level of activity.

☑ Capital assets to be purchased during the budget period should be budgeted as to type, amount, and timing, just as with any other demand on the company's resources.

☑ Every operating budget should include a cash flow plan to ensure that all intended activities for the year produce and maintain an acceptable cash level so the company can conduct its business without either running low on cash or having excess cash balances that aren't being put to work.

☑ Remember these magic questions for getting the most benefit from budget variance reports:
- Why did it happen?
- What immediate action should we take?
- What are we learning that will make the next budget a better management tool?

**Chapter 13**

# Financing the Business: Understanding the Debt versus Equity Options

Throughout this book we've referred to the investment in a business that provides the cash to begin operations. We've also looked at a balance sheet that shows debt owed by the business—money borrowed for some corporate purpose. But we've yet to talk about how that money is raised and how the debt or equity gets onto the books.

While there are many books on this subject, we only need to preview this important area. In these final chapters, we look at both debt and equity financing: what they are, how they work, and why an owner or CEO might choose one or the other or both to meet the company's financing needs.

## The Strategy of Borrowing Money

Recall from earlier chapters the concept of leverage, using borrowed money to increase the amount of capital available to a business. As discussed in Chapter 3, leverage is useful to virtually every company, in part because much of it—trade credit—is interest-free. The part that isn't free is money borrowed through formal agreements such as bank loans. This chapter covers long-term and short-term borrowing, plus various forms of equity. But first a few comments on the nature of interest rates may be useful.

To begin, a word about competition: Lending is a competitive business, particularly among commercial banks. Large and small banks compete for your business, just like the TV ads proclaim. Every bank offers a range of borrowing options. Even though banks pay similar rates for the money they receive in deposits and federal loans, they often have different goals in terms of the kinds of loans they want on their books. Bank A may have only 40 percent home mortgage loans when its target is 50 percent, so it will likely offer favorable rates to attract more home mortgage borrowers. Bank B may have reached its goal with mortgage loans but is behind target on construction loans, so it will offer favorable financing to builders to bring in that kind of business. Thus their respective home mortgage rates may be quite different, even though they both pay the same rate for their money. It pays to shop around, whether you're an individual, a small business, or a mega corporation. Then there's the interest rate "market" itself that affects banks, and by extension every borrower from a bank. During the recovery from the financial markets crash of 2008, the U.S. Federal Reserve (the Fed) chose to keep interest rates at near-historic lows, and as this book was written, rates were still closer to zero than to historical averages. What does that do for borrowers? It gives us an opportunity to convert all our credit needs to low-cost loans. So it's good for borrowers. For banks, not so much. Here's why:

Banks only make money when they put their money to work, and that means making loans. Their profit comes from the *spread*, the difference between the rates they pay—primarily to the Fed—and the rates they charge to borrowers. Low rates mean their spreads are smaller. That's the equivalent of a gross margin squeeze in business, and we all know that's bad for profits. So if you're a bank and your margins are being squeezed, your best solution is to sell more stuff or lend more money. And that's what creates competition among banks.

**KEY TERMS**

**Spread** A banking industry term that refers to the difference between the rate a bank pays for its money and the rate at which it can lend that money. If a bank borrows from the Fed at 2 percent and lends out that money for 4.5 percent, the spread is 2.5 percent, or 250 basis points.

**Basis point** A banking industry term that means 1/100 of a percentage point. Thus, 100 basis points is another way of saying 1 percent, and because many transactions are set in fractions of a percent, the use of basis points became common shorthand.

Then there's the *yield curve,* the difference over time between long-term and short-term rates. We can learn a lot from the yield curve at any point in time, and the savvy business owner can save money by observing what it says about interest rate trends. Interest rates as this is written are near historic lows because central banks around the world—led largely by the Fed—use low rates as a way to help their economies grow. It's expected that rates will rise over time to more normal levels. But what does "normal" look like? And why do we care?

> **Yield curve** A line on a chart that plots, at given points in time, the interest rates of bonds of equal credit quality but differing maturity dates. The most frequently reported yield curve—that of U.S. government debt—compares the rates on **KEY TERM** 3-month, 2-year, 5-year, and 30-year U.S. Treasury debt. This yield curve is used as a benchmark for other debt in the market, such as mortgage rates or bank lending rates. The curve is also used to predict changes in economic output and growth. Yield to a lender is what the interest rate is to a borrower.

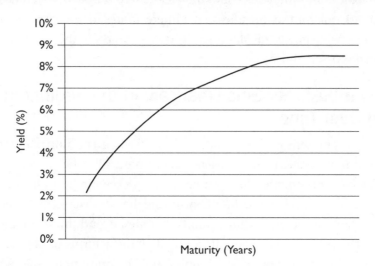

**Figure 13-1.** Normal yield curve

Figure 13-1 shows a normal yield curve in which short-term rates are lower than long-term rates because of the greater risk perceived by lenders when committing funds for a longer term. In a normal economy, short-term lending rates are lower because lenders don't have to wait so long to get repaid, thus those loans are assumed to bear less risk. Sometimes, however, this curve becomes inverted, with current rates higher than longer maturities' rates.

This is often the case when the market sees economic downward pressure in the future, as would be the case if a recession were anticipated. This was true in 2007, for example, when long-term rates were actually lower than short-term rates. As we now know, a major global recession followed a year later. By 2013 the yield curve had reversed and again was in the normal pattern, with long-term rates higher than short-term rates. Now to the "Why do we care?" part.

First, because of the historical reliability of the yield curve, having an advance warning that an economic downturn may be in the offing should give you good reason to line up any financing you'll need over the next few years, preferably at long-term rates, because it may be harder to borrow in a downturn when banks themselves are trying to preserve capital. It could be a good time to convert your short-term credit line into a long-term loan, for example. Second, the yield curve is a ready reference for where to look for the most favorable interest rates for a company's normal borrowing needs. All of that, of course, is subject to the bank competition discussed above.

## How a Business Gets Financed: In the Beginning and Over Time

A company obtains working capital either by selling a portion of the company to investors (which we discuss in Chapter 14) or by getting a loan from a bank or other lending source. There are seemingly endless variations of debt, from basic forms of borrowing that we discuss in this chapter, to more exotic borrowing options that are beyond the scope of this book. The principal common attribute of all these forms of debt is that they require repayment at some point, unlike equity financing, which involves the permanent sale of a share of ownership. That seems simple enough, but there are exceptions: Convertible debt may, under certain circumstances, be exchanged for equity and not repaid, and sometimes equity ownership in an emerging company carries a condition that the company may repurchase it, again under certain circumstances.

That said, let's look at the principal kinds of debt you're most likely to encounter and not concern ourselves with the exceptions.

> **Convertible debt** Money loaned under an agreement that gives the lender the right under certain conditions to forego payment of part or all of the debt in return for some other asset, typically ownership—shares of common stock—in the borrower company. These agreements may have other conditions, such as the conversion rate, the length of time that conversion is permitted, etc.

**KEY TERM**

## Short-Term Debt: Balancing Working Capital Needs

Every company has short-term debt of one kind or another, obligations that it must repay some time in the next 12 months. Its purpose is to extend the company's working capital resources and to put more money to work earning for the company, so the owners don't need to put more of their own cash into the company's bank account. Short-term debt includes both short-term bank loans and traditional trade credit.

The most common kind of trade credit is accounts payable to suppliers, typically extended for 30 days at a time and without formal loan agreements. However, many companies also have formal arrangements to obtain additional short-term debt in the form of loans from banks or other lenders. Here are some examples of working capital needs that may be relieved by short-term borrowing:

- Increasing accounts receivable balances, perhaps to finance rapidly growing sales on credit or a slowdown in receiving payment of open customer balances;
- Building inventory due to a planned new product introduction, preparing for a heavy selling season, or avoiding an upcoming supplier price increase;
- Covering a temporary cash shortage caused by operating losses the company has incurred but expects to recover from soon, provided it can rebuild its working capital in the meantime; or
- Preparing for a business cycle that inherently includes alternating periods of negative cash flow (incurring costs to manufacture products for sale) and positive cash flow (to sell what was manufactured).

The following examples show the variety of short-term borrowing that's possible.

---

**TRICKS OF THE TRADE**

## USE SHORT-TERM DEBT ONLY FOR SHORT-TERM NEEDS

Business owners squeezed for cash to expand sometimes make a big mistake. Because short-term financing is often easier to get than long-term financing, they borrow short-term money, then renew or stretch out their repayments, using the money to satisfy long-term needs such as multiyear marketing programs, new product development and introduction, and so on. If the long-term plans take longer to bear fruit than management expected, the businesses may be strapped for cash to repay short-term debt that can no longer be delayed, and working capital can be negatively affected.

The key: Use short-term debt for working capital that will generate the funds to repay the loan when it comes due, and use long-term debt to finance long lead-time projects for which the timing of a return is either long term or uncertain.

---

## Revolving Credit Line

A *revolving credit line* is a promise by a bank (typically) or other lender to provide cash on demand up to a certain maximum, the *credit limit*. The borrower obtains a revolving credit line based on the projected need for short-term cash and the available collateral. The company then borrows—or draws against the line—as it needs the cash, and repays it when the need is past. Thus, actual borrowing fluctuates over time, and the cash advanced by the bank revolves; in other words, money is borrowed, repaid, and reborrowed as the borrower's cash needs change. The lender typically charges a variable rate for the amount outstanding and may charge other credit line fees as well.

**KEY TERM** — **Revolving credit line** An agreement by a bank or other lender to provide cash on demand up to a specified limit and then, as the borrower pays back all or part of the loan, to allow the borrower to borrow up to that limit again, as often as needed. Also known as a *revolver*.

Revolving credit lines may be collateralized by liens on the company's assets, such as accounts receivable, inventories, equipment, or property. Typically a lender extends credit up to 70–90 percent of eligible receivables and perhaps 50–70 percent of eligible inventories. These credit lines may be unsecured for the lender's financially strongest customers. Most companies with short-term credit needs try to satisfy their needs by using revolving credit lines, either secured or unsecured, because these lines enable them to obtain cash when they need it and to limit their interest expense when they don't.

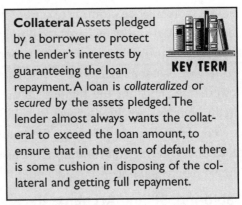

**Collateral** Assets pledged by a borrower to protect the lender's interests by guaranteeing the loan **KEY TERM** repayment. A loan is *collateralized* or *secured* by the assets pledged. The lender almost always wants the collateral to exceed the loan amount, to ensure that in the event of default there is some cushion in disposing of the collateral and getting full repayment.

Revolving credit lines are widely used to meet temporary working capital needs. Such lines provide easy and flexible borrowing, and allow a company to control borrowing costs. Loans are for working capital purposes and can be used for any business purpose, as long as the lenders are protected (usually) by adequate collateral.

## Accounts Receivable Loans: Collecting Before You Collect

Companies that don't have the cash to finance their operations while waiting for their customers to pay them and companies that have the cash but want to use it for other purposes may borrow from a bank or other lender, pledging their accounts receivable as loan collateral. This is a variation of the revolving credit line, in that the lender advances a certain percentage of eligible receivables in the expectation that the company will repay the line when it collects the accounts. Terms and conditions vary widely, including limitations on which receivables are eligible, what constitutes a good credit risk, how quickly advances must be repaid, and so on. Advances against receivables enable the company to retain control of its collection activities and its credit risk (unlike factoring, discussed below, in which both control and risk often—but not always—pass to the lender).

Accounts receivable lending works much like the revolver (the loan, not the gun), except that accounts receivable are the only assets used to calculate how much may be borrowed. Advances are usually limited to 70–90 percent of the value of the eligible collateral. Depending on the lender, there may be monthly or quarterly statistical reporting and quarterly or annual audits by bank accountants to satisfy the lender that the company is properly handling its paperwork and collection activities. Borrowing cost for such loans is best characterized as medium—not the lowest rates and not the highest. Actual rates depend on the lender's credit policies and the borrower's creditworthiness. Even though these are considered collateral loans, the lender's willingness to lend and its flexibility on terms and conditions are also influenced by the overall relationship between borrower and lender.

## Factoring: Selling Accounts Receivable and Passing Along the Risk (Sometimes)

For companies whose credit rating is not strong enough to warrant other forms of borrowing, there's the option of *factoring*, which is selling the company's accounts receivable balances for immediate cash. This is a widely used but relatively high-cost option—typically from 15–30 percent APR—so companies generally don't choose factoring if another option is available.

Here's how it works. A factoring company, or factor, purchases the customer invoices individually, following a detailed review to identify accounts and invoices that qualify. The factor pays the company for each invoice, after deducting a discount, usually 3–5 percent of the invoice amount. The discount compensates the factor for two things: (1) interest on the money from the time it's paid to the borrower until the customer pays the invoice, and (2) a premium for assuming the collection risk of the customer. The company typically notifies its customers that its invoices should be paid to the factor rather than the company. When the customer pays in due course, the factor receives 100 percent of the balance due and thus gets its money back plus fees. The factor periodically pays the remaining balance from what it has collected (after fees) back to the borrower. This process involves a lot of paperwork in selling the individual invoices and in documents flowing back and forth, often daily—from the borrower to support amounts sold and from the factor to document amounts collected, advanced, charged back under recourse agreements, and so on.

Besides their fees and account-by-account scrutiny, the factor may build in additional safeguards against loss. It may, for example, purchase invoices "with recourse," meaning it has the right to sell the invoices back to the borrower if it has not collected from the customer within a certain time, thus protecting the factor from a loss of prin-

> **Factoring** The selling of a company's accounts receivable at a discount to a business (a factor) that **KEY TERM** assumes the credit risk of the accounts and receives cash as the customers pay their invoices.

cipal. There may be other fees and restrictions that effectively increase the cost of the loan.

Certain kinds of companies use factoring as a normal business tool, perhaps because they are not sufficiently well financed from the beginning or because margins are so thin that they are unable to earn enough profits to build a working capital base. The U.S. garment industry, populated by many small, creatively driven businesses, is an example.

---

## DON'T LET INTEREST COSTS EAT THE COMPANY'S LUNCH

Factoring is a good example of borrowing that's so costly that it can adversely affect profitability if not used with care, especially by companies with marginal profits. For example, a cash-strapped company with a hot product may feel it makes sense to pay a factor to get early access to cash so it can continue to expand sales. But factoring charges add up fast.

**CAUTION**

Let's suppose a company factors $1.2 million of sales under a plan that charges 4 percent per invoice (a midrange price), and customer balances are outstanding for two months on average. That means the company borrows, repays, and reborrows $200,000 six times a year, paying $8,000 in fees each time ($200,000 x 4%). In a year, the company pays $48,000 in factoring fees ($8,000 x 6)—but has the use of *only $200,000* of the factor's money at any one time. That's an *effective interest rate of 24 percent!* If the company nets 10 percent pretax profit from sales, its pretax profit of $120,000 has been cut by *40 percent* to gain access to that cash.

Factoring may be a good decision, but only in special circumstances. Managers should do their homework before choosing this option. Any decision to use factoring for financing should be reviewed with your financial advisor and should be accompanied by a plan to systematically remove the need in the future.

## Honorable Mention of Some Other Short-Term Borrowing Techniques

**Flooring.** *Flooring* is buying inventory without paying for it until it's sold. This is a little like consignment buying, commonly used years ago to induce retailers to carry products they didn't want to pay for until they were sold. The difference? Flooring is a financing method for high-ticket items like cars and boats. Dealers cannot typically afford to pay for a showroom full of inventory, so they borrow against the inventory, item by item, and pay off the loan when they sell the item. They pay the lender—such as GE Capital, a bank, or a finance company—interest (the *flooring charge*) based on how long they held the item on their premises. Financing plans can include only inventory, or a combination of inventory and receivables.

**Inventory financing.** *Inventory financing* is another way to use inventory as collateral. It's possible to obtain financing using the company's inventory as collateral, but it isn't easy. It must be possible to sell the inventory readily if necessary, which means that only certain kinds of raw materials and finished goods qualify. Even then, the loan amount is limited to 50 percent or so of the inventory value, and the lender often wants additional collateral. Inventory can be hard to liquidate if the borrower defaults, so the lender has a greater risk of loss, so the lender protects itself against potential losses by setting a conservative inventory lending limit. This kind of lending is less common today than it used to be.

**Purchase order financing.** *Purchase order financing* goes one step beyond factoring. A company that wins a large customer order it doesn't have the cash to fulfill can borrow money on the strength of the purchase order to enable it to manufacture the products to fill the order. This is very high-risk lending, because the lender is betting the borrower will be able to make the product and successfully deliver it. As a result, the requirements for this kind of borrowing are even stricter than for factoring: strong customer, firm purchase order, borrower with a good track record of completing its work, and so on. Only the smallest companies with the weakest working capital position or those with unusually large, one-time orders typically seek this kind of financing.

# Long-Term Debt: Semipermanent Capital or Asset Acquisition Financing

## Term Loans the Old-Fashioned Way

A *term loan* is the kind of loan you and I use to purchase real estate or to finance a college education. We borrow the money, use it for its intended purpose, and repay it in installments over several years.

How does it work? To get such a loan, a company applies to a bank or other lender. Upon approval, the company signs documents promising to repay the loan over some number of years in monthly installments, including principal and interest, and the bank advances the money. The bank usually requires a pledge of collateral to make the loan. This might be a specific asset or it might be all assets of the company not already encumbered with debt. If the loan is for real estate, the real estate is always pledged as the loan collateral. If the company is privately held, collateral might also include a personal guarantee by the owners. Interest costs for such a loan are typically moderate, as a company must be in reasonably sound financial condition to be approved. Such borrowers are in demand, and banks often compete for the business of solid business borrowers.

Who uses a term loan? A company might do so to finance the acquisition of another company, to develop or improve products for its market, or to obtain funds to buy or build a factory. The idea is to put a large amount of money to work immediately and repay it over time as the company receives the benefits of the front-end investment. The company expects the additional earnings or other benefits to more than cover the cost of servicing the debt, including principal and interest, for the life of the loan and hopefully beyond. The challenge for many companies is, before they take on the long-term debt obligation, to do a thorough enough analysis that the return is reasonably assured. The risk is that a company won't be able to repay the loan, which means a painful series of meetings and negotiations with the lenders as everyone tries to work out a win-win solution to the dilemma. This is the stuff of which corporate turnarounds are made.

## Equipment Purchasing or Leasing: Two Paths to One Goal

Equipment purchasing is what you do when you buy a new car. You pick the car, negotiate the loan, and buy the car; the lender pays the seller; and you make installment payments to the lender until you've paid off the loan and you finally own the car. In the same manner, a company buys manufacturing equipment or computers or, for that matter, new cars.

The business purpose of an *equipment purchase loan* is to extend the cash outlay for the equipment over a period of time that relates more closely to the length of time the purchase provides a benefit to the company. Such loans are typically paid off in three to five years, well before the equipment is worn out, so the benefit continues after the loan is repaid, and the strain on the company's cash balance is minimized. This is particularly valuable to rapidly growing companies that, as we've noted earlier, have a constant need for cash to finance their growth. The cost of such loans is typically related to the borrower's creditworthiness and the expected value of the collateral over the life of the loan. The interest rates charged vary, but are higher than loans secured by stable collateral and lower than loans with greater risk, like accounts receivable financing.

Payments are structured to provide a level payment of principal and interest each month. That means, of course, that earlier payments are mostly interest with little principal reduction. (Have you ever looked at your home loan statements a year or so after buying or refinancing? You're not paying down much principal, are you?) The level payment makes repayment manageable for the borrower, but the downside is the low rate of principal reduction until late in the life of the loan. One option: shorten the life of the loan. Principal reduction increases in shorter-term loans, and total interest cost correspondingly decreases.

A variation on the equipment purchase loan is the equipment lease. The cash management objective is the same, but the money is often easier to find because the lender/lessor has a stronger hold on the collateral until the company has paid the full amount of the loan. In an equipment purchase, the lender has a lien on the equipment, but the borrower actually owns the equipment. Thus, legal action in the event of default can be involved. Under an agreement for an *equipment lease,* by contrast, the equipment lessor, not the borrower, owns the equipment. The lessor remains the legal owner until the lease obligation has been satisfied in full, at which point the lessee either purchases the asset or returns it to the lessor. Collection action is simpler in event of default. Because the risk is less, a lease is often easier to obtain than a purchase loan.

The cost of equipment leasing is typically higher than the cost of an equipment purchase loan, if for no other reason than there's usually an intermediary (the lessor) between the buyer and the seller. This cost comparison rule-of-thumb is not always valid, because there are other considerations that affect cost. Tax benefits can accrue to a lessor who continues to own the equipment which might be partially passed through to the lessee/borrower, resulting in lower net lease rates. But companies looking into leasing should meet with their financial advisor and do their homework before they sign on the dotted line.

---

### Don't Believe It!

Don't believe that an equipment lease conveys unique tax benefits. It's not true!

We often hear radio ads touting the tax advantages of leasing over buying—cars, for example. They tell us we can deduct the lease payments, a unique advantage over buying. Well, guess what? It's not true.

The cost of a car—or any other asset—is tax-deductible if the asset is used for a tax-deductible purpose, regardless of how you pay for it. Any difference? In a lease you deduct the lease payments, and in a purchase you deduct the depreciation and interest. In the end, the difference to you is which one costs you more money after taxes—and that's usually the one that cost you more money *before* taxes.

---

One more variation is worth mentioning here: a *sale and lease-back arrangement*. A company that owns its equipment and property outright, but needs to raise money, can sell its equipment to a financing source and then lease it back from the source, without anything changing physically. The company sells ownership of the property and then leases it for a period of years, just as if it were an original equipment lease as we've already described. Since the equipment is used, the interest cost is usually higher, but the transaction effectively frees up cash invested in plant and equipment to be used for another purpose.

## Small Business Administration Will Guarantee Your Loan

A source long known to entrepreneurs and seasoned business owners is the Small Business Administration (SBA), a federal agency that exists to support the growth of small business in this country. One way the SBA does that is by helping small businesses obtain loans by guaranteeing a portion of those loans made by commercial lenders, principally banks. For the lender, this means making a loan with less risk, because the SBA guarantees a large part of it if the borrower defaults. For the borrower, this is an excellent way to get long-term, relatively inexpensive access to growth capital.

The SBA guarantees a variety of loan types for business purposes. While details of these programs are available at *www.sba.gov/content/ sba-loans*, the most common among them are:

- A term loan called the *7(a) program*, which can be used for a wide variety of business start-up or expansion purposes, including the purchase of equipment, the purchase or construction of business real estate, or acquisition of a business, with negotiated fixed or variable rates and loan amounts up to a maximum of $5 million.
- The *CDC 504 loan program*, available for the purchase of land, the construction or renovation of buildings, and related purposes, with fixed rates, terms up to 20 years, and a loan limit generally up to $5 million.
- The *Microloan program*, providing loans up to $50,000 for small start-ups and available through local nonprofit SBA intermediaries for terms up to six years.

A company owner wanting to obtain long-term, lower-cost financing for an approved purpose can file an application with the SBA or, more commonly, any of the hundreds of banks designated "Preferred SBA Lender." A small business owner has a good chance of obtaining such a loan provided the company meets the bank's own lending standards, such as having collateral for the loan, an apparent ability to repay the loan in accordance with its terms, and so on.

Because the SBA guarantees the repayment of up to 90 percent of the loan, minimizing the bank's risk, loan rates should be lower than those for loans lacking an SBA guarantee. Over time that has not always been the case, however, and business owners should always shop around. Most authorized banks will assist business owners with their application or refer them to independent "loan packagers," who—for a fee—will complete the lengthy application paperwork and help the borrower *who has not read this book* understand things like cash forecasts and balance sheets.

## Convertible Debt: The Transition from Debt to Equity

When a company needs to raise cash, an initial choice must be made: do we borrow or do we sell stock in the company? Borrowing costs money in the form of interest payments, but selling equity dilutes the ownership interests of the present stockholders. A company in financial difficulties might have to sell a substantial piece of ownership to raise the needed funds while adequately compensating investors for taking the risk. Yet management doesn't want to be saddled with interest payments for a long time, particularly since a downtime for a company usually means the interest rate it must pay to attract lenders is also high. What to do? (For a brief comparison of borrowing methods see, Figure 13-2.)

The answer for some companies is to sell debt that is convertible to equity at some future time when it's beneficial to both the company and the lenders. This financing tool is called *convertible debt* or *convertible debentures*. By any name, the instrument is a convertible bond that pays the lender interest only for some period of time, thus conserving the company's cash and enabling management to make the most of its cash

---

**Bond** A negotiable instrument that's typically sold by public companies, which pays interest quarterly and is usually publicly traded during its life (like company stock). Bonds are not collateralized, but are often issued with insurance (purchased by **KEY TERMS** the issuing company) that guarantees payment of principal and interest by an insurance company in the event the issuer defaults. This provision typically gives such bonds the highest investment grade rating because it removes essentially all ownership risk except interest rate fluctuation.

**Debenture** A bond that may be sold publicly or privately, but that has no collateral to back it up except the strength of the issuing company. These instruments are similar to bonds and are often enhanced by being convertible into the issuing company's common stock under certain circumstances. Typically only the largest companies can successfully sell debentures.

resources. The lender may later choose to convert the debt into shares of stock at a predetermined conversion ratio. Result: The company stops paying high interest and surrenders a reasonable amount of ownership.

Here's how it works. A borrowing company issues a convertible debenture with provisions that call for interest to be paid periodically, usually quarterly, but no principal. At some future time, the bond is *callable*, meaning the company can buy it back (usually at a premium over its face value) and retire it, in effect paying off the loan. In the interim the bond can be converted into stock at any time, at a conversion rate advantageous to the borrowing company.

---

**FOR EXAMPLE**

### THE BIRTH, LIFE, AND RETIREMENT OF A CONVERTIBLE DEBENTURE

A convertible bond is issued with a conversion price of $25, meaning that a $1,000 bond can be converted into 40 shares of stock. But when the bond is issued, the market price of the stock is only $15. The lender (the bond buyer) won't consider converting, because buying shares on the open market would cost less than converting the bond. So the lender waits and collects interest on the loan, in this case 10 percent per year.

Over time the company prospers. The stock price rises to $30. Now the lender has a choice: collect $100 interest per year and in the future be repaid the $1,000, or convert the bond into 40 shares of stock and then sell the shares for $1,200 (40 x $30). The lender's decision will depend on his or her individual financial objectives, but there's a good chance the lender will convert. If so, the company ceases paying interest and does not have to repay the loan. However, it must issue 40 shares of stock to satisfy the conversion request and accept a slight dilution in its earnings per share. The lender gets a return greater than 10 percent on the money loaned. Everybody wins.

---

# Capital Stock: Types and Uses

## Common Stock: Fundamental Ownership of the Corporation

*Common stock* is the basic form of corporation ownership. In the classic scenario, a company's management issues stock to investors in return for their cash, then uses the cash to start and operate the business. A share of stock represents a unit of ownership in a company, but the size of that unit depends on the number of stock shares issued. A small com-

| Terms of Borrowing | Duration of Loan | Collateral | Use | Cost |
|---|---|---|---|---|
| Revolving Credit Line | Credit line one-year renewable, but borrowing revolves indefinitely | Accounts receivable, inventory, other assets owned, not pledged elsewhere | Temporary cash needs; replacing the cash tied up in receivables and inventory until they can again become cash | Low |
| Accounts Receivable Loan | Credit line one-year renewable, but borrowing revolves indefinitely | Accounts receivable | Early access to cash tied up in receivables, similar to revolving credit line | Medium |
| Factoring | Invoice by invoice 30--90 days, revolving as new sales are made | Accounts receivable | Getting cash from receivables, passing on risk of collection to the lender | High |
| Flooring | 1–3 years renewable, borrowings revolve indefinitely | High-priced inventory, such as cars and boats | Financing showroom inventory of items for sale, which are also the collateral | Low |
| Term Loans | Various annual terms depending on type of loan and life of asset financed 1–30 years | Various, from collateral being purchased to all assets the company owns | Long-term purchase of assets or real estate or to provide capital for long-term projects to companies without adequate internal cash generation | Medium |
| Equipment Loans and Leasing | 3–5 years or longer, depending on life of the asset | The asset being acquired, or refinanced in case of sale-and-leaseback | Acquisition of large pieces of equipment or large amounts of equipment | Medium to High |
| Bonds | Variable, with lengths to 30 years and more | None, although some are mortgage-backed and others are insured as to default | Major long-term projects for large companies, including expansion and acquisition programs | Low |
| Convertible Debt | Variable, with lengths to 30 years and more | None, although conversion privilege adds value, especially in a good market | Major long-term projects for large companies, including expansion and acquisition programs | Low |

**Figure 13-2.** Summary of common business borrowing methods

pany owned by a handful of people might only have a few hundred shares outstanding, that is, owned by its stockholders. Microsoft, by contrast, has over 5 *billion* shares outstanding. So percentage of ownership is not only about how many shares you own; it's about how many shares

**KEY TERM**

**Common stock** Equity ownership in a corporation that entitles the stockholders to dividends and/or capital appreciation and the right to vote. In the event of liquidation, common stockholders have rights to corporate assets only after bondholders, other debt holders, and preferred stockholders are paid. In other words, common stockholder liquidation rights come last, after every other claim on the company's assets. As a result, most liquidations leave common stockholders with nothing or nearly nothing.

everybody owns. Thus we arrive at a key observation of stock ownership: The more shares there are, the less your shares are worth. This is called dilution, as we discussed in Chapter 4.

**FOR EXAMPLE**

### GOOD FOR THE COMPANY, BAD FOR THE SHAREHOLDERS

Issuing stock to raise cash helps the company, but it can hurt the shareholders.

Consider the example of Wonder Widget, our rapidly growing company. It's publicly owned now, under the understated symbol WOWI. The company is profitable, earning $1 million in net income last year. You own 1,000 shares, out of 500,000 outstanding. The company's earnings per share (EPS) were $2 ($1,000,000 ÷ 500,000). The market thinks WOWI's shares are worth 20 times earnings (price/earnings ratio), meaning the company is valued at $20 million. Your shares would bring $40,000 (1,000 x $2 x 20) if you sold them today.

But Wonder Widget is still growing, so the next year it sells more stock in a "secondary" stock offering: It sells 100,000 shares at $20 to raise $2 million in cash. WOWI is better off now, but how about you?

You still have your 1,000 shares, and the company earns $1,050,000 that year, a 5 percent increase over the prior year. But since there are now 600,000 shares outstanding, EPS is down to $1.75 ($1,050,000 ÷ 600,000). The market still thinks the company is worth 20 times earnings, so valuation is up to $21 million (20 x $1,050,000). Your shares, however, are now worth only $35,000 (1,000 x $1.75 x 20).

The company has more cash and is making more money. You did nothing different—and lost $5,000 in market value. That, dear reader, is *dilution*.

Common stock is the basic ownership unit, as noted before. The common stockholder is the *residual owner* of the company's assets. That means the common stockholder gets the remaining value when all the debts are settled, which may be a great deal or may be nothing. It's this risk/reward relationship that has enabled public stock ownership to become the best investment for growth in the long term—and a risky investment in the short term.

## Preferred Stock: Ownership with Perks ... and Limitations

There's a way for the investor to mitigate the risk without entirely losing the potential for appreciation. If a company needs additional equity capital and wants to avoid diluting the value of its common stock, it could elect to issue a separate class of shares such as preferred stock. *Preferred stock* typically carries a stated dividend rate, in terms of percent of face value or dollars per share.

Preferred shares are a separate class of stock, with privileges and restrictions different from common stock. And they're called preferred shares for good reason. When the board of directors declares a dividend to the shareholders, the preferred shareholders must get their entire dividend,

> **Preferred stock** Equity ownership in a corporation that entitles the stockholders to a specified dividend **KEY TERM** before any dividends are paid on common stock. In the event of liquidation, preferred stockholders have rights to corporate assets after bondholders and other debt holders, but before common stockholders.

based on the stated dividend rate, before any dividends can be paid to the common shareholders. In some cases, the preferred shares are also *cumulative*, meaning that dividends not paid in one year accumulate as obligations of the company and must be paid in full before common stock dividends can be paid. For some companies, that can mean years of paying preferred dividends in full while giving common stockholders little or nothing.

For example, following the 2008 financial crisis and the federal government's bailout of large banks, these banks were only allowed to pay common stock dividends of $0.01 per share for years. One of these, Bank of America, had 16 classes of preferred stock outstanding during this period, and the preferred stockholders got their full dividend every quarter.

In the event of a company's dissolution, with both preferred and common shares outstanding, the cash raised from liquidating the assets is first used to repay creditors. What's left goes to the stockholders, with the preferred stockholders coming first. If there's enough money to satisfy 100 percent of the preferred stockholders' claims, then the balance goes to the common stockholders. If there's insufficient cash to satisfy both groups of owners, there's no pro-rata sharing between them. The preferred shareholders get all of theirs, and the common shareholders get what's left, which may be nothing.

That, simply, is the meaning of the word "preferred."

Why doesn't every investor buy only preferred stock? The downside of preferred stock ownership is the limitation on participation in the extreme good fortune of the company. If a company does very well, it can declare a handsome dividend for its common stockholders or give them additional shares (*stock dividends*) or both. Generally, however, such extras need not be paid to the preferred shareholders. The tradeoff for the preference is the restriction on enjoying the fruits of success. These restrictions have the effect of also restricting the market price appreciation of preferred shares, since they cannot participate in a company's dynamic growth as much as common stockholders.

One feature is sometimes added to preferred shares to offset this limitation: A company can issue *convertible* preferred stock. These shares act like preferred shares until their owners decide to convert them, under provisions similar to those built into the convertible debt discussed earlier. Once the holders convert their shares, the preference ends and they participate like other common stockholders, for better or worse. Typically, as with convertible debt, strong success is the best inducement for preferred shareholders to convert their shares. Once the preferred shares are converted, the company no longer has to reserve earnings for preferred dividends. It can pay out those dollars as common stock dividends or retain them for expansion, debt repayment, or other corporate purpose.

# Manager's Checklist for Chapter 13

☑ Borrowing rule No. 1: Lending is a competitive business. Always shop for a loan, even if your favorite banker has made you an offer you think you can't refuse, unless saving money is not an important objective.

☑ Borrowing rule No. 2: Borrow short-term money only for short-term needs. Don't get caught with an overdue loan because the long-term project it was financing has taken longer than expected to pay off.

☑ Perhaps the most expensive form of short-term borrowing is factoring, the sale of accounts receivable to a lender. Rates can go as high as 5 percent a month, and paperwork requirements are substantial.

☑ Leasing equipment and buying equipment on installment are two ways to finance equipment acquisition. Leasing and buying differ mostly in the strength of the lien held by the lender, the size of the monthly payments, and the net borrowing cost. Again, shop around.

☑ Dilution lowers the value of your investment even when things are going well. Pay attention to the potential dilutive effects of the actions of any company in which you hold stock. The most common examples are stock options and new stock sales.

☑ Preferred stock differs from common stock in that preferred stock owners are paid dividends before common stockholders and receive similar preference in the event of liquidation. Conversely, those preferences limit preferred stock market price appreciation when the issuer's business is successful.

# Attracting Outside Investors: The Entrepreneur's Path

T he United States is without question the entrepreneurial capital of the world. More people start businesses here than anywhere else on the planet, and more of them succeed here than anywhere else. Of course, it's also likely true that more of them fail here than anywhere else. But entrepreneurs keep trying, because that's the kind of capitalist system we have. People know that if they try and succeed, they'll be rewarded, both financially and socially. Even if they try and fail, they know they won't be ostracized. On the contrary, they might even get another chance.

Some entrepreneurs tell stories of several failures before they finally achieved success, and they tell those stories with understandable pride— pride in their own perseverance and achievement, and pride in a capitalist economy and political system that not only permit but encourage that kind of effort. Some professional investors even give special credit to entrepreneurs who've had a failure, feeling that it makes them smarter and less likely to repeat their mistakes.

Most major universities have undergraduate education programs designed specifically for would-be entrepreneurs, and many universities provide opportunities for students to form companies while still in school. Icons Bill Gates, Michael Dell, and Mark Zuckerberg were high school entrepreneurs. All started their businesses while in college and all left school before graduation to build the companies that would revolutionize the personal computing and social media industries.

Many start-up businesses, notably the technology-related companies that popped up so prolifically over the past 15–20 years, have needed financial support from outside investors to get started and get their first products to market. Others needed outside investors to expand their companies. Yet today the game has changed dramatically as a result of the investment bubbles during that same period. Results are expected sooner and more reliably, both in profit and cash flow.

Dave Berkus, the entrepreneur/investor first mentioned in Chapter 5, noted in a blog post that

> The days of being able to trust that there will be an investor or lender on the other end of a call or email whenever needed ended with the 2000 and 2008 bursts of those respective bubbles. *It's entirely possible that Amazon could not be created and funded today with its planned seven years until profitability.*

**KEY TERM** **Entrepreneur** A businessperson who starts a company with the intention from the beginning of (1) growing it to be much larger than would be necessary to simply provide an income to the owner, and (typically) (2) selling it at some point—either to the public through a stock offering or to another company—for a substantial profit.

Many sources for investment capital are potentially available to the promising or proven entrepreneur. Sometimes the money comes at first from the founder's own pocket, from savings or borrowing against the house or raiding the kids' college fund. But often the money comes from others who have heard about the entrepreneur's dream and want to be a part of it.

This chapter is an overview of investment capital sources for the entrepreneur, from the first dollar invested to the last dollar before the entrepreneur sells what he or she has built. The discussion generally follows the order in which the entrepreneur would tap those sources of capital. Keep in mind that a particular company may not need all these stages to reach profitability and cash self-sufficiency, and some need them all, depending on the enterprise's complexity and the difficulty in establishing a successful market position.

When an entrepreneur wants to start a company and needs more money than he or she has in the bank or can borrow, here are the places to go knocking with that exciting, well-written business plan in hand. These are the investors.

## The Start-Up Company: Seed Money and Its Sources

Regardless of how difficult it is, the entrepreneur starting a company from scratch must almost always put up the initial money from his or her own resources, for several reasons:

- There may be no one else who believes the idea can work until the entrepreneur proves it and can attract investments.
- The founder wants to keep as much of the stock ownership as possible and believes, or at least hopes, to succeed without outside funding.
- Potential investors have suggested to the entrepreneur that they may invest, but only if the entrepreneur first invests meaningful personal funds. This is referred to as having "skin in the game." (Don't ask how the analogy arose. I don't think either of us wants to know!)

So, the entrepreneur calls on savings, talks his or her spouse into refinancing the house, or asks the parents, aunts and uncles, and close friends to invest. Such sources are typically, and usually accurately, referred to as *friends and family*. These people are usually good sources for initial capital (*seed money*), because they have known the entrepreneur a long time and have faith in him or her or because they feel enough empathy for the entrepreneur's efforts to be willing to take more risks than more objective investors might.

This initial injection of money enables two important changes to take place:

1. The entrepreneur becomes a founder, president, and CEO who now has the opportunity to begin to prove that his or her idea is good enough to attract investors.
2. The entrepreneur can move from idea to reality. He or she can set up an office, develop the business, hire employees, and create a business plan to serve as the brochure for the next round in the continuing search for capital.

# Professional Investors: Angels on a Mission

Once the start-up company has a little momentum, perhaps with a pro-totype of an invention or a product, some interested potential buyers, and a few paying customers, the founder may be in a position to tell a compelling story to potential investors. These may be individuals who've made some money beyond what they need for their personal and business use and have set aside some of that money to invest in other people's new ideas. These investors are called *angels* because they often come to the rescue of the entrepreneur and invest when no one else is willing or able.

One thing to keep in mind about professional investors that might not have been as true during the wild ride of the early 2000s: The expectation of actual revenue as the real "proof of concept" is more a requirement today than ever before. Investors burned by concepts that never attracted revenue are unwilling to be burned a second time. They've learned that the best proof of an idea's viability is when customers pay for it.

> **KEY TERM**
>
> **Angel investor** An individual who invests in start-up or emerging companies on his or her own account, rather than as part of a formal organization or company. Usually an individual with some personal wealth and prior management or investing experience. These "angels" may seek investment opportunities on their own or they may join angel groups in an informal "angel network," similar to an early-stage investment club, to find opportunities that appeal to several group members.

Angels don't do this because they are foolish, but because they have a greater risk tolerance than other folks and because their background often makes them uniquely able and willing to assist a start-up company with ideas, introductions, and advice in addition to money.

## What Angel Investors Want to See

How does an entrepreneur attract the interest of angels? These potential investors typically are attracted by:

- A reasonably well-written business plan outlining the concept and the investment premise;
- A founder with sufficient business management experience to con-

vince the investor that he
or she can carry out the
plan's promise;

- A demonstration in some
form of the product or
service that allows angels
to judge the likelihood
that the entrepreneur will
achieve what the business
plan defines as success;

**Proof of concept** The evidence an entrepreneur accumulates to prove to potential investors that the **KEY TERM** entrepreneur's business model is viable, meaning it's good enough to attract customers, revenue, and profits. That's harder to do for very early-stage development companies than it is for companies that have progressed sufficiently to have some satisfied customers.

- An organization with a
reasonable management team in place and ready to carry out the
plan, and at least a few paying customers to help prove market potential; or
- As many of the things on the venture capitalists' list (in the next section) as possible.

The first professional investor to take a chance on a company is typically able to obtain a substantial ownership percentage in the company in return for the investment. The early-stage investor commands a strong ownership position because he or she is taking a chance very early in the game, when the risk of loss is correspondingly higher and when some parts of the idea are yet unproven.

A first-round professional investor often takes an active role in helping the company grow. The early investor serves on the board of directors and/or advisory board. He or she may help the founder attract key executives to the management team or, if the need is acute and the company is not ready for high-level employees, strategic management consultants. The investor typically provides guidance; many are seasoned executives or entrepreneurs.

For some companies, these early-stage investors provide all the outside capital needed to reach profitability. A start-up company that does not require huge cash infusions for R&D may be able to build sales momentum early on and use much of its investors' money to establish market position and put a sales organization in place. This investment strategy hastens the climb to profits and self-sufficiency, and enables the investors to earn a good return on their money in a shorter time than might otherwise be possible.

A successful launch without any additional investment beyond the angels' contributions is not the normal situation, however, as start-up companies typically take five to seven years or more before their investors can convert their investment back into cash. The more typical start-up that requires investor capital needs several infusions or rounds of capital before it's self-sufficient in terms of cash flow. Early-round money may be needed to prove the soundness of the business concept, to begin the development of the product or service, and to start building the organization.

Perhaps most important to the founder who will need more money as the company gains momentum, first-round investors may facilitate introductions to later-stage investors willing to invest larger amounts of money based on the company's results, thus enabling further progress toward profitability and a handsome return for all. Prominent among these next-stage investors are the money managers known as venture capitalists.

## Venture Capitalists: What You Need to Know to Attract Them

When more money is needed than angels can provide or when angels want others to invest to support their early stakes, a young company may seek out institutional investors, the folks known as *venture capitalists* (*VCs* to those inclined to buzzwords).

A manager for the institutional investors, usually also a VC, evaluates the investment opportunity, makes the investing decision, and monitors the investment's performance over time, with the hope of selling the shares at a profit for the investors (and for the VC him- or herself, since these folks usually accumulate shares for their personal accounts along the way, sometimes by direct investment and sometimes in the form of options or warrants for their services). In one outsized success story, Facebook raised over $1.3 billion in venture funding before its momentous $16 billion IPO. Virtually every start-up company in the Internet technology space whose name you've heard of raised millions from investors before they were able to support themselves from profitable operations.

> **Venture capitalist (VC)** A member of a firm that invests in emerging companies, many in start-up mode, typically for others rather than for their own account, often by starting an investment fund and convincing other institutions, corporations, or wealthy individuals to passively invest in the fund, and then finding good investment opportunities. VCs also guide the growth and subsequent funding of their portfolio companies until they are either sold to other companies or to the public in a public offering of shares (see "The Initial Public Offering" below).
>
> **KEY TERM**

## What Venture Capitalists Want to See

Venture capitalists are attracted by:

- All the things on the angel list above;
- A polished business plan demonstrating solid thinking with regard to all the key success factors, the inhibitors to success, and the advantages of the proposed product or service;
- A large potential market, so that even a small market share will produce a big sales volume;
- The new company's ability to gain a foothold in the market that will inhibit competitors, otherwise known as *barriers to entry*;
- A distinct competitive advantage over all the alternatives that customers have or might have;
- For a technology company, a compelling new technology that's difficult for potential competitors to copy, circumvent, or make obsolete—more barriers to entry—and
- The potential to grow to a valuation at least 10 times greater than the valuation at which the investors purchase their shares.

*Valuation* is the term that defines the venture's proposed total market value, which in turn defines the amount of ownership interest the investors will receive. By way of an example, a venture may

> **Valuation** The venture's proposed total market value, which determines the amount of ownership interest any investor will receive. Since this valuation is an estimate of a company that typically has little value in traditional terms (sales and earnings), it's as much a negotiation between the company, the underwriters, and the venture capitalists as it is a calculation.
>
> **KEY TERM**

be valued at $5 million by the founder, who might want to raise $2.5 million. The founder's calculation might go as shown in Figure 14-1:

| | |
|---|---|
| Value of the venture before the investment of $2.5M ("pre-money valuation") | $5 million |
| Value of the venture after the investment of $2.5M ("post-money valuation" = pre-money valuation + investment) | $7.5 million |
| Value of the investor's $2.5M in terms of ownership percentage ($2.5M ÷ $7.5M) | 33 1/3% |
| Percent of the firm the entrepreneur offers to sell for $2.5M | 33 1/3% |

**Figure 14-1.** The entrepreneur's calculation

he venture capitalist, on the other hand, might look at it as shown in Figure 14-2:

| | |
|---|---|
| Value of the venture before the investment of $2.5M ("pre-money valuation") | $2.5 million |
| Value of the venture after the investment of $2.5M ("post-money valuation" = pre-money valuation + investment) | $5 million |
| Value of the investor's $2.5M in terms of ownership percentage ($2.5 ÷ $5.0M) | 50% |
| Percent of the firm the investor wants to own for $2.5M | 50% |

**Figure 14-2.** The venture capitalist's calculation

The difference between the two views is one of perspective. Since both are estimating future value in their negotiating, neither is right and neither is wrong. The person in the stronger negotiating position usually gets more of what he or she wants. When a company approaches a VC firm for an initial investment, the VC firm is usually in the stronger position. Once the company has proven its ideas, attracted customers, and perhaps even piqued the interest of other VC firms, the founder may be in the stronger negotiating position.

Venture capital firms typically prefer to keep a low profile. Despite that preference, their names are published on lists that are eagerly purchased

**NEGOTIATING WITH CLOUT**

A company that has attracted the interest of VC firms may be in a strong position to negotiate funding. I once served as the CFO of a start-up technology company that had VC firms aggressively competing for the right to provide the next round of investment capital. The company actually turned away money, effectively rationing the next investment opportunity to those firms the owners felt could be most beneficial to the company's strategic agenda. Now, *that's* negotiating leverage!

by entrepreneurs, and they receive hundreds of unsolicited business plans every year, only a small fraction of which are read. It's generally acknowledged, although seldom stated as an absolute, that a business plan has little chance of receiving serious attention unless it's been introduced by someone known to the venture capital firm, someone whose opinion they value or at least feel comfortable with. Thus, when it comes to getting attention from these investors, it's truly a matter of who you know.

Venture capital firms account for only a small portion of all the investment funds poured into new businesses every year. Entrepreneurs who have had VC investors on their boards tell a mixed bag of stories, ranging from masterfully insightful guidance to self-serving decisions designed more to protect the VC investment than to foster the venture's success. Yet because of their reputation, their ready pools of cash, and their skill in identifying and backing some of the most successful start-ups in memory, nearly every entrepreneur who starts a new venture seeks—or at least covets—the views, the money, and the support of venture capitalists.

For their part, despite their skill at evaluating new ventures, these investors expect to be wrong most of the time. In fact, traditional wisdom says they will lose money on four of five investments they make, but getting a 10-to-1 return on the fifth makes the efforts worthwhile. If you think about it, would you make your living doing something at which you expect to fail 80 percent of the time? Perhaps that's why these investors ask for *and typically get* the valuation leverage they want, even when it seems unfair to the hard-working founder.

## Avoid the Top 10 Lies

Guy Kawasaki, a serial entrepreneur and speaker whose affiliations have included Apple, The Motley Fool, and currently Google, once warned against the following statements that entrepreneurs most commonly use with venture capitalists.

1. **Our projections are conservative.** Venture capitalists know that entrepreneurs are optimistic. They won't take your projections at face value, and they certainly won't believe "conservative."

2. **ABC [Consulting Firm A] predicts our market will swell to $X by 20XX.** Refrain from giving such numbers. Anybody can predict almost anything.

3. **XYZ [Huge Company B] is about to sign a sales contract with us.** Entrepreneurs may interpret even a polite rejection as a sign of real interest. VCs know better.

4. **Key employees will join us as soon as we're funded.** VCs have telephones and can call those key prospective employees.

5. **We have first-mover advantage.** Two problems. One, "first-mover advantage" doesn't matter, not as much as "first to scale." Two, it's easy for VCs to check out claims to an advantage.

6. **Several VCs are already interested.** VCs can check out this claim; if it's untrue, you lose a lot of credibility.

7. **MNO [Big Industry Leader C] is too slow to be a threat.** VCs will read in such a statement a lack of market awareness.

8. **We're glad the bubble has burst.** OK, so it's good that investors and entrepreneurs are more rational and realistic, but what sane entrepreneur would be pleased that investment money is harder to obtain?

9. **Our patents make our business defensible.** Be realistic: Outside of medical devices and biotechnology, patents mean very little. If an idea is worth money, somebody will copy it.

10. **All we have to do is get 1 percent of the market.** Leave the worst-case scenario to the VCs. Aim at a figure you consider realistic—and show how you intend to hit it.

# The Initial Public Offering: Heaven or Hell?

As we've already mentioned, the pot of gold at the end of the rainbow—the goal of long-term strategies for the entrepreneur who doesn't want to run a company for the rest of his or her working life—is to sell it for a lot of money and retire to a beach in Tahiti or a golf course in Florida. While there are several ways to do that, selling the company to the investing public through a public offering of stock will typically bring the largest return to the sellers. The first time the company sells its shares in the public market is called the *initial public offering* (*IPO*). For the classic entrepreneur, the IPO is the ultimate exit strategy.

**Initial public offering (IPO)** The first sale of equity in a company to the public, generally in the form of shares of common stock, through an investment banking firm.

**KEY TERM**

Unfortunately for the entrepreneur with beachfront dreams, the IPO isn't as simple as selling all the shares and walking away, dragging a bag of money. The U.S. government, through the Securities and Exchange Commission (SEC), long ago decided too many owners were selling a pig in a poke to unwary public investors who found out too late their shares weren't worth what they paid for them. Today, all the owners, including the professional investors, must remain owners after the IPO, and their fortunes will rise and fall with the public stock price, making everyone interested in the same goal: consistent price appreciation.

The SEC aside, the prospect of selling shares over time, along with the likelihood that the company's continued success will raise the stock price still further, makes the IPO the preferred exit strategy if the company can get it. That's a big *if*, because not every company with investor backing makes a big enough splash to interest investment bankers. Remember the 8 in 10 companies that don't make it? And the 1 in 10 that makes it big? Well, that means that roughly 90 percent of the start-ups that are funded by professional investors are probably not good enough to become IPO stocks—the actual numbers are even more daunting. And of those that do succeed with their IPO, many will deliver less stellar performance than projected in their IPO offering

**Investment banker** An individual or firm that assists companies in raising money by finding private **KEY TERM** investors, acquiring companies, or selling a company's shares in the public market, such as an IPO. All major securities firms (*stockbrokers* to most of us) also conduct investment banking activities, a situation that has raised charges of conflict of interest in the last few years because they sell stock in companies that they've also recommended to their clients. This has led to changes in this segment of the marketplace.

literature. Some of them will sink to market prices below their IPO price, while others will languish with modest returns and sort of disappear into the haze without ever making a significant market impact.

For those reasons, along with the financial crash of 2008, the high cost of an IPO, and the general mood of professional investors since the 2001 tech collapse, IPOs have not been the exit strategy they once were. Today, more successful ventures are sold to a larger company with strategic interests than go public in a splashy debut.

Still, the exhilarating prospect of making it big in the breathtaking IPO game gives company owners hope. Along the way, they are aided by the coaches and advisors, the investors, consultants, accountants, lawyers, and others because everyone wants to play in the big leagues. Every entrepreneur believes it can happen to them—and no one knows for sure, until they take their shot.

---

**CAUTION**

### DON'T COUNT ON AN IPO

It would be simple if any company could go public. Unfortunately, it takes more than that—and few succeed. The most likely IPO candidates are companies in industries that are hot—according to the whims of the stock market—and companies that are expected to reach revenues of $100 million or more quickly. As we've seen the past few years, those will often be Internet-based companies with truly innovative technology in unfilled niches. Facebook, eBay, Amazon, and Google are all names that come to mind for their dramatic rise and phenomenal valuations. While they all had successful IPOs, each has since purchased numerous smaller companies to broaden their reach, companies owned by entrepreneurs and investors who opted for that type of strategic exit rather than an IPO.

---

## Strategic Investors: The Path to a Different Party

Let's do a little guessing here. There are an awful lot of companies that start up every year. Even if only 5 percent of them stay in business, that's still a big number. If only 10 percent of these survivors hit it big, that would still be far more than the published statistics of IPO success rates. What happens to all the rest—the companies that succeed but don't go public?

Well, many of them simply become successful privately owned companies. In fact, many of the most successful U.S. companies are quietly owned by private interests. Many privately owned companies had great ideas and grew to be successful but still didn't get there by using venture capital money. Many of them were started by entrepreneurs who had the same dream of a rich exit, like their IPO counterparts. Do they just give up and go home? Not by a long shot. Many of these companies go the other route—teaming up with an existing company that appreciates the value of their ideas and hopes to improve its own business through the success of the start-up.

Such companies often become *strategic investors* by investing in promising start-ups in return for both stock ownership and the first opportunity to receive the benefit of the start-ups' innovations. These strategic investors may want the rights to sell the venture's products as their own, to incorporate the venture's products into their own, or to purchase the start-up and merge it into their business. That benefit is mutual, if it's done right:

- The venture gets access to the technical expertise of the larger company to help it solve issues.
- The investor gets innovation it likely is not nimble enough to create by itself, except at an exorbitant cost.
- The venture gets a partner with more marketing muscle than it would have alone, perhaps even getting its products into the strategic partner's sales force offerings, producing a built-in distribution channel.
- The investor gets to offer new products, perhaps including state-of-the-art technology that it didn't know how to develop or wasn't prepared to take the risk of developing.
- The investor may be able to purchase this company and its products and innovation for a fraction of the cost of buying a more established company, if it even could find an established company willing to be acquired.

## Acquisition: The Strategic Exit

Suppose you're the founder/CEO of a company that didn't get angel funding, didn't get VC funding, didn't get strategic partner funding, but *still* managed to build a company that's making it on its own. The company is self-sufficient in terms of cash flow and modestly profitable, but lacks sufficient resources to take full advantage of its market position. Let's further assume that your company isn't an IPO candidate because it's not exciting enough to sizzle the pages of a prospectus. Finally, let's suppose the company was built on some innovative technology that's likely to be seriously challenged in a few years. This is a fair assumption because technology moves pretty fast these days, particularly if a company has demonstrated there's a ready, profitable market for it. Or, let's suppose the owners are in their 50s or early 60s. They managed to survive the bruising recession of 2008–2010 and have firmly decided they don't want to go through that again. I believe there are thousands of business owners who will exit their companies in the next 5–10 years with exactly that mindset.

Many founders look at the prospect of running such a company for 5–10 more years to make only an adequate living and say, "No more!" Others are ready to go the distance, but fearful of their chances against bigger, well-financed competitors, and they're worried that they might lose it all. Their options? Fold the tent and go home, hang on and hope for the best, or find a big brother to protect the company from intruders.

In financial circles, finding a big brother doesn't mean going to some charity event or calling long-lost relatives. It means finding a large company that wants to acquire the young company and is perhaps willing to pay off the owners/managers after a transition period or to offer them jobs running their company from inside the newly acquired big brother.

Without a strategic partner, the management team must find a prospective buyer and convince the company that acquiring the venture would be a good idea. The venture owner(s) might do that by hiring an investment banker or by initiating their own search, but the idea is to find a friendly 800-pound gorilla they know and like before an 800-pounder they don't know or don't like knocks on the door. The young company would be looking for:

- The possibility of making a friendly deal at a better price for the owners' stock than might be available later, in more challenging times;
- Jobs for the venture's employees, including the CEO if desired, which might not be so easy later with an unfriendly buyer, especially if the CEO resisted their overtures; and

■ The ability to pick the time to look for a deal, when the venture looks its best, prospects are looking good, there's cash in the bank, and the venture isn't facing an immediate threat.

By contrast, the potential acquirer has a different list, which might include:

■ Maintaining or increasing a growth rate that stockholders have come to expect, particularly if the acquisition is in a growth area expected to become "hot" soon;

■ Protecting itself from inroads into its market by younger companies with the kind of innovative products it lacks;

■ Putting excess plant capacity to work building products for the young company at a favorable incremental cost because it's already paying for the capacity;

■ Putting excess cash to work earning a better long-term return than it can earn sitting in the bank; or

■ Developing complementary products (e.g., lawn tools for a lawn-mower company or computer printers for a computer company).

There are some distinct differences in an acquisition under these circumstances and the kind of deal that might be made with a strategic investor. For example, a company that acquires a venture rather than investing in it early on doesn't bear the added cost *or risk* of nurturing the young company to self-sufficiency. For coming late to the party, however, it must likely pay more for the company because there's less risk and a higher certainty of a good ROI. The selling stockholders are generally entitled to a better price because they rode out the rough times and carried all the risk.

Of course, like any acquisition transaction, the outcome is the result of negotiation more than calculation and logic. Each party tries to present his or her case and convince the other to accept it, or something close to it. For this reason, CEOs wishing to buy or sell typically enlist the services of negotiating experts, such as investment bankers, mergers and acquisitions (M&A) consultants, or lawyers skilled in deal making.

# Manager's Checklist for Chapter 14

☑ Angel investors are often the first step for entrepreneurs to obtain outside financing, after they have exhausted their "friends and family" resources. Angels typically accept the highest risk and make the smaller investments that very early-stage companies need to get started.

☑ Venture capital investors are often the second stage for the entrepreneur. VCs invest larger amounts, but typically ask for larger stakes in the company and expect it to make more progress before they invest. That means greater actual sales, among other things.

☑ Valuation of a company when it's not yet earning a profit—or even bringing in revenues—is a challenging task that's crucial to the company wanting investment capital, yet the lack of real data typically reduces the decision to a negotiation rather than a calculation.

☑ While the initial public offering is often the pot of gold at the end of the rainbow, few companies realize the dream. Many more are acquired by strategic partners, sold once they have matured, or simply run under private ownership until the owners retire.

# Index

# About the Author

**Gene Siciliano** is a financial management consultant. His business helps companies increase profits and enterprise value by developing and implementing more effective operational financial strategies. He collaborates with CEOs to develop, implement, and manage financial strategies that will improve profitability, enterprise value, and owner peace of mind. His tools of the trade include interim and part-time financial management, business planning, management effectiveness audits, due diligence and quality of earnings reviews, management workshops in financial management, and executive coaching. His Controller for Rent™ service provides interim financial executives to manage finance departments on an interim basis—for a few weeks, a few months, or even a few years.

An active writer, speaker, and trainer, Gene is also the author of *Financial Mastery for the Career Teacher* and *Finance for Administrative Assistants*. His articles on financial management, business planning, and cost control have been published internationally. He also publishes print and electronic newsletters for advisors, managers, and owners of privately owned companies.

Following graduation from Penn State University's Smeal College with a business degree in accounting, Gene spent several years on active duty as a Naval Reserve officer. He carries the permanent rank of Commander,

U.S. Navy–Retired. Returning to civilian life, he joined Alexander Grant & Company (now Grant Thornton), a large international public accounting firm. In 1986 he founded Western Management Associates, the consulting business that he owns and operates today. In his practice he often serves as the part-time chief financial officer for client companies. From that experience grew the trademark of his business, Your CFO for Rent®.

When not in the office, Gene has served nonprofit organizations— both professional and charitable—as board chair, president, board member, and treasurer. He's most often drawn to organizations that help children and adults with special needs. In his spare time, he enjoys tennis and the theater, both available in abundance near his home in Redondo Beach, California. He can be reached at (310) 645-1091 or by visiting his website at www.CFOforRent.com.